Library of
Davidson College

LANGUAGE AND PSYCHOLOGY
Historical Aspects of Psycholinguistics

PERSPECTIVES IN PSYCHOLOGY

WILLIAM KESSEN   GEORGE MANDLER   General Editors

GEORGE A. MILLER
  Mathematics and Psychology

JEAN MATTER MANDLER AND GEORGE MANDLER
  Thinking: From Association to Gestalt

WILLIAM N. DEMBER
  Visual Perception: The Nineteenth Century

WILLIAM KESSEN
  The Child

ANNE ANASTASI
  Individual Differences

ARTHUR L. BLUMENTHAL
  Language and Psychology

LANGUAGE AND PSYCHOLOGY
Historical Aspects of Psycholinguistics

Arthur L. Blumenthal
Harvard University

John Wiley & Sons, Inc.
New York · London · Sydney · Toronto

401
B658l

Copyright © 1970, by John Wiley & Sons, Inc.

All rights reserved. No part of this book may be reproduced by any means, nor transmitted, nor translated into a machine language without the written permission of the publisher.

Library of Congress Catalogue Card Number: 78-123738

ISBN 0-471-08400-X Cloth 74-9291

ISBN 0-471-08401-8 Paper

Printed in the United States of America

10 9 8 7 6 5 4 3 2 1

FOREWORD

Perspectives in Psychology is a series of original books written for psychologists and students who are concerned with the history of ideas in psychology.

It is our intention to present fresh and thoughtful assessments of the current psychological scene in the context of relevant historical changes. Many authors of the *Perspectives* books will examine a selected slice of the history of psychology by way of selected and annotated readings. This is not to say that *Perspectives* is a uniform or systematic encyclopedia of the history of psychology. Psychologists, by disposition and training, are reluctant to work their ideas into a standard weave—homespun or exotic—and *Perspectives* represents well the happy diversity of the discipline.

Some books in the series are scholarly disquisitions on the historical antecedents of a current problem in psychological analysis, some books move—after a brief glance at historical antecedents—directly toward a discussion of contemporary psychology and its future, some books deal with the past largely as a platform for polemical exposition. And, occasionally, *Perspectives* will present an original work in psychology that escapes the historical definition altogether.

Perspectives in Psychology, by using the avenues of documented history and informed discussions of current as well as classical issues, will emphasize that psychology has a history as well as a past and that it advances as it grows.

William Kessen
George Mandler

PREFACE

This book is primarily about the history of modern psychology and is specifically restricted to one thread of interest throughout that history—psycholinguistics. The term "psycholinguistics" appeared a few times in the English-language literature in the earlier history of psychology, but it had not rallied a following nor captured much attention. Most academicians were quite content with the longer phrase *psychology of language*, which stood for a loose conglomeration of interests in and out of psychology. But our English tongue does not easily permit us to convert that longer phrase into the designation of an active agent or an academic specialist.

The appearance of the hybrid expression in the early 1950s was sudden. In 1951 and 1953 the formal adoption and promotion of *psycholinguistics* took place at interdisciplinary conferences organized and supported by the Social Science Research Council. Conferees representing a perplexing forest of diverse interests—information theory, word-association, speech pathologies, linguistics, social psychology, verbal learning, and others—all with competing claims on the new discipline, posed the confusing question, "What and who is a psycholinguist?" In the years following that conference, sections of psychology libraries blossomed with psycholinguistic literature. It now appears that the parent disciplines were too optimistic about what they could offer the newly christened field. Moreover, a revolution in linguistics has upset the very foundations of that field.

Today some solid elements have settled out of the initial flurry of activity, and it is possible to see that the connotations attached to the term "psycholinguist" have narrowed and are more specific. In particular, many psycholinguists have distinguished themselves from those psychologists who have only a secondary interest in man's capacity to use language. For example, most research in the area of social psychology or verbal learning that involves the use of language is not necessarily psycholinguistics. In these and several related fields, language performance per se is not of primary interest. Instead, language behavior is used as a measure of some nonlinguistic event or it is used as a stimulus for eliciting a variety of behaviors. It may be true, for instance, that a certain dialect elicits emotional reactions in a prejudiced individual, but that observation may not be very interesting to one who investigates the nature of the language skill. Today most psycholinguists are doing just that. They are working toward a theory of language *performance*. They ask: How do humans acquire language? How do they compose utterances or understand them? Answers are sought to describe the psychological processes that enable humans to use language.

One fact inspired the present volume: American psychologists are seemingly unaware of an illustrious earlier history of psycholinguistics.* And recent statements such as, "psycholinguistics is a field of specialization that is very new," belie historical fact. During the last quarter of the nineteenth century there was a monumental rise and by the 1930s there was a sharp decline in a tradition of psycholinguistic research. None of the earlier work is associated with the recent resurgence of the field in America. On examination of the early literature a striking relevance is found—there once was a very close collaboration between early experimental psychologists and linguists and a self-conscious investigation of the overlap of their two fields. The early findings were prolific in the form of experimental investigations and theoretical writings. And the viewpoints of that day were often quite similar to those developed during the past ten to fifteen years.

Any student of the psychology of language today can enrich his own work through the perusal of the early material. For the student who wishes to undertake such study, I hope this book will furnish a helpful beginning. The topic of "language and psychology" is formidably a broad one, and the reader will soon

---

* In America the most eloquent, although least known, recent plea for establishing the field of psycholinguistics came from the late A. A. Roback, *Destiny and motivation in language* (1953). Besides Roback, J. R. Kantor, E. A. Esper, and John Carroll have made seldom noticed brief references to this earlier tradition in their writings.

notice that this short book does not survey it completely. There are certain popular aspects of the subject that have been adequately summarized elsewhere, and where relevant, I have referred to them giving only brief mention of that material here. In a final chapter I have included several influential contemporary selections to help the reader make comparisons between early and recent work. The introductory chapter on nineteenth century backgrounds is somewhat limited; it seems impossible to capture the complexity of nineteenth century linguistics in a few paragraphs. Yet this section may prove helpful to the psychologist who has little acquaintance with the history of linguistics. Most of the relevant German and French literature has never appeared in English translation. Several selections included in this book appear in English for the first time.

This work then does not attempt to examine all the aspects of language that have interested psychologists during the past century. However, there are several developments that run through the early period and that show interesting similarities to present work. One is the study of *the psychology of the sentence*. Because this is a particularly fundamental issue today its history should be better known.

I have encountered little trouble in organizing this type of historical study of psycholinguistics. It would make little difference whether one focuses on great men, great works, or great ideas. The same story would be recognized in each case. The author can only accent certain parts, lessen others, and inject opinions through side comments. My initial opinion is that the earlier psycholinguistics and its relevance to the present is largely unknown. This may be a reaction to the common belief that language is a process so complex that only recently have psychologists been barely able to study it. I hope this volume will be enough to dispel that unfortunate view even though I present just a sampling from a vast literature.

In brief, I have attempted to fill in a gap in the writings on history of psychology as well as to stimulate further psycholinguistics research. As in the other volumes of the "Perspectives in Psychology" series, selected historical excerpts will appear in what follows. But perhaps a larger portion of this text is devoted to commentary and summary. Thus the number of influential personalities and the works that are covered is considerably more than those listed in the table of contents. The latter were selected primarily as historical moments around which trends could be charted. On the other hand, I have given little emphasis to the often reviewed fields of verbal learning and conditioning, word association, articulatory phonetics, speech pathologies, and mass communication studies—all or some of which are occasionally classified as psycholinguistics. Also, some well-known theorists are given little mention because they were not directly related to the historical movements considered. For an historical review of the study of the biological bases of language the reader may see the survey by Otto Marx, which appears as an appendix in Eric Lenneberg's book *Biological foundations of language* (1967). This includes mention of the classical aphasiologists such as Jackson, Pick, and Head.

In this book I emphasize the history and development of psycholinguistic theory. I have devoted more attention to summarizing early experimental results in my monograph "Early psycholinguistic research: a review" which appears in *The structure and psychology of language* edited by T. G. Bever and W. Weksel. Yet many comments made in that paper also appear here.

I acknowledge my gratitude to friends and colleagues who have been quite helpful with this work. George A. Miller first urged me to undertake the project. George Mandler edited the entire text and made many important suggestions. Morris Halle and Noam Chomsky provided support and office space at the M.I.T. Department of Linguistics for one year when most of the text was written. Others who have read and made useful comments on parts of the manuscript are Herbert Rubenstein and Carol Chomsky. Several people have given valuable assistance on problems of translation, particularly Jim Lyon of the Harvard German Department, and also Judith Goodman Barisonzi and Inez Hedges. I also thank my typist Ann Cura.

Work on this manuscript was supported in part by a grant from the Department of Defense, Advanced Research Projects Agency (SD-187) to the Harvard Center for Cognitive Studies and also by a grant to the Department of Linguistics, M.I.T., from the National Institutes of Health (HD00111).

Cambridge, Massachusetts *Arthur L. Blumenthal*

CONTENTS

1. INTRODUCTION: Nineteenth Century Backgrounds 1

2. WILHELM WUNDT: The Master Psycholinguist and His Commentators 9
   Wilhelm Wundt, *The Psychology of the Sentence* 20
   Hermann Paul, *Synthesis Rather than Analysis* 34
   Anton Marty, *Sentence Types and Transformations* 44
   Karl Bühler, *The Functionalist Viewpoint* 58
   Jacob Robert Kantor, *Expression vs. Stimulus Response Adjustment* 72

3. LANGUAGE ACQUISITION: The Most Frequently Studied Problem 79
   Clara and William Stern, *The Language of Children* 86
   Margaret Morse Nice, *The Child as a Language Creator* 107
   Paul Guillaume, *The Emergence of the Sentence* 117
   Floyd Henry Allport, *Control of the Verbal Response* 133

4. THE PSYCHOLOGY OF READING: Early Contributions to Psycholinguistics 143
   Edmund Burke Huey, *Language, Perception, and Reading* 147
   Guy Thomas Buswell, *Reading Sentences* 161

5. THE NEW PSYCHOLINGUISTICS: A Renewal of "Sprachpsychologie" in America 172
   Karl Spence Lashley, *The Problem of Serial Order in Behavior* 183

Noam Chomsky, *Transformational Generative Grammar*   200
  George Armitage Miller, *The Psychology of the Sentence*   211
  Eric Heinz Lenneberg, *Language Acquisition*   226

6. RETROSPECT   237

   INDEX   245

LANGUAGE AND PSYCHOLOGY
Historical Aspects of Psycholinguistics

CHAPTER 1

INTRODUCTION

Nineteenth Century Backgrounds

If one were to determine the behaviors that humans engage in most often, it would not be surprising to find that most human activity employs language. Perhaps for this reason the study of language has no historical beginning but is, instead, a science that stretches back to prehistoric times, to the Tower of Babel legends, and to the sophisticated observations made by the grammarians of ancient India. After reading through the Hellenic, Roman, Arabic, medieval, and renaissance literature on the nature of language, a linguist may understandably identify with one of the most time-honored fields of research and scholarship. Moreover, linguists have frequently impressed other social scientists with their significant and successful advances in the analysis of the structure and nature of language. It is surprising that good English language reviews of the history of linguistics have been scarce until quite recently. The reader is strongly urged to see R. H. Robins' *A short history of linguistics* (Indiana University Press, 1968) for a broad and readable account.

The present book concerns a narrower aspect of more recent history—specifically, a body of language research developed in conjunction with the appearance of psychology as a specialized discipline a century ago. First, we shall consider briefly the nature of nineteenth century linguistics. An earlier age of exploration and discovery revealed the diversity of human languages, and after 1800 a new generation of language scholars, known as philologists, attempted to put their expanded information about world languages into some order.

At the risk of historical oversimplification, two spheres of influence can be specified underlying both the development of psychology and linguistics. One tradition tended to be atomistic and dealt more with associationist psychology, sensations, and external factors. This is widely described as the tradition of *empiricism*; other terms frequently related to it are sensationalism, associationism, and later, positivism. The second tradition, on the other hand, was more often holistic and tended toward intuitionism, innate properties, and speculation about a priori internal mental principles. We shall designate this trend broadly as *rationalism* including here certain other philosophies that were related in various ways—nativism and idealism.

These doctrines represent differences that have come into conflict many time in the history of philosophy. In the nineteenth century the rationalist tradition was more prevalent east of the Rhine in German idealism; empiricism was stronger west of the Rhine in Anglo-French associationism and functionalism. The two were by no means neatly divided—there were significant incursions of each philosophy into the other's home provinces.

The empiricist influence, with its emphasis on pure description and inductive method, is reflected in the vast compendia of language data and in a number of provocative discoveries. Rasmus Rask (1818) and Jacob Grimm (1822) showed that it was possible to write precise descriptive statements of regular differences in sound structures between related languages. For instance, Rask pointed out the extent of regularity in the sound shifts between European languages. Where English words begin with an *f*, Latin words generally have a *p*:

English	Latin
father	pater
foot	pes
few	pauci

Discoveries of such frequent regularities between widely separated languages led to the recognition of language "families" and to some exciting conclusions about prehistoric human migrations. Soon numerous nineteenth century scholars of all backgrounds became obsessed with the idea of discovering mankind's original language.

During these times social sciences were often pursued with the optimistic vision that they would some day assume the form and exactness of physical sciences. Newtonian physics had commanded considerable reverence within the empiricist tradition, and all the happenings of nature, including language, were submitted to an analysis in terms of attractive and repellent forces. Comparative philologists were especially tempted to adopt biological models in an imitation of a physical science. In writing the first great summary of comparative language investigations, Franz Bopp (1816) stated his intention "to give a comparative description of the organism of the languages . . . a compendium of all their related features, and an inquiry into their physical and mechanical laws." Later in the century, the Darwinian theory of evolution was directly adopted for language study. In Germany, August Schleicher initiated the movement with his book *Die Darwinische Theorie und die Sprachwissenschaft* (Darwinian theory and linguistics), 1863. The language family corresponded to the species of a genus; the dialects corresponded to the subspecies; subdialects corresponded to the varieties; the speech of particular men corresponded to individuals. In fact, language was considered to be an organism that grows, dies, and evolves new forms. The strategy of nineteenth century language research was thus heavily historical; one could not hope to understand a language unless one studied its historical development.

Schleicher had also been a biology professor. Taxonomy was his linguistic method of research; each language "organism" was dissected so that its parts and functions could be categorized and its "genealogy" traced. The legacy of this movement was an emphasis on word-forms and sound units to the neglect of other aspects of language; and often, within this tradition, thought and speech were regarded as identical. At Oxford, the German-born professor Max Müller became the best known popularizer of these biological borrowings, described in England as *biological naturalism*. Müller is especially remembered for promoting the theory of thought-language identity (see his *Lectures on the science of language,* 1864).

In the studies of syntax, formalisms of logic were applied directly to observed speech. However, within empiricist work investigations of abstract or syntactic aspects were few (the opponents of this trend referred to it as the "negative syntax" movement). The study of word-forms had captured more interest.

The importance for psychologists of the empiricist viewpoint, as passed down through the philosophical tradition of Locke and Hume, is the analysis of human mental life and behavior into elementary sensations and external causes. Psychological events were viewed as governed by certain mechanical principles, essentially external to the mind of man. These, of course, are the classical doctrines of associationism including such notions as frequency-of-occurrence, intensity, and contiguity of sensory or mental events.

Consider now the idealist tradition. In sharp contrast to the views of the "sensationists," the German "apperceptionists," in the tradition of Leibniz and Kant, built on an internal analysis of cognition prior to consideration of external sensation. The classical doctrines of this tradition are the universal laws of judgment and perception that predetermine experience. A judgment, for instance, is not merely the association of two sensations; it is an elementary cognitive phenomenon itself. The parts of a judgment, the *subject* and *predicate,* are not contiguous associates, but instead are the parts of an elementary relationship where the predicate *belongs* to the subject.

One philologist, Wilhelm von Humboldt, working early in the 1800s was especially under the influence of this second tradition; in turn, his influence formed a distinct trend in nineteenth century linguistics. When Humboldt was appointed minister of public instruction for Prussia he used his authority to establish professorships in linguistics in the universities. There were major differences between the Humboldtian linguists and those who closely followed Rask, Grimm, and Schleicher. Most obvious is Humboldt's position that language is not a substance spread out before us ready for dissection and classification. He argued that language was an *activity* that could be described by a finite set of principles according to which infinite varieties of speech are produced, and he concluded that all human languages were "variations upon a single theme." While nineteenth century language researchers, especially in England, were occupied with the physics of language sounds, the Humboldtians were more impressed with the psychological aspects of language.

Humboldtians believed that all sentences were reflections of underlying subject-predicate judgments; many scholar-hours were spent in parsing and diagraming sentences or in wrestling with ambiguous sentences.* Sometimes the subject-predicate logic was applied to the unobserved mental act of judging, at other times it was applied directly to observed speech. In the latter case, as was certain to happen, sentences were found that had no subjects or only indefinite subjects as in the sentence, *It's raining* (Miklosich, *Subjectlose Sätze*, 1880). What is the subject here? Does *rain* rain? If not, who or what is *It*? A number of psychologists, including Wilhelm Wundt and Franz Brentano, also became involved in the search for the "lost subject."

Curiosity about language spread rapidly and into many related disciplines during the 1800s. There were important advances in articulatory phonetics brought about by the interdisciplinary conjunction of physics, physiology, and linguistics. An interdisciplinary approach was also fruitful for studies of syntactic structure through the work of philosophers who examined formal logic, psychologists who studied judgment, and grammarians who analyzed syntax. The early twentieth century fostered an attitude of reaction and rejection of the often confusing nineteenth century natural language scholarship. Many later scholars shifted their interests to the more pristine puzzles of artificial and mathematical languages or to the communication systems of animals.

By the 1870s the comparative and historical philologists' zealous pursuit of an exact science of language was well underway. A new generation of scholars then claimed that languages must be studied only as "natural objects" and the laws by which they develop must be physical science laws admitting no exceptions as did many of the laws for sound shifts written earlier by Rask and Grimm. This generation became known as the *Junggrammatiker* (neogrammarians),† and its members con-

---

* For an early description of and negative reaction to this see Benjamin H. Smart, *Thought and language: an essay having in view the revival, correction, and exclusive establishment of Locke's philosophy* (London, 1855).

† This term was invented by the then older generation of linguists who had originally applied it to a young group of phonologists at Leipzig in a derogatory way, with the accent on *Jung* to emphasize their immaturity. But the title was received enthusiastically at Leipzig and became their banner. The customary English translation of "neogrammarian" is misleading.

stituted a youthful, aggressive group centered at the University of Leipzig. Their influence has continued into the twentieth century through their students, most notably Ferdinand de Saussure who later broke through many of the rigid constraints of the *Junggrammatiker* viewpoint. That viewpoint was also noted for its opposition to theory construction and for its emphasis purely on data collection.

The increasing specialization of psychology had a striking influence on nineteenth century academic circles. The philosopher-psychologist Johann Herbart had begun his program to give psychology the structure and appearance of mathematics. His demonstration that mathematical description could be applied to the study of mental life was for a while immensely persuasive.* The psychological theory that he offered was a mechanical analysis of mental life into atomic elements that pushed and pulled each other forcing some elements into consciousness and others out. The success of the exact psychophysics of Gustav Fechner and Ernst Weber was related to Herbart's popularity. Thus some linguists of the *Junggrammatiker* group at Leipzig were tempted to base language study more closely on these developments in psychology. A linguist related to this group was Hermann Paul whose opinions on the psychology of language were under the direct influence of Herbart, and whose work appeared to some scholars as a precise science of psycholinguistic mental chemistry.† (Paul classified psychology along with mathematics as an exact science.)

Important for psychology was the *Junggrammatiker* adoption of the *principle of analogy* as an explanation of language evolution. It is an extremely old notion that was given a dramatic rebirth shortly after it was discussed in 1876 by William Dwight Whitney, an American philologist trained at Leipzig who used the term "false analogy" to explain regular errors often found in the grammar of child speech. False analogy for example, is

---

* For a summary of Herbart's mathematical psychology see George A. Miller, *Mathematics and psychology* (New York: John Wiley and Sons, 1964).

† Paul differed from the *Junggrammatiker* linguists in that he was mentalistic while most in the movement opposed this and adhered strictly to "physicalism." In other ways, however, he was quite close to them.

when a child says "foots" instead of "feet" using as his model the more common form of final *s* pluralization for English nouns. The *Jungrammatiker* group showed that this principle was not only useful in discussions of child speech, but also might be useful for discussing patterns of change and development in the history of a language, that is, as a mechanism of language evolution. And with this device they attempted to explain many historical language changes not accounted for previously. Thus the analogy principle was partly responsible for the new fervor among the young (1880s) linguists. That principle was also to reverberate through the succeeding generation of psychologists who studied language.

But the new optimism was soon shaken. In the summer of 1875, an eighteen-year-old French-Swiss student, de Saussure began his graduate work in linguistics at Leipzig. Today many linguists look back to him as the father of twentieth century linguistics. He could not accept one basic premise of nineteenth century philology: the premise that language is understood only through its historical development. In radical opposition he reasoned that a complete description of a language as it exists at the present moment is logically prior to the study of how it got that way. Similarly, speakers of a language need not know the etymology of a word in order to use it. De Saussure claimed that his ahistorical or *synchronic* approach was more representative of a true scientific analysis than was the historical or *diachronic* approach. Language is a social fact, something that can be studied without reference to history. In this one respect de Saussure turned the clock back to the way things had been prior to the nineteenth century, and before the Darwinian model had influenced linguists. According to de Saussure, we need only to segment, define, and describe language units as they exist. Although he published less than 600 pages during his lifetime, de Saussure made many other fundamental contributions to linguistic thought.

In 1860 a psychologist-turned-linguist, Heyman Steinthal, along with a linguist-turned-psychologist, Moritz Lazarus, founded the *Zeitschrift für Völkerpsychologie und Sprachwissenschaft* (a journal of "social psychology and linguistics"), the first journal largely devoted to the psychology of language. Steinhal, well-trained in both Humboldtian and Herbartian studies, was renowned for his view that a science of psychology is necessarily impossible without a science of language. Accordingly, the primary access to the mind of man was to be through the innate laws of language, not the senses. At Leipzig, Steinthal proceeded to write an introductory psychology textbook that began with a chapter on linguistics. Several of the *Junggrammatiker* linguists believed that the new empirical mathematical psychology was prior to linguistics, and they predicted that psychophysics would be relevant to speech perception and that the laws of association would help explain the phenomena of analogy formation. Unfortunately, these hopes eventually led to bitter disputes and to the total rejection by many psychologists and linguists of each other's studies.

In 1875 a chair for a professorship in philosophy was open at Leipzig, and the University decided to divide the new position between a linguist and a psychologist. Wilhelm Wundt, an ex-physiologist accepted the new half-chair appointment in psychology and arrived in the same summer of 1875 as did the young de Saussure. Years later, Leonard Bloomfield, the leading figure in American behaviorist linguistics who had studied at Leipzig, wrote in his book *Language* (1933) that Wundt's psycholinguistic work represented the culmination of a major tradition in nineteenth century linguistics, namely, that begun by Humboldt. This is the same tradition recently renewed by Noam Chomsky and his collegues in America.

Wundt's goal as a psychologist was to give an explicit characterization of the principles that govern the functioning of cognition in humans. It was his belief that the study of human language would provide one of the best means to knowledge about the mind. We shall now focus on Wundt.

CHAPTER 2

WILHELM WUNDT

The Master Psycholinguist, and His Commentators

It was Wilhelm Wundt (1832–1920)—the physiologist, psychologist, philosopher, philologist, anthropologist, politician, moralist, and villian of behaviorism—who founded experimental psychology. He also had the paternal claim to psycholinguistics because no psychologist wrote as much nor on as many aspects of language performance as did Wundt.* Furthermore, in his late years he remarked that if he had received better training early in his career he would have become a linguist instead of a psychologist. In America, Titchener discounted this comment attributing it to the infirmities of Wundt's old age. Nevertheless, Wundt's statement does not contradict his own development.

Before coming to Leipzig, Wundt had been an assistant to Helmholtz in physiology at Heidelberg. That period seems to have been somewhat less than successful; he had been overlooked for promotion and had been given minor teaching assignments. In 1874 he left Heidelberg and went to Zurich where he lectured for the first time on language. His move to Leipzig the following year initiated a rebirth in Wundt's academic life. Although Leipzig journalists were critical of the University for appointing the relatively undistinguished Wundt to this new position, several linguists welcomed him warmly by attending his first lectures and greeting him with their optimism for the future of *Sprachpsychologie* (psycholinguistics) research. In his memoirs, Wundt tells of the significance and stimulation of these first encounters: "The encouraging approval of a man [Leskien, a *Junggrammati-*

---

* A possible exception to this may be the more recent five-volume *Psychologie der Sprache* by Friedrich Kainz of Vienna. However, Kainz often wrote as an encyclopedist although not always. Also, Kainz was more concerned with language pathologies and less concerned with linguistics than was Wundt.

ker] who was for me the first authority in his field, aroused my hopes that I might be able to derive psychological explanations for the new linguistic discoveries. . . ." Leskien must not have suspected what Wundt would produce because in Wundt's first (1875) Leipzig lecture, which concerned thought and language, the discussion of language development revealed the strong and popular Darwinian influence. But then Wundt immediately turned to formal logic, and here he moved toward the Humboldtian tradition. The first volume of his *Logik* (subtitled "Universal Logic And Cognitive Theory") appeared in 1880, the year after Wundt formally opened the first laboratory for experimental psychology.* The book contains the fundamentals of his approach to language as part of a general theory of cognition. Significantly it shows that Wundt believed basic work was necessary in the psychology of logic before language study could advance. The *Junggrammatiker* linguists, on the other hand, moved away from this view with slogans such as "linguistics must free itself from the dark regions of formal logic"; work such as Wundt's was sometimes considered a regression to "medieval scholarship."

It helps to understand Wundt if we consider his opposition to various forms of materialism, a cause that was a theme in most of his intellectual pursuits whether in his writings on psychology, logic, ethics, or politics. Throughout his life he was active in politics—writing popular pamphlets, delivering speeches, and even holding an elective office. Before coming to Leipzig he had been involved in the German workers movement. In a speech delivered in the 1860s he described the goal of the movement as the freedom and independence of the working classes and "their deliverance from a machine-controlled form of life." He concluded that, "The power of the arm and strength of conviction are dependent on no privilege and they are better than money and materials." Wundt left this movement when it turned toward a materialist and anti-idealist course.

Wundt was nationalistic and was dedicated to keeping what he considered to be certain English and American traditions out

---

* Although he founded the first formal "psychological institute," Wundt always opposed the notion that psychology should be separated from philosophy as an independent discipline.

of Germany, which is ironic in view of the fact that he actively recruited large numbers of students from America. What he opposed was Anglo-American "egoistic utilitarianism" and materialism. The same theme occurred in his opposition to certain trends in Anglo-American and French scholarship. Thus we find him in opposition to materialist views in psychology. The following is an illustration from his *Ethik*, Vol. 2 (second edition, 1892, translation by M. F. Washburn, p. 46):

Matter is a hypothetical conception which we ourselves, impelled by the relative constancy of some impressions and by logical forms of thought, have manufactured. To suppose that this hypothetical substrate which we have constructed among other of our ideas can exert any influence on those other ideas or on our thoughts in general . . . is perfectly absurd. It is a supposition that could arise only as a result of first transforming a product of conceptual thought into a being independent of thought, and then, to complete the absurdity, to regard mental activity itself as a phenomenon similar to its own product.

Thus for Wundt notions of matter are products of conceptual thought and can hardly be independent from it. "Physics" is the product of mental activity. A similar theme underlies his criticism of associationism in his *Introduction to psychology* (translation by R. Pintner, 1912, p. 121–122):

The succession of two independent ideas, only joined together by outward similarity or by habitual contiguity, was made the basis for a scheme for all psychical processes. And thus the view was formed that each idea was an unchangeable thing, very similar to the object from which it arose. If we take an unprejudiced view of the processes of consciousness, free from all the so-called association rules and theories, we see at once that an idea is no more an even relatively constant thing than is a feeling or emotion or volitional process. There exists only changing and transient ideational processes. . . .

In truth, Wundt opposed the strict empiricist tradition.* However, his psychological works represent a serious attempt to ameliorate the recurring idealist—empiricist dispute.

---

* This is perhaps the basic reason why Wundt is little known today, not because he "wrote too much to read," nor because his work was supposedly disorganized. American textbook accounts of Wundt now present highly inaccurate and mythological caricatures of the man and his work.

Wundt was prominent among those German scholars who adhered to a distinction between natural science (*Naturwissenschaft*) and mental science (*Geisteswissenschaft*). The former he considered to be the area of description and explanation characterized by fixed laws and the latter area was to be described by normative rules. His work in psychology drew on both areas. But psychology was to be based on what he felt was the most certain reality we know—that of immediate experience. By this he did not mean external sensation. And because of this Wundt has been mistakenly described as proposing that the mind can observe itself. In fact he opposed that notion in disputing John Locke's *reflection* psychology, which considered the mind as capable of observing itself as though looking into a mirror. Wundt proposed that *knowledge* of the mind was not immediately or directly available but must be built up through inference and theory-construction using any and all data.

Before discussing Wundt's psycholinguistics we will first outline his system of psychology. Although he felt that the study of language was an important source of knowledge of the workings of the mind, Wundt was in opposition to Steinthal and argued that certain psychological assumptions must be made prior to any theory of language.

Wundt's Psychology

Especially after his move to Leipzig, Wundt's psychology grew out of reactions to psychological atomism, particularly that of Herbart, and to the views of empiricist philosophy.* For his alternative, Wundt borrowed (in a loose way) the notion of apperception from Kant. The basic outline of his ideas is found in the

---

* The fact that Wundt's work has often been called atomistic is again a caricature put forward by certain later anti-Wundtians or is a reading out of context. Wundt has often been cited but apparently seldom read. There is yet a more striking reason for misinterpretation of him in America. For years Titchener reigned as the chief spokesman for Wundt's psychology. Titchener's influence was great in this regard. However, he held to the mental mechanics of British empiricism in which he had been thoroughly trained before ever meeting Wundt. And he passed on only those aspects of Wundt's psychology that he could filter through his own particular empiricist views. Even before Titchener's time in America, William James had openly and bitterly opposed Wundt. See Chapter Six.

works of the German idealist, Johann Gottlieb Fichte, a follower of Kant. Specifically, Wundt developed the aspect of Fichte's philosophy that concerns the processes of consciousness. As Wundt's work matured it became holistic and configurational; thereby representing traditional trends in German philosophy. In his memoirs Wundt acknowledged this debt to earlier German philosophical ideas, particularly Fichte's ideas.

Many of the central topics in Wundt's cognitive psychology are again emerging today. Such notions as creative synthesis, rhythmical grouping, attention span, preattentive processes, volition, and similar conceptions of psycholinguistics, may be found, for example, in Ulric Neisser's recent book *Cognitive psychology* (1967).

Wundt's goal was not to form a science of mental life that would rely on a nonmaterial mental substance as conceived in dualist philosophy. Contrary to some textbook accounts, Wundt did not propose either the Cartesian mind-body dualism, nor the isomorphic mind-body parallelism as proposed in Spinoza's philosophy. Wundt described his approach as a "relativity theory." That is, how one describes psychological phenomena depends on the momentary observation point from which one operates. This is methodological. The psychical and the neurological were taken as two separate fields of discourse concerning one and the same phenomenon. This dichotomy is forced on us, according to Wundt, because we seem unable to explain mental phenomena in the terms of neurology; but more importantly, such an attempt might lead to laws that are hopelessly complex and that would not readily lead us toward principles of mental life that are within our grasp now. To eliminate one or the other type of data would needlessly restrict psychological investigation. In his writings on the philosophy of science (*System der Philosophie*, 1889) he also argued that it is necessary for psychologists to go beyond their data in order to develop scientific theory.

Soon after starting this work Wundt gained much disfavor from William James, the most prominent psychologist at that time in America, who abhorred formalisms and theory construction and who had no sympathy for Wundt's technical analyses of mental events. In return, Wundt was hostile toward James, whose writings Wundt found to be vague, superficial, and mystical. But it was Wundt's analysis of "inner" as well as "outer" events, the anathema of behaviorism, that was to cause more dispute and misunderstanding among American psychologists.

Wundt's study of mental events had yielded a divided system of the "inner" and the "outer." In this he was able to profit from both the associationist and the idealist schools of thought. In the inner system of cognitive processes are the idealist principles involving apperception and judgment. In the outer system, of sensory motor function, we find principles of association, concerning the effects of frequency, contiguity, and intensity of events. So Wundt's psychology did involve the "parallel" operation of two systems. Wundt did share with Descartes the problem of how dual entities interact. But it was the problem of the relation between sensory motor events and cognitive events where the two realms were often governed by different principles, and where the relation between them was viewed as a complex and indirect one, and further, where the methods of study often had to be different for each.

Wundt employed the term *apperception* to refer to the focus of attention within the field of consciousness. Just as the fovea of the eye may move over the visual field and bring each point to the place most favorable for seeing, so does Wundt's inner (mental) fixation point move over the range of thought taking various points into clearer consciousness. Early experiments indicated that the "span" of this mental fixation point was about six or seven items or groups. Research on short-term memory and perception has produced supporting data. It was important to Wundt, as we shall see, that the act of apperception embraced not only successive events but also simultaneous ones. Associated with the phenomenon of apperception were "creative resultants" or those aspects of experience organized and constructed (created) internally. Apperception meant the selecting and structuring of internally directed experience. Perception referred to externally directed sensing and detecting.

The course of "active" apperception is determined by subjective (that is, inner) causes, such as the individual's innate mental characteristics, motivation, memories, affect, and the structure of judgments or concepts. These events tend to conceal if not counteract the effects of momentary external conditions that become dominant only during "passive" apperception. Thus in the passive state the individual's consciousness is more under the control of associational effects—frequency, contiguity, or intensity of external events. Although external sensation may sometimes be effective in controlling attention, active apperception easily dominates as seen when attention is directed to weak external stimuli when much stronger stimuli are present. Thus apperception may focus on a certain idea or event under external conditions that have, at other times, given rise to other events.

According to Wundt, the structures that are the products of the cognitive system are quite different from those that are the product of the external system. Every part of an external structure remains essentially independent so that when it becomes dissociated from other elements it retains its identity and remains recognizable. But with events of internal origin the case is very different. The significance of the individual element is now entirely dependent on the whole impression (*Gesamtvorstellung*) of which it forms a part. Wundt considered memory not as consisting of "traces" nor stored copies of input, but instead as consisting of stored "principles" or means for regenerating previous experience. His descriptions of concept formation were sometimes similar to those of memory in that he viewed a concept as a rule for specifying members of a class rather than as collected and stored attributes and instances of class membership.

The number of constituents in any phenomenon of consciousness, whether of inner of outer origin, is limited to the degree that the mental content lacks structure. For example, a list of words grouped into connected phrases is grasped more readily than it would be if the words were unrelated. Many of Wundt's empirical facts are based on such everyday observations. But he and his students produced considerable experimental and observational data relevant to these conclusions. Elsewhere, Wundt himself preferred dialectical over experimental methods in the study of the inner or "higher" cognitive processes that involve concept formation and language. The higher processes, he felt, might be understood by their products, most notably language. And that led him into linguistics and anthropology.

One of Wundt's most ambitious and controversial research programs was the attempt to identify subjective feelings accompanying apperceptive states. We must be careful here in the translation of the term *Gefühl* which did not mean feeling as arising from peripheral external sources. *Gefühl* applies to an underlying basic affective level from which emotions, attitudes, and certain other cognitive functions are derived. For instance, there are feelings of activity, strain, and expectancy that accompany the train of thought. Wundt claimed that the most prominent *Gefühle* during apperception were those of activity (*Thatigkeitsgefühle*) that come with willful acts of the mind. The study of this phenomenon received extensive treatment in Wundt's Leipzig laboratory and resulted in a tridimensional classification of rudimentary feelings: *pleasantness-unpleasantness, strain-relaxation,* and *activity-passivity.* This may remind one of the three dimensions of the "semantic differential" developed more recently by Osgood, et al. (1957).*

Wundt's Psycholinguistics

The theory of language performance developed by Wundt closely follows his psychological analysis and is divided into two aspects: (1) the outer phenomena of sound production and perception and (2) the inner phenomena of the train of thought. Wundt's analysis of the complex relations between inner and outer systems for psychology in general relies heavily on linguistic phenomena. He proposed that through the study of the structure of language this interaction might be better understood.

To understand language *performance* in Wundt's terms it is necessary to trace the mental processes that precede, accompany, and follow utterances. The first difficulty is that these processes are usually extremely rapid and seem automatic. Nevertheless, a person often censors his own speech and revises it while in progress. Thus speech is often retarded by preparatory activity in producing appropriate words and inflections.

According to Wundt, we may say that the act of natural speech begins with the apperception of a general impression (the *Gesamtvorstellung*). Then attention isolates some aspect of this impression. It is not strictly the isolation of a mental "element,"

---

* C E. Osgood, G. Suci, and P. Tannenbaum, *The measurement of meaning* (Urbana: University of Illinois Press, 1957).

because the object of attention must retain a sense of relation or belonging to the general impression. In this way (of relational structuring) the mental content is further organized and analyzed into features or constituents all retaining certain structural relations to one another. From this we derive the basis for the relational structure of sentences. Wundt adopted the device of the tree-diagram in his *Logik* of 1880 to describe these mental events —the judgments made and the relations applied between constituents by the apperceiving individual in the act of preparing his thought for representation in speech. To simplify, consider a speaker who is viewing a white house. He may first divide the impression by focusing attention on one and then another aspect.

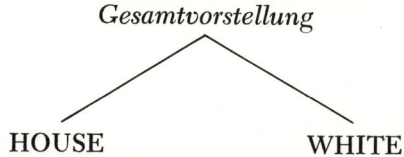

This type of apperceptive division, when including the elementary logical relation of the subject-predicate judgment, enables humans to make their unique representation in speech sounds, or gestures, or by whatever means—for example, *"The house is white."* These means are social conventions and they are simply signals and cues from which a listener may recreate a similar *Gesamtvorstellung* or whole impression for himself. However, this example is too simple when compared to Wundt's involved analysis of grammatical relations and his sequential ordering (*Gliederung*) of the words or the elements of expression.

In the act of rapid conversation, the analysis-for-production process is often diverted by the responses of listeners. A listener, on the other hand, may believe that he detects an error or may find a point of disagreement with the speaker. This feeling may be vague, but the listener becomes conscious of the nature of a correction or counterargument. An impulsive person might break in when his own thought is unanalyzed and thus will find himself for a moment conscious of what he wishes to say but unable to say it. Or, if interruption is not possible and we continue to listen to the speaker, the germinal concept may be lost, such as when one says, "I forgot what I was going to say." If we see a child doing something dangerous the impulse to interfere is at first no more than a willed negative: "No!" or a prohibition: "Don't!" And only subsequently the process of analysis of the situation into a fuller utterance begins. In a similar manner the germinal form of a question may show itself before the *Gesamtvorstellung* analysis, or prior to the production of a full sentence. Many interrogative states need only the slightest analysis as shown in the output, "Huh?" indicating, "What did you say?" or, "What is it?"

The apperceptive function of applying grammatical relations (subject of X, object of X, and so forth) to aspects of general impressions are basic tools in the preparation of thought for expression in human language. They influence the direction of the analysis and retain the sense of sentence unity. The aim of the whole process is to enable a listener to use the ultimate end of the analysis, the speech sounds, as cues for organizing and creating his own cognition. We may observe listening and speaking simultaneously in one individual when he censors his own output by matching it with his own germinal concepts. That is, when he stops and exclaims, "That's not what I intended to say," or "Let me start over."

Approaching the study of language comprehension from the physical utterance and the listener, apperception is again the basis of Wundt's approach. The listener must recombine sound sequences into the *Gesamtvorstellung* quite rapidly or he is lost. For this reason the very attentive hearer's long-term retention of exact words may be very poor, although at the same time he may understand the speaker perfectly. Wundt asserted that this same ability enables the speedreader to grasp whole sentences at a glance. A person with superior reading ability dispenses with detailed analysis and instead catches words and phrases here and there as cues to reconstruct the thought. His apperception skill, the ability to synthesize internal impressions, is superior. The attention of the interested listener just as that of the speedreader is actively at work anticipating what is to come, and it may regress to revise or complete interpretations of what has already been heard. But Wundt notes that where the subject matter is unfamiliar or where the language is foreign and imperfectly understood then the reader or hearer is forced into a piecemeal, detailed analysis of the utterance.

It is important for Wundt's approach to language that it entails the priority of the *sentence*, which he defines psychologically as the transformation of a simultaneous mental representation (the *Gesamtvorstellung*) into sequentially ordered speech segments that are logically related to each other according to the rules of language. Because the *sentence* is primary and the *word* is secondary, word-forms are seen as the somewhat arbitrary results of the sequential organizing activity.

The following translation of a portion of Wundt's writing is an excerpt from Chapter Seven of his *Die Sprache* (Language). The original text first appeared in 1900 and was revised in 1904 and again in 1912. It eventually composed the first two books of a much longer series devoted to social psychology and anthropology, the ten-volume *Völkerpsychologie* (Ethnic psychology).[*] For his illustrations Wundt often drew on exotic as well as Indo-European languages. His analysis of sign language is perhaps still one of the best treatments of that topic. We cannot, of course, illustrate the breadth of this work by including all that material here. It is significant that the study of language constituted the first volume in the series, for Wundt's whole approach to "ethnic psychology" was based on the analysis of language, and the nature of language underlies much of the content of the later volumes which concern other social institutions such as customs, religions, and mythology. The entire series was completed during and shortly after World War I. Thereafter it was seldom read outside of Germany.

There have been some very poor translations of portions of Wundt's writings. We can sympathize with the translator if we appreciate the nature of the task. One's goal should be to make the English sentences mean the same as the German sentences. A translator should elaborate at points to make the meaning clear, and he should vary the terms he chooses according to their context, all this with the goal of writing clear English. One can

---

[*] The study of "ethnic psychology" was initiated earlier in the mid-nineteenth century by Steinthal. However, Wundt's holistic-organic approach was quite different from Steinthal's which had been based on Herbart's mechanistic psychology. Wundt's *Völkerpsychologie* has been repeatedly confused, in American reviews, with his *Elements of folk psychology* (translated by E. Schaub, 1916). The latter is a different, one-volume work which contains very little about language.

never be sure of perfection. The only hope is that overall accuracy of the translated passage will counteract any distortions of particular terms.

The first of several translations presented in this volume follows. It is fundamental in that many of the succeeding writings are based on it or are reactions to it. Wundt held the sentence to be the basic form of language, so naturally he was quite concerned with sentence definitions. The selection begins just after Wundt has analyzed and criticized past attempts to provide such definitions dating back to antiquity. He concludes that the sentence can never be adequately understood in terms of the physical utterance, that is, as an acoustical event. Instead, the sentence must be analyzed as a cognitive process. The relation between these two processes (cognitions and speech sounds) is not a direct nor isomorphic one, and the nature of that relation should be the object of sentence study.

WILHELM WUNDT · *The Psychology of the Sentence*

1. The Sentence as a Transform of a Simultaneous Cognition into a Sequential Structure

1.1 Conceptual Components of Sentences. Although definitions may differ widely when grammarians, logicians, and psychologists describe the universal characteristics of sentences, there is agreement on one point. This is that a sentence is some sort of a linking of a succession of words or concepts. But this common assumption is the very one that cannot stand up under a more rigorous examination of grammatical as well as psychological definitions. Its questionable nature is perhaps more apparent in psychological analyses than in grammatical ones. A sentence certainly can be conceived as an

SOURCE. Wilhelm Wundt, *Die Sprache,* sections from Chap. 7, "Die Satzfügung," Book 2, Vol. I of the *Völkerpsychologie* series, 1912. (First edition, Leipzig: Engelmann, 1900; later editions appeared in 1904 and in 1911–1912.) Translated by A. L. Blumenthal. In this, and in all other selections, original section headings, figures, and footnotes have been renumbered for clarity in the present context.

association of words. But whether it is also a simple association of separate concepts is very questionable in view of the fact that it is clearly impossible to describe individual sentence parts as independent concepts. This is especially so when we attempt to refer purely formal sentence features to concepts.

When I construct a sentence, an isolated concept does not first enter consciousness causing me to utter a sound to represent it. That it cannot be this way is shown by the phenomenon of phonetic induction which occurs when a vocal element on the verge of being expressed is already affecting the form of a sound being spoken at the moment. And similarly, an articulation that has just occurred influences the succeeding sound. Whether the regressive or the progressive effect dominates depends on other, secondary factors. Actually both effects are present at the same time.[1] This is true not only for the individual parts of a word but also to a certain degree for the succession of words in a sentence. The sentence, however, is not an image running with precision through consciousness where each single word or single sound appears only momentarily while the preceding and following elements are lost from consciousness. Rather, it stands as a whole at the cognitive level while it is being spoken. If this should ever not be the case, we would irrevocably lose the thread of speech.

Naturally, the word being spoken at any particular moment is as a rule in the focal point of attention. Yet in the wider span of consciousness the other constituents are there—at least those that are essential for the structure of the whole configuration. For this reason the ability of man to think in sentences is closely related to his attention span. Because of this capacity, one can be aware of the principle parts of a sentence even before beginning to express them.

From a psychological point of view, the sentence is both a simultaneous and a sequential structure. It is simultaneous because at each moment it is present in consciousness as a totality even though individual subordinate elements may occasionally disappear from it. It is sequential because the configuration changes from moment to moment in its cognitive condition as individual constituents move into the focus of attention and out again one after the other. The claim that the sentence is a "chain of word concepts" is as psychologically untenable as that it is merely a "chain of words." On the contrary, it is

---

[1] See Wundt, *Die Sprache*, Book 1, Chap. 4.

the dissection of a totality present as a whole in consciousness. If one characterizes this as a linking process, then the outer grammatical form is taken as the inner mental form. And it is thus assumed that the outer form is from moment to moment a faithful picture of the psychological process underlying it. This of course it is not. The outer form is only the result of the process. It is, moreover, an end product which shows by its nature that the psychological factors determining a grammatical utterance are themselves distinct from the utterance. The sentence as an *inner* psychological construction must have a simultaneous nature in addition to the sequential one. Without this quality it could not be a coherent totality.

If we study the psychological conditions that accompany sentence formation, and then study the relations existing within sentences between individual constituents and their actual meanings, then this dual psychological nature of sentence structure becomes clear. Its simultaneous existence is revealed by the sentence unity. Its sequential course is revealed in the successive prominence of particular components in the focus of attention. In this sense the construction of the sentence is at once an analytic and a synthetic function. But it is mainly an analytic process. Sentence unity appears to us primarily as a whole mental impression that includes individual constituents, even though these are relatively less apparent. This cognitive configuration is then formed into successive segments by the process of apperception.

. . . .

1.2 Toward a Universal Conception of the Sentence. We can now define the sentence according to its objective and subjective characteristics. It is the linguistic representation of the voluntary sequential ordering of a simultaneous mental impression into logically related segments. In addition, it should be expressly stated that although *words* derive from this process of sequential structuring, words can themselves in turn contain several logically related parts representing the various structures that word forms display. It is the rule in most languages that the process of sentence formation continues within individual words. A word, then, is also a sequentially formed unit and is subordinated to the sentence. From this it is at the same time apparent that in certain extreme cases word and sentence can coincide.[2]

---

[2] Ottmar Dittrich has to some extent narrowed and to some extent broadened the above sentence definition, in that on the one hand he limits it to

Just as the structuring within the word determines word form, so sentence form is thus produced by arranging words into sentences. These similarities again show that it is not possible to draw an absolute boundary between the sentence and the word. Sentence formation proceeds in a way that depends on the primary segments of the underlying configuration. This always depends on the particular restrictions that determine and organize the primary aspects of the underlying whole impression and thus the primary constituents of language; these restrictions precede the actual construction of sentences. Words divide a sentence only into those segments that are relatively stable in that they regularly form parts of other sentences and maintain similar forms. From this derives the relationship of word form to sentence form which can become a further criterion for the distinction between word and sentence.

Depending on the situation, a sentence may be formed in a variety of ways using the same words. In each instance certain words are given different positions. Within the single word, however, the arrangement of the parts is less changeable. Thus the formation of words is generally more constant, while the formation of sentences is a more variable characteristic of language. However, this characteristic is somewhat dependent upon the nature of particular languages, and the distinction between word and sentence always remains indefinite. In some

---

phonetic speech, and on the other, he includes the condition of hearing and understanding. He thus says, "A sentence is a modulated closed articulation by which the hearer is asked to test a relatively closed apperceptive (interrelated) sequential formation of a meaningful state of affairs recognizable as correct by the speaker." (O. Dittrich, *Philosophische Studien*, Vol. 19, p. 93 ff., & *Grundzüge der Sprachpsychologie*, I, 87 ff.) I do not misjudge the practical motives which are the basis for this narrowing of the previous definition. Nonetheless, I think that it is not permissible from a psychological point of view to limit the general definition of the sentence to the phonetic level of language, since even in sign language complete sentences are possible in the psychological sense. I also consider the inclusion of the hearer—as well as that of a recognition of "correct" meaning—to be an unreliable restriction of the notion. Even though the conjunction of speaking and hearing is psychologically indispensable for the initial formations of sentences in phonetic speech, once linguistic thought is there it is no longer bound to this requirement. A universal sentence definition must be as applicable to the sentence formed in solitude as to that formed in conversation. No less, the "recognition of correctness" places a restriction on cognition which to me seems unnecessary. See here the observations about the relationship of speech to expressive gestures in *Die Sprache*, Vol. 1, Chap. 1, p. 43.

languages sentences have a compact and fairly stable composition that is usually found only in words.

It should be noted that the conditions determining sentence and word formation fall within two limiting cases. One extreme is the case of the isolating languages where the formation of a sentence to represent a cognitive configuration is carried to the point of such segmentation that words cannot be further subdivided, and the analytic process is accomplished by extensive dissection into words. The other extreme case is that of the highly agglutinative languages in which word and sentence are totally identical, or where the word carrying the main content of the sentence undergoes only minor supplementation from added words. Yet both extremes are still very close to one another with respect to the underlying structure of the sentence. Their essential difference is that the segments into which the sentence totality is sequentially arranged are clearly separated in one case while in the other case they remain thoroughly bound up with one another.

. . . .

2. Constituents of Sentences

2.1 Subject and Predicate in the Simple Declarative Sentence. Among the unfortunate results that came about through the mixture of logical, grammatical, and psychological points of view, there is hardly one that has brought more confusion to the understanding of the real facts of language than the transfer of the logical components of the judgment to the division of grammatical constituents in sentences. . . .

Since the declarative sentence can be viewed logically as a judgment, the concepts of *subject* and *predicate* may be directly applied to it. One can then view the relation between subject and predicate as the expression of the fundamental principle in the structuring of the mental configuration underlying the sentence. Because this structure is a binary one the subject and predicate designate the major segments into which the expression divides. And thus these constituents remain distinct in a simple sentence.

But how can this hold for other sentences such as exclamatory and interrogative sentences, which are not simple affirmative propositions? And what relations do the principal segments of the propositional sentence have to one another if the sentence undergoes any grammatical transformations that leave its sense unchanged? If I transform the sentence *Caesar crossed the Rubicon* into *the Rubicon was crossed by Caesar,* is then the subject *Caesar* changed into the object? Does the former object, the *Rubicon,* become the subject? Or further, if I say *The crossing of the Rubicon was successfully accomplished by Caesar,* has the original predicate now changed into the subject?

2.2 Dominating Concepts in the Sentence. . . . . We can most accurately conform to the usual psychological terms by considering the dominating impression to be that part of the sentence standing in the center of attention during speech. Here there is an important characteristic regarding the logical categories of subject and predicate. It is that they don't divide merely into two sentence segments in consciousness, one dominating and the other relatively diminished. Rather, several further gradations are often found. Frequently three are found. This can be seen in the simple sentence, "Today is my birthday." It may divide into only a more and a less stressed member (*today* and *my birthday*). But this can also be true of the second of these parts so that either *my* or *birthday* is relatively more stressed.

With that we come to another point. The theory of the so-called psychological subject considers in a narrow way that word order is the product of this gradation of subjective emphasis. It is true that the sentence part standing in the focus of attention frequently claims the first position in the ordering of the sentence constituents. Very often, therefore, dominating concepts are followed by subordinated ones where only gradations of this sort occur. Indeed, this ordering appears with the signs of gesture language (see *Die Sprache,* Chap. 2, p. 216 ff.). But in the case of phonetic language there are other forces that work in a different way to determine sentence structure, namely the application of determinate rules of positioning in addition to the logical aspects of sentence structure. Language processes of stress and tonal modulation are still other forms of expression that can vary the emphasis on sentence parts. They are primarily able to bring about the correct cognitive emphasis on sentence constituents according to the logical or so-called deep grammatical base which cannot prevail over word positioning when that has been associatively fixed. This occurs in the simple sentence, but occurs to a much higher degree in exclamatory and interrogative sentences, because for these the general rule that the dominating concept always claims the first position in speech does not apply. [At this point Wundt discusses numerous syntactic structures such as eliptical constructions, verb phrases, pronoun constructions, particle placement, etc.—A.L.B.]

3. Predicate Sentence Forms

3.1 Simple Predicative Sentences. . . . . We may classify as the grammatically simplest sentences all those that consist of only one assertion with a single subject and predicate, although either subject or predicate or both may divide into further segments. The criterion for the simple sentence is thus not the number of concepts contained in the sentence, but the basic unity of subject and predicate. To describe sentence structure let us designate the whole mental configuration symbolically as *G*, [for *Gesamtvorstellung*], the subject and predicate as *A* and *B*, and the possible other segmentations of these principal parts as *a, b, c, d,* etc. Thus all forms of such binary-segmented simple sentences are enclosed groupings. In addition, nothing is changed if either the subject or predicate or both consist of several impressions copulatively connected to one another, as long as these form a unified segment that was represented in the original cognitive configuration. In the same way no substantial change of the relations is involved if in the growing number of parts or secondary structures many specifics are but dimly discerned in the original total impression. The closed nature of the structure necessarily implies that they all be represented in it beforehand. In the present psychological sense every closed thought content is a simultaneous one, which does not exclude a varying clarity and opacity of the individual parts which change in clearness from moment to moment during the utterance of a sentence. As principal types of simple sentence with varying intricacies of structure consider the following three. The third could be represented by numerous other modifications.

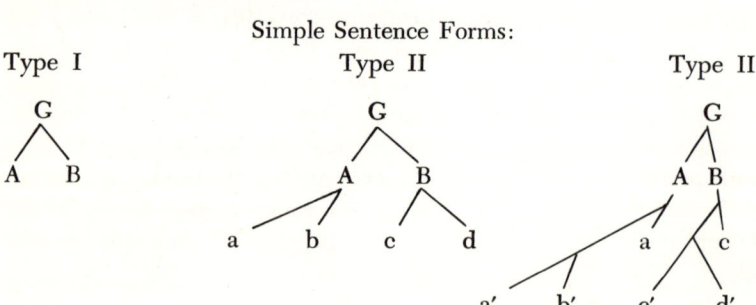

3.2 Complex Predicative Sentences. The complex sentence differs from the simple one in that it consists of several simple sentences related to each other in a way similar to the parts of the simple sentence, so that the whole combination forms a new sentence unity as a result. The simplest and most common structure is here again the binary one in which the members are not sentence segments but are independent sentences. The main distinctions among these complex forms depend on the strength of their internal connections and correspondingly on the nature of the relationship that joins the constituent sentences to one another.*

. . . .

4. The Sequential Ordering of Sentence Parts

4.1 Typical Forms of Word Positioning. In the sequencing of individual words in a sentence as well as in the ordering of the various constituents of complex sentences (the main and the subordinate clauses) we observe certain regularities. These vary partly from one language to another and partly within one single language. The reason for such variations are usually linked to conditions of historical development whose psychological significance is obscure, or where only vague suppositions are possible. This influence of an historical nature whose causes can no longer be traced appears clearly in those cases where syntactic structures that express psychological relations have different forms in otherwise related languages. Here we have no reason to assume a corresponding difference in the underlying psychological nature of the relation in question. Thus in German an adjective attributively related to a noun regularly precedes it. In the romance languages the position is variable; sometimes orderings have become established that are similar to the German, and sometimes they are dissimilar. Consider the expressions for "a poor man," which have the same word order in German (*ein armer Mensch*) and in French (*un pauvre homme*). These are not more closely related in their inner

---

* Later in the original text (Vol. 2, pp. 339, 355) Wundt diagramed more complex structures where other G terms may be reintroduced within the same sentence at lower points in the tree-diagram. He also asserted that the best way to uncover the true nature of the relations that hold between constituents is to transform the sentence into various other forms (e.g., active to passive, etc.) thus to observe how the relations and constituents behave under these variations.—A.L.B.

thought form than are the German and the French phrases for "a very lovable woman" (*eine sehr liebenswüdige Frau* and *une femme très aimable*) which have dissimilar word orderings. In such cases linguistic tradition exerts a force, and a consistent particular sequential ordering appears to be the result of such tradition.

Two classical languages, Greek and Latin, offer better examples of the dependence of word order on psychological motives, for in these languages the force of tradition on the positioning of words is less. Word position is much freer. Thus it can more easily follow momentary prevailing psychological themes. It is possible, then, to test in an experimental way the psychological significance of various word orderings by virtue of this capacity for free variation. In German we can express the sentence *Romulus gründete Rom* (Romulus founded Rome) in this one way, unless we wish to undertake changes in the word forms or make use of helping pronouns—such as *Rom wurde von Romulus gegründet,* or *Es gründete Romulus Rom,* and so on. In Latin on the other hand, the three words that compose this sentence can be used in every possible permutation of their positions. Thus we derive the following six sentence forms where we may call the first three the main types (1, 2, 3), and the three following ones secondary types (1a, 2a, 3a):

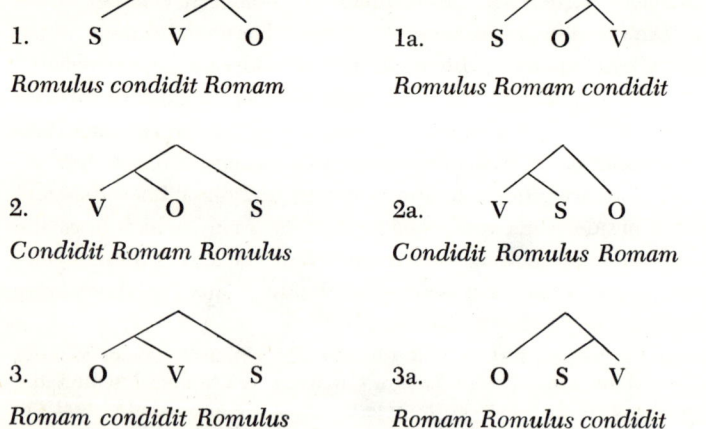

1. S V O
Romulus condidit Romam

1a. S O V
Romulus Romam condidit

2. V O S
Condidit Romam Romulus

2a. V S O
Condidit Romulus Romam

3. O V S
Romam condidit Romulus

3a. O S V
Romam Romulus condidit

The significance of the differences among these particular simple sentences may be seen when we examine the corresponding interrogative sentences to which each constitutes a reply. We can then see that the three principal types are answers to questions whose object in each case is one of the three concepts contained in the simple sentence. If the question concerns the subject of the sentence, then type 1 is the appropriate form: "Who was Romulus?" answer: "Romulus was the founder of Rome" (*Romulus condidit Romam*). If on the other hand the verbal predicate is the object of the question, then type 2 results: "What happened then?" answer: "The founding of Rome by Romulus" (*Condidit Romam Romulus*). If, finally, the question concerns the object of the statement, then type 3 results: "What was founded?" Answer: "Rome" (*Romam condidit Romulus*).

. . . .

4.2 *The Principle of Placing Emphasized Concepts First.* If one looks for changes in the sense of the utterance that correspond to changes in the above six permutations of the three sentence constituents, it is obvious that the sentential relational structures are of an identical nature in each case. They can be analyzed under the general principle that where word positioning is free, not bound by a hard and fast traditional rule, etc., then the words follow each other according to the degree of emphasis on the concepts. The strongest emphasis is naturally on the concept that forms the main content of the statement. It is also first in the sentence. In many cases it is the subject of the sentence, in others it can be the verbal predicate or the object.

The psychological significance of this law is easy to understand; word positions do not first appear in the center of consciousness as they are added to the sentence, but rather in a sense they are there from the beginning in the preceding whole impression as a less apparent psychological theme that has a determining influence on attention. The theme is successively apperceived in an order that reflects its emphasized aspects. The speaker confronts his cognitive configuration just as a perceiver faces a complex external object where he first perceives those parts that make the strongest impression on his attention, so long as there are no other distracting events. Where there is free word ordering the principle of positioning is simply a special application of the general psychological principle of the *successive apperception of aspects of a whole according to their proportionate effect on cognition.*

. . . .

5. Inner Linguistic Form

Wilhelm von Humboldt introduced the concept of "inner linguistic form" into the study of language. He returns to this notion repeatedly in his general discussion of linguistic problems.[3] According to him, inner linguistic form is related to outer phonetic form as, in his manner of speaking, the mind relates to the body. It is the "intellectual side" of language activity that dominates language using phonetic form for its ends and working through the "laws of perception, thought, and feeling." A natural classification of languages, or the solution to the problem of whether such a classification is at all possible, seems to him feasible only on the basis of a closer examination of inner linguistic form. He claims further that one could probably even expect that inner linguistic form must be generally relatable to the endless variability of phonetic forms since it comes from one and the same mental nature of man. But to this point he replies that the intellect can surely choose different means for the same end. And in addition to intellect, the imagination and emotion may be active in language and may reveal mental characteristics peculiar to certain nationalities.

Humboldt's original concept of inner linguistic form did not go beyond these uncertain general claims, since on the whole he wanted to give more of an indication of a task to be solved in the future than of an already carefully defined notion. But in place of his examples another viewpoint has appeared in the comparative study of language diversity that stands disturbingly in the way of the attempt to get closer to his notion. The problem is that an *ideal* form has been associated with concepts of inner linguistic form. This ideal would supposedly yield the most exact expression of thought and would be attained to greater or lesser degree by different languages. Such a description might have been appropriate enough at a time when ideas of universal and perpetual laws of thought were more deeply rooted than today. However, in application to real language this notion has come to imply that some particular form of language, for example Greek, is taken to be the model by which other languages are measured.[4] Recently, this was often related to the attempt to distinguish languages according to their degree of form or formlessness.

Now the concept of inner language form, in the original sense

---

[3] See especially *Ueber die Verschiedenheit des menschlichen Sprachbaues*, section 11, *Werke*, Vol. VI, p. 92 ff., as well as the discussion of comparative language study, *Werke*, Vol. III, p. 241 ff.

[4] *Ueber die Verschiedenheit*, op. cit., p. 96.

established by Humboldt, is surely a correct and indeed a necessary one that we are led to by the study of the structural and relational characteristics within a language. But if this is to be a useful concept, it must be freed from the corollary linked with it ever since Humboldt's time—that there is one ideal language by which other individual languages are to be measured. Moreover, just as the outer form of the language can only appear as an actually existing language, so the inner form implies only the actual psychological characteristics and relations that bring about specific outer forms by their effects. The concept of inner form is in this sense by all means attached to that of outer linguistic form, and is just as concrete and real, for it is impossible to understand anything else by it except the complex of psychological relations, particular principles of association and apperception, which become apparent in the construction of word forms, the distinction of parts of speech, and the division and structuring of sentence constituents.

. . . .

As here conceived, the inner linguistic structure has an immediate bearing on the surface structure of language. The former is simply understood as the psychological themes that bring about the external form as their result. Of all the things that belong to the external side of language, only the phonetic aspect is relatively separated from these psychological motives, or at least it is only indirectly related to them. Similarly, on the cognitive side this is true of the conceptual array and the related processes of the construction of meaning. Inasmuch as these are the shared cognitive structures encompassing the mental content of a speech community they are the cognitive material that will be formed into language. And the internal linguistic constructions must naturally be adequate for the task, but still they are only indirectly related to the mental content. The store of concepts and the formation of meaning are more ultimate conditions and are not themselves the immediate terms of the internal language form. Forms of word organization and the relational structure of sentences constitute the internal structure of language.

It may be tempting at this point to begin making comparisons between Wundt's writings and recent developments in linguistics. But that would leave at least half of our story untold. We shall therefore delay modern comparisons until more of the early work is presented.

Wundt's psycholinguistics was a major part of the background for early psychological investigations of language performance. But the good rapport between psychologists and linguists that began in the 1870s was doomed and Wundt figured highly in this turn of events. One of the monumental arguments that should be cited in any historical account of psycholinguistics concerned the nature of the sentence and sentence production. It was an extended dispute between Wundt and the philologist Paul. We have already mentioned Paul in connection with the *Junggrammatiker* movement (Chapter 1). His major work was *Prinzipien der Sprachgeschichte* (Principles of language history) which went through five editions from 1880 to 1920. As that book's title illustrates, Paul's fundamental principle was that linguistics should be historical. His book became the standard work on methods of historical linguistics. As mentioned before, Paul had great faith in Herbartian mathematical psychology, which he described as "the science of the relation borne by ideas to each other." Paul and Wundt might be classified together because they both held to a psychological interpretation of language, but Paul differed in relying heavily on the notions of *analogy* and *association* as the principles of language evolution, language learning, and language performance in general.

The controversy, which generated much heat at least in German academic circles, centered on the nature of sentence production. It may have begun as early as 1880 when both men first published their basic views about language, and it continued off and on until nearly 1920—the date of Wundt's death and the last revision of Paul's book.*

According to Paul, a sentence reflected the association of two or more ideas in the mind of a speaker. In contrast to Wundt, he viewed the verbal expression as being isomorphic to the mental constructs. Speech production was thus possible through the formation of associations between individual speech elements

---

* The first published expression of Wundt's opposition to Paul and the *Junggrammatikers*, of which I am aware, appears in *Philosophische Studien*, 1886, Vol. 3.

(words) and individual mental elements (ideas). However, Paul's difficulty was in the many problems of sentence analysis, such as the effects of word order, that were presented to him as contradictions of his explanations. Paul's position was often designated as the *synthetic* theory of sentence production. Wundt's was known as the *analytic* theory.

Paul studied problems quite similar to those of Wundt, as we shall see in the following selection. This writing actually appeared before Wundt's *Die Sprache,* and many of Wundt's ideas were based on direct reactions to it. Paul's later replies to Wundt will be cited below.

Paul immediately became popular in England and America. Henry Strong, a philologist at University College, Liverpool, hastily prepared a translation. The resulting English text, titled *Principles of language history* (1880), was highly imperfect and in places incomprehensible. It contained the English words but also the idiosyncracies of German syntax. Negative reaction to the inferior quality of the work prompted Strong to undertake a corrected edition almost immediately; however, the results were not much better. Strong then collaborated with W. S. Logeman, a philologist at the University of Utrecht, and B. I. Wheeler, a philologist at Cornell University, in what they described as a "rewriting" of Paul's notions for an English audience. It was titled *The history of language* (1891). The text follows Paul quite closely and is very readable. The nonreader of German who wishes to study Paul would probably do better with this book than with Strong's earlier word-for-word translation. The last edition (1920) of Paul's book has been revived and was reprinted in Germany in 1966. His basic ideas remained essentially unchanged in the later editions.

What follows is a new translation of a small portion of Paul's book covering his fundamental conception of syntax in terms of psychological associationism.

HERMANN PAUL · *Synthesis Rather than Analysis*

The Sentence as the Expression of the Combination of Several Ideas

All linguistic activity involves the formation of sentences. The sentence is the linguistic expression, or symbol, which indicates that several ideas or groups of ideas have been joined in the mind of the speaker. It is also the means for reproducing the same linking of ideas in the mind of a listener.

. . . .

The way that ideas may be connected to each other is determined to some degree by the frequency and intensity of the events involved. This applies to the methods of combination as well as to individual ideas. Speech does not need to be equivalent to the psychical relation as it exists in the mind of the speaker, and as it is produced in the mind of the hearer, because it may be less definite.

Every sentence consists of at least two parts. These are related to each other not as equivalents but are distinguished by their function. They are termed subject and predicate. Such grammatical categories refer to a psychological and a logical relation. No doubt we have to distinguish between the psychological and the grammatical subject or predicate because the two are often different, as we will see later in detail. Yet it remains true that grammatical relations are built up solely on psychological foundations.

The psychological subject is the idea that is first present in the consciousness of the speaker; then a second idea joins this and is the psychological predicate. The subject, according to Steinthal, is the apprehending portion. The predicate is the apprehended. Von der Gabelentz[1] is correct in defining both from the viewpoint of the hearer.

SOURCE. Hermann Paul, *Prinzipien der Sprachgeschichte*. Halle: Niemeyer, 1886, Chap. VI, "Die syntaktischen grundverhältnisse." Translated by A. L. Blumenthal.

[1] *Zeitschrift für Völkerpsychologie*, Vol. VI, p. 378.

The psychological subject, according to him, is whatever the speaker wishes the hearer to think about and attend to. The psychological predicate is whatever he wishes him to think about it. Such a definition of the predicate may be falsely restricted to a conception still current in our common grammars. But we must strictly follow the principle that one idea always gets joined in consciousness with another idea.

. . . .

The claim that there must be at least two constituents to make up a sentence seems contradicted by the fact that we find sentences of only a single word or of a group forming a single unit. This is explained by the fact that one member of the sentence (as a rule the logical subject) may be taken for granted with no expression in speech. It may be present in what has been said before. In particular, we observe that in the course of conversation this element often must be found in the words of the other speaker. For example, a reply often consists of a predicate alone; the subject is either contained in the question, or the whole question is the logical subject: (1) *"Who struck you?"*—*"Max."* (2) *"Was it you?"*—*"Yes"* (*No, Certainly, Surely, Of course*). Similarly, remarks like the following may serve as the predicate for a sentence spoken by another: *very possibly, strange enough, no wonder, nonsense,* etc. . . . In other cases, it is the situation or object of perception common to speaker and hearer that forms the logical subject, and attention may even be more effectively directed to it by gestures. This object of perception may be the speaker or the listener, *e.g., your most obedient servant; welcome; why so sad?* Besides these we have many exclamations of astonishment and alarm and appeals for aid like, *fire! thieves! murder! help!* or challenges like, *Friend or foe?* or questions like, *Straight ahead? Right or left?* . . . .

In the case of sentences that consist of a single member as far as mere expression is concerned, the psychological predicate of the speaker becomes the subject for the hearer. The man who sees a house on fire calls out *"Fire!"* and this is the subject. On the other hand, the common idea *fire* is the predicate for the man who hears *"Fire!"* before he himself sees a fire. The idea of fire is the subject, and the situation is the predicate. Of course, sentences also occur where what is uttered is the subject and the situation is the predicate for both speaker and hearer. Suppose, for instance, that someone sees a child in danger. He naturally alerts the person entrusted with its safety merely with *"The child!"* Here an object alone is denoted. Attention is called to it as a logical subject. The predicate, on the other hand, must be inferred by the person addressed from what he sees when he attends to whatever is named.

. . . .

If we define the sentence as the outward indication of a linking of two ideas, then negative sentences seem to contradict this since they denote a separation. However, such a separation finds no expression unless the ideas in question have first occurred in the consciousness of the speaker. We may define the negative simple sentence as expressing the fact that an attempt to establish a relation between two ideas has failed. And further, the negative sentence is of later development than the positive one. Most likely negation is everywhere a very special case of linguistic expression. One might, however, very well imagine that negative sentences were formed at a primitive stage of language development in which the negative sense is indicated by nothing other than stress and accompanying gestures. . . .

We customarily regard the affirmative sentence as the normal one. The "demand" sentence is at least basic if not more primitive. The earliest sentences uttered by children have reference to their needs —the very earliest of course consist only of a single word. They express demands or affirmations that indicate a need that must be satisfied. It may be assumed that such circumstances held for the earliest stage of speech development. Thus once no special device was needed to form demand sentences. The simple connection of subject and predicate sufficed in this case as well as for affirmative sentences. Voice stress was once the only means of indicating the difference. Even now we use demand sentences frequently where the demand feature is in no other way present. These are sentences without a verb such as, *Eyes right! Attention! Hats off! This way! All aboard!* . . . . etc. Then there are sentences composed of a single member, as far as their expression in language goes, such as: *Hush! Quick! Slow! Forward!* . . . . etc. Demand sentences occur especially in this primitive form. As a rule this does not hold for most sentences. It is owing to this contradiction that these sentences are immediately recognized by us as demands.

Still there are instances that may permit either interpretation, such as *"Fire!"* as a cry of alarm and *"Fire!"* as a command.

. . . .

The subject-predicate relation in the broad sense indicated above is the relation from which other syntactic conditions arise. The one exception is the copulative connection of several elements into a single sentence constituent. This connection may in the case of developed languages be denoted by a particle, but mere collocation of a series suffices. Thus it is not surprising that in a primitive stage of language it was possible to dispense with any special linguistic expression for coupling.

All other means of extending sentences are brought about by recurrences of the subject-predicate relation. Two main cases may be distinguished. First, two elements may join with a third, that is, two subjects attach to a single predicate or two predicates to a single subject. This may be represented by the formula $(a+(b)+c)$. Secondly, subject and predicate may be placed in relation to a further member. This is represented by the formula $(a+b)+c$. The further member may of course be compounded again.

In the 1909 edition of his *Prinzipien* Paul added a preface that contained a statement on Wundt's writings. One important charge against Wundt's notions was that he had underrated the principle of speech formation by analogy (see Chapter One). In Wundt's view this principle had little explanatory value. The mere occurrence of a new language sequence that is analogous to an older one does not explain how it came about. It might be the reflection of some deeper process to which the notion of *analogy* in no way makes reference.

Paul sought evidence in the performance of the *hearer*. In this case, he maintained, sentence understanding clearly arises according to his view since the one who listens to speech can only receive words consecutively. But Wundt argued that the mind of the hearer is just as active in transforming and creating as the mind of the speaker, and that a listener arrives at comprehension by matching and correcting his own whole cognitions according to the cues the speaker provides. The outer system of associational processes provides the mental material that the inner system—the apperceptive, constructive process—organizes into a "total impression." Yet the two systems work simultaneously, sometimes in conflict with each other, such as when misperception or misunderstanding occurs. There are also "schemata of apprehension"—the anticipation of a sentence that may be derived from a single initial word, or there may be the recognition of a sentence-encompassing grammatical relation before it is fully expressed, such as may be signaled by the *case* of a noun or the *form* of a verb.

The following is Wundt's explicit reaction to Paul's explanation of sentence production.

If one compares Paul's definition to those of the ancient grammarians, it is immediately apparent that he revives the oldest of these which views the sentence simply as a chaining of words, and in drawing the psychological state from the speech act, or substituting the idea for the word, his definition is seemingly rendered more sensible. Certainly this transfer to the psychic realm is based on the justified notion that descriptions of the sentence as mere orderings of words is much too superficial. On the other hand, there is the question of whether much is gained if one substitutes the linking of ideas for the linking of words. Whether I express the twelve signs of the zodiac in words or think of them as concepts, in either case they too are joined to a whole, but they are no more a sentence in one case than the other. Paul's definition would also fit any random, purely mechanical association of concepts.

In one respect it must be admitted that the old grammatical formulation is superior to this newer psychological one, namely, because it is a simple external one; it at least does not make false assumptions concerning what is going on in the mind of the speaker. The psychological (Paul's) definition does this when it characterizes the sentence as "a linking of ideas" and thus necessarily implies that the connected concepts in the sentence existed independently prior to the sentence. If I define the sentence, "The grass is green," as a chain of words, then this description is not deep, but it is at least not wrong. If on the other hand I define it as a chain of concepts, then this definition is surely wrong. For the ideas *grass* and *green* did not first exist separately from each other so that I subsequently connected them to form a whole. Rather, they are both present simultaneously at the outset. The image of *grass* is given together with the quality *green* in the immediate perception. In order to create the connection one does not need the sentence at all.*

Wundt's refutations of Paul's notions are essentially reactions to the Herbartian psychology that had influenced them. In this regard Wundt also objected to the simple *dualism* expressed here. Further, he felt that the taxonomic approach, sometimes based on analogies to biology, was too weak for the phenomena it must treat. And finally, he believed that the omission of any serious discussion of volitional processes was another weakness. His own analysis of the language skill included volition as an important factor in the process.

A common response among linguists early in the twentieth century was to react as though Wundt's intrusions into their field was a threat. The high priest of psychology was claiming linguistics as part of his own discipline. Wundt was a challenge in another way: his data were often drawn from exotic and distant languages. This freedom in dealing with non-Indo-European languages was, ironically, somewhat rejected by many philologists of that day. Paul's examples had been restricted to the Indo-European group. Philologists sometimes held these to be the only ones worth consideration for making basic and important generalizations; the reason was, perhaps, that they were the best understood languages by those scholars.

Most language scholars soon abandoned the argument between Paul and Wundt and followed the opinion of Berthold Delbrück. In his widely read book, *Grundfragen der Sprachforschung; mit rücksicht auf W. Wundt's Sprachpsychologie* (Basic questions in language research—in view of Wundt's psycholinguistics), 1901, he argued that it makes no difference what theory of psychology a linguist follows because linguistics, the study of abstract formal systems, is independent of psychology. As this statement shows, Delbrück was not closely involved with the

* *Die Sprache*, Book 2, 1912, pp. 237–238.

work and views of the *Junggrammatikers*. His review of Wundt was quite laudatory and gentlemanly—in contrast to other exchanges that were occurring in the journals of that day.

Wundt's reply to Delbrück, later that year, also took the form of a short book: *Sprachgeschichte und Sprachpsychologie; mit rücksicht auf B. Delbrück's Grundfragen* (Language history and psycholinguistics—in view of Delbrück's basic questions), 1901. The reply was also quite warm and was thankful for Delbrück's accurate and perceptive account. Wundt then reasserted several strong claims about linguistics and philology, namely that whenever a linguist presents language as a mental process and attempts to explain the changes in language by performance factors, he has thereby become a psychologist. And further, those linguists who treat sentences as the outward form of the psychological judgment also deal in psychology. The way language is acquired by the child might be important for language theory as well, according to Wundt, but is seldom taken into account by linguists. In America generations later and far removed, such issues once again produced monumental interchanges between linguists and psychologists during the 1960s. The interchange between Wundt and Delbrück has not been completely forgotten like much of the literature of that earlier period. Recently, it has been reviewed by Erwin Esper.*

There were several linguists in prebehaviorist America, particularly of the Yale school, who were notably influenced by Wundt. This can be seen in the following American works: Hans Oertal, *Lectures on the science of language* (1901); E. P. Morris, *Methods and principles of latin syntax* (1907); A. D. Sheffield, *Grammar and thinking* (1912); and Leonard Bloomfield, *Introduction to the study of language* (1914). The latter work must not be confused with Bloomfield's 1933 book which is based on the radically different behaviorist orientation.

Another important Wundtian critic, whose background differed from Paul's, was Anton Marty of the University of Prague. Marty was one of the few early figures known strictly as a psycholinguist (a "*Sprachpsycholog*"). He had been a student of Franz

---

* Erwin A. Esper, *Mentalism and objectivism in linguistics* (New York: Elsevier, 1968).

Bentano who had an important influence on psychological thought during Wundt's formative years.

Brentano's masterpiece *Psychologie vom empirischen Standpunkte* (Psychology from the empirical standpoint) 1874, was important in convincing philosophers that psychology could be a *science* of the mind. Yet the notion of psychology as an experimental science was not proposed. Nor did Brentano's student, Marty, ever undertake experimental investigations. Brentano's viewpoint was quite evidently that of neoscholasticism. As a former priest, he had the bias of the Catholic theology and an immense acquaintance with Aristotle and Thomas Aquinas. He wrestled with the medieval problem of "Can the mind know itself?" but did so in relatively modern terms. His belief in the rationality of men led him to the affirmative answer. Therefore he settled on the method of self-observation and introspection, and on observations of another's experience as shown through speech or other forms of self-expression. To Brentano, the application of experimental techniques or of physiological studies was a hopelessly tedious and indirect way to understand the human mind. Brentano's technique was the application of formal logic to immediate experience. Concerning this procedure for research on language and cognition Wundt differed very little from Brentano. We shall delay our discussion of Wundt's attitude toward experimental psycholinguistics until we consider the work of Karl Bühler.

Brentano was a phenomenologist. But unlike Wundt, his basic reality was that of external objects instead of immediate internal experience. Brentano's psychology was the study of how man makes mental reference to external objects. His major contributions were in the area of logic; and we could well cite the historian Brett's understatement that "the experimental psychologist is inclined to regard him (Brentano) as reactionary."

Brentano's "psychic act" is what psychologists have often studied as *judgment*. Usually we describe the simplest judgment as taking the form, "A is B," where B says something about A. But Brentano finds that the consciousness of A as A is itself the most fundamental judgment; thus we have here a more microscopic analysis of conscious experience. As a direct result, Marty later disagreed with Wundt about the nature of one-word sentences.

In Marty's view a single word cannot reflect a subject-predicate judgment, but instead reflects the judgment that consists only of a single element. His approach to sentence production resembles Paul's in being more "synthetic" than "analytic."

In his linguistics, Marty remained fairly close to some of the ideas of Humboldt and was fundamentally concerned with linguistic universals, perhaps more so than Wundt. He argued that Wundt's system improperly conceives of the organization of language as a part of the psychological process. Such a distinction is the basis of the following comment, which appeared in Marty's essay, *Satz und Wort* (Sentence and word), 1914:

> We shall see ... that predication is not tied to "verbal" expression, and that the so-called verb is not class-structured according to the semantic viewpoint but rather according to the distinction of external and internal language form. Further, when Wundt posits "an essentially different form of thinking" for the nominal and verbal modes of expression and even insists that "the increasing predominance of the predicate sentence form (i.e. the verbal sentence form) is one of the greatest revolutions in the history of human thought", it is only based on a transfer of language peculiarities to the thought process.

But Wundt did make a sharp distinction between the psychological events that determine a sentence content and the factors that determine its acoustic form. Wundt sought the universal principles of human language in the psychological characteristics that govern it. Marty, in agreement with the seventeenth c and eighteenth c century ideal of a "universal grammar and philosophy of language," sought universality in the formal structures of language, the tradition of scholasticism passed on by Brentano. Yet Marty's works show that in the final analysis his primary recourse was to modern psychology. He indeed began with the assertion that the meaning of linguistic forms is concerned both with the expression of the psychological states of the speaker and the stimulation of appropriate reactions in the listener. His writings on language are now little known. They were once heavily criticized for misinterpretation of Wundt. Nevertheless, he is of interest here because he replied in great detail to Wundt, and especially because of his role in initiating other reactions to Wundt.

Marty first found scholarly recognition with his 1876 volume on the origin of human language: *Ueber den Ursprung der Sprache*. He listed and described all the theories of language origin since antiquity and then classified them as either *nativist* or *empiricist*, that is, as relying on either innate causes or environmental causes. The classifications did not escape the criticism of Wundt who, for one thing, had come to regard nativism versus empiricism as a misunderstood opposition in psychology. Wundt described his own viewpoint as "genetic"—in a way a compromise as mentioned above (we shall return to this in Chapter Three concerning language acquisition). Most of Marty's subsequent writings took the form of polemics directed either at Wundt or Steinthal. He is a generally unrecognized but significant influence in the movement of a group of German empiricist psychologists (mostly Brentano's students) in opposition to Wundt. Erwin Esper (1968, cited above) considered Marty's writings to be "protobehavioristic."

Again, Wundt considered Marty as having too much faith in the "reality" of the perceived external world. In his rambling and vague *Untersuchungen* (Investigations) of 1908, Marty makes a number of notable errors in his description of Wundt. One is the equating of Wundt's notions with those of Steinthal (note the differences cited in Chapter One). Marty also made the distinction between inner and outer language form, but for him inner form was simplistic associations between sound and meaning. Similar to Paul, Marty also left volition out of his system in contrast to Wundt.*

It is apparent in Marty's writings that he either had little understanding of the fundamentals of Wundt's psychology (such as the distinction between passive and active apperception) or that he did not consider these notions seriously. The following excerpt is taken from his essay *Satz und Wort* which appeared shortly after his death. It is in part a critique of Wundt's categorization of certain sentence types. Wundt's discussion of sentence types had not been as significant for his psycholinguistics as it was for a new generation of psycholinguists of which Marty

---

* For a more detailed description of the three-way arguments between Wundt, Paul, and Marty see Otto Broens, *Darstellung und Würdigung des sprachphilosophischen Gegensatzes zwischen Paul, Wundt und Marty* (Betzdorf: Ebner, 1913).

was an early member. Sentence classification schemes were soon to be greeted with a new enthusiasm by several of Brentano's students and by other later psychologists who called themselves "functionalists." Although, partly because of his confused and convoluted writing style, Marty's writings had little direct effect, some younger psychologists who studied them became much more prominent.

ANTON MARTY · *Sentence Types and Transformations*

Wundt contends that an accurate description of differences in sentence forms must be derived from basic psychic functions (as was done by the early scholastics). This leads to three types: (1) the exclamatory sentence, which he subdivides into sentences of emotion and of desire, (2) the declarative sentence, and (3) the interrogative sentence.

The first two apparently correspond to a classification of speech into declarations and into attention provoking utterances. But how does Wundt arrive at the third? Is it basically as different from the first two as they are from each other? Wundt does not seem to claim this, though the foregoing leads one to expect it. Instead, he seems to assign it a medial position. In fact in *Die Sprache* II, p. 264, he says that the interrogative sentence is generally "a transformed declarative sentence." But on page 254 he says again that an asking person wants a declaration about something; thus the question includes a wish. If I understand correctly, the relationship that the interrogative sentence still has to the declarative sentence (in contrast to sentences expressing desire) is that each question involves and presupposes declarations.

This must be admitted without doubt. But it certainly does not establish a special relationship between interrogative and declarative sentences that cannot also include sentences of emotion or desire (which Wundt distinguishes from declaratives as "exclamatory sen-

SOURCE. Anton Marty, excerpts from *Satz und Wort* (1914) (Reichenberg: Stiepel, 1925). Translated by Jim Lyon and A. L. Blumenthal.

tences"). Even an imperative sentence (even emotional exclamations) implicitly express judgment (*"What good fortune!" "Come here!"*). From a semantic viewpoint I can only categorize interrogative sentences as sentences of desire and as imperatives; I cannot distinguish them as a third class separate from the others. When Wundt maintains elsewhere (*Die Sprache*, II, p. 132) that they are distinct because declarative and imperative sentences contain expressions of opinion and volition this is an artificial contrast constructed between a question and a command by confusing the points of view necessary for division, as I have shown elsewhere.[1] A question is a challenge to react with correctness. But so is a command. If one asks for its meaning, the answer is that it means the person addressed should do something. The command also expresses the will of the speaker. But the question does so as well. It expresses the desire or will of X to determine something.

Therefore, I see no reason for a triple division. For support one might call on the three punctuation marks used to close sentences: the period, exclamation mark, and question mark. This is indeed what Wundt does in *Die Sprache*, II, 249. But apparently his excessive trust in the parallelism between the symbol and the symbolized again deceives him. . . . It is sufficient if there is a so-called difference in content. Consider the question *"Isn't two times two equal to four?"* Can this be called a question or rather a declaration which merely assumes the linguistic form of a question? Or if I give the polite command, *"Mr. X and Mr. Y are requested to meet with me tomorrow,"* and thus do not use the emphasis or punctuation of a command but use a period instead, does this make it a declaration? Only the shading has changed; the meaning remains the same.

This change in shading is the element of truth in Wundt's remarks on such transformations (*Die Sprache*, II, p. 217). At the end of his discussion of the relations between the three sentence forms he says,

> Just as these linguistic devices reveal relationships among the various types of sentences which ultimately have their source in cognitive states underlying them, so can the one sentence form be completely transformed into another without producing a basic change in the fundamental intention of the sentence (especially in highly developed languages). This occurs most frequently when a wish or command is transformed into a question:

[1] A. Marty, *Untersuchungen*, p. 377 ff.

"Come to me!" and *"Do you want to come to me?"* The doubting question makes the command milder (though only in form) by appearing to leave it up to the addressee whether to follow it. The question can be made milder in a similar way assuming the form of a declarative sentence with the expression of doubt and retaining the nature of a question only in its tone: *"Did the clock strike?"* and *"The clock struck?"* The direct question demands an answer and is therefore still not free of the underlying tone of a command. In the form of a declaration it leaves it up to the person addressed whether he wants to answer. These are transformations that occur in all areas of language expression and that, though apparently only a matter of form, are still motivated by definite affects under whose influence they occur automatically.

When Wundt speaks here of "cognitive states" and "motivating affects" as the initiators of these transformations,* he could only mean what I have designated as "shading" of linguistic expression. Yet I cannot understand how he can speak of a transformation as though the wish or command changed into a question and say repeatedly that one type of sentence is completely transformed into another, for he himself admits that the basic intention of the sentence undergoes no essential change.

Therefore, if the division of the three parts of speech† is taken from clearly observed basic psychic functions, how can one let the three sentence types fuse into each other without totally abandoning that semantic viewpoint. Here Wundt must mean the form and not the content when he makes his division of sentence types.

The notion of "sentence types" is quite old. At the turn of the nineteenth century it was the subject of frequent discussions. William James referred to sentence "schemes" as the "verbal skeletons" that hold words together. One of Marty's colleagues at Prague, Arnold Pick, applied the notion extensively in his influential studies of aphasia. Karl Bühler, Otto Selz, and others attempted to classify sentences according to a small number of sentence frames or schemes, but the attempts were doomed because of the infinite number of different sentence types.

Marty had doggedly followed Wundt with critiques and com-

---

* The German word used here was indeed *Transformationen*. Sometimes in other places in Wundt's and Marty's writings the terms *Umwandlungen* and *Umformungen* were also used with this meaning.—A.L.B.

† Noun, verb, and modifier.—A.L.B.

mentary, but in this case Wundt seldom replied, at least to Marty's later works. It had been the opinion of Wundtians that Marty's work needed little refutation. Nevertheless, his efforts were an encouragement to those who wished to break the Wundtian influence in psychology. Marty was also a leader in taking issue against Wundt's acceptance of innate principles in language. His opposition here was based on his own philosophical empiricism. Similarly, he disputed Wundt's inclusion of volition in the analysis of apperception (see Marty's *Gesammelte Schriften*, Vol. 1, 1916).

In the late nineteenth and early twentieth centuries the University of Leipzig had been the center for language scholars of all sorts. Wundt's foremost psycholinguistic student, Ottmar Dittrich, organized the Leipzig "Sprachpsychologie Gruppe" (sometimes awkwardly translated as the "glottopsychology group"). Dittrich's own *Grundzüge der Sprachpsychologie* (Fundamentals of psycholinguistics), 1903, was a massive text that reviewed in detail the physiological and psychological foundations of language. The 700 pages are accompanied by an atlas of 114 figures of the nervous system and organs involved in speech, as well as diagrams of apparatus and charts of data. A projected second volume which was to be more concerned with linguistics never appeared. However, Dittrich did publish another interesting short book, *Die Probleme der Sprachpsychologie* (Problems of psycholinguistics) 1913, in which he presented some of the unique problems that arose in the attempt to join the disciplines of psychology and linguistics. He discussed the distinction between a surface structure and a base structure in the syntax of language. This was the continuation of Humboldt's distinction between "inner" and "outer" form.

But Dittrich's work came at an unfortunate time; the *Zeitgeist* was deserting him. And one notices that Dittrich's writings are programmatic and have an unfinished character. The Wundtian School was aging, reactions to it were intensifying, and with World War I, cataclysmic changes took place in German psychology. But during the period from the beginning of the century to the War, commentators on Wundt's psycholinguistics were profuse and prolific in the tradition of Paul, Delbrück, and Marty, with protagonists as well as antagonists.

Ludwing Sütterlin in his *Das Wesen der Sprachlichen Gebilde*

(The nature of linguistic structures), 1902, goes through the entirety of Wundt's *Die Sprache* and critically summarizes, in order, each section in a clear writing style and all in less than 200 pages.

Jacques van Ginneken in *Principes de linguistique psychologique* (Principles of Psycholinguistics), 1907, was the supreme eclectic; he cites nearly 600 authors. His work is filled with observations, but too often they are of an independent character, and the book is a labyrinth of postulates and scholastic divisions. Nevertheless, it is an all-out attempt to psychologize linguistics. In this respect van Ginneken had hoped to *surpass* Wundt.

C. A. Séchehaye, a student of de Saussure's, attacked Wundt vehemently in his *Programmes et méthodes de la linguistique théorique* (Programs and methods of theoretical linguistics), 1908. He proposed a psychology of language that was to be strictly *descriptive* (avoiding Wundt's explanations) and based on the notion of habit and statistical analysis. This was five years before A. A. Markov published his famous study of the transitional probabilities in textual material, and it appeared 20 years before E. V. Condon's statistical study of vocabulary. These interests eventually led to G. K. Zipf's statistical analyses of language in the 1930s and to Claude Shannon and Warren Weaver's mathematical model known as "information theory" in the 1940s.

Karl Vossler, in *Sprache als Schöpfung und Entwicklung* (Language as creation and evolution), 1905, disputes Wundt's psychologizing as well as the earlier *Junggrammatiker* trend in the late nineteenth century. He appealed instead to aesthetics and cultural history as the only means for understanding language, and he claimed that the history of language is part of the history of art. Vossler's influence can be noted in the work of some of the later Prague Circle linguists.

With so much work on language theory, the hegemony of the Leipzig School was soon to be seriously challenged. A Slavic linguist, Vilém Mathesius, who had studied with Marty, provided a formal basis for such a challenge by founding *The Linguistic Circle of Prague* in 1926. Among the group of original members were two young Russian refugees, N. S. Trubetzkoy and Roman Jakobson, who were destined to revolutionize the study of phonetics. Trubetzkoy obtained a professorship at Vienna where he met and encouraged the young German psychologist Bühler, who had begun his own revolt against Wundt's *Sprachpsychologie*. Soon Bühler became a member of the Prague Circle. After Wundt's death he succeeded to the position of the leading authority in Europe on psychology of language.

Bühler became a prominent figure in German psychology through his contributions to the Würzburg school's famous break with the Wundtian tradition.* Wundt believed that the higher mental processes could best be understood through studies of the products of those mental processes. Thus the psychology of language was best approached through linguistics, language history, and logic. Only external or sensory motor events were considered to be amenable to experimentation; Wundt held to very strict standards for experimental work, essentially those of measurement, replicability, and experimental control. The inner phenomena such as linguistic structure seemed to him not accessible, in any profitable way, with his laboratory apparatus.

The Würzburg group, founded by Wundt's former student Oswald Külpe, deviated from Wundt's standards and methods. They treated pure introspection as experiment. At Cornell, Titchener and his students also moved in this direction although their introspection studies showed more of the influence of the mental mechanics of British empiricism. The Würzburgers soon embroiled the Titchenerians in the notorious "imageless thought" controversy. Titchener viewed cognition as being composed of images that are faint copies of external reality. In disagreement the Würzburgers noted the existence and significance of imageless thought. Their movement was supported simultaneously in France by Binet, in England by Stout, and in America by Woodworth. The whole issue had relevance to language phenomena because it was in processes of so-called verbal reasoning that identification of mental imagery was especially difficult.

During a decade of experimentation in their own "liberal" style the Würzburgers made several contributions, particularly to the vocabulary of psychology, for example, the notions of "set" and

---

* For this history see J. M. Mandler and G. Mandler, *Thinking: from association to Gestalt* (New York: John Wiley, 1964); also, G. Humphrey, *Thinking* (London: Methuen, 1951).

"determining tendency" in problem-solving activity and in perception. The Würzburg movement* culminated in Bühler's experiments on thought processes which were described in three papers appearing in 1907 and 1908. These articles fomented a bold confrontation with Wundt who immediately refuted Bühler at great length because of his "mock experiments." But Bühler replied with a stirring defense of his techniques of introspection. In the simplest terms his "experiments" involved the use of language as a tool for probing the workings of the mind. Bühler's tests consisted simply of "talking" with his subjects in careful ways. This was dubbed the *Ausfrage* method and it was an attempt to produce interesting and relevant data by communicating with subjects in a highly constrained situation. In one sense this is what any psychologist does when he conducts an experiment; he arranges a situation for communicating with an experimental subject whether by means of controlled discriminative acts or by verbal responses. In other words, an experimenter controls certain events to which a subject reacts in a particular way that gives information to the experimenter. And as follows from Bühler's argument, *language* itself should thus be our most powerful tool in the study of human psychology. However, Wundt argued that Bühler's experiments were simply not controllable, not replicable, and were open to all kinds of bias.

In the course of his early studies, linguistic phenomena held strong interest for Bühler. His test had consisted of observing the comprehension of, and memory for, complex sentences and proverbs. The "trained" introspectors had relied on their own intuitions to analyze their own experience in search of the "constituents of the thought process," or for irreducible thought units. Bühler claimed to have found "moments" of consciousness characterized by a collection of features. A consistent feature of a thought-moment was said to be the consciousness either of a rule,

---

* This group also developed the base out of which grew the Gestalt psychology of Wertheimer, Köhler, and Kofka. Bühler, highly critical of the Gestaltists, accused them of borrowing their notions from earlier German psychology. The Wundtians also intensified their interests in these matters and moved further toward holistic psychology. However, instead of using the term *Gestalt,* the later Wundtians (Krueger, Sander, and Volkelt) referred to their movement as *Ganzheit* (holistic) psychology.

a relation, or an intention. These were described as "automatic events" in that they usually pass unnoticed, and one must subtly contrive to demonstrate them or notice them.

In the act of understanding a sentence, Bühler found that there was always a pause, a processing time, before his subjects grasped phrase meanings and relations between sentence parts. And then comprehension would appear in a sudden way. For such language-related experiences, Bühler introduced into psychology what was to become widely used jargon: "the Aha-experience." For Bühler it meant the grasping of a relation, the very moment within the hearer when he becomes conscious of a relation between constituents. The importance of grammatical relations, as Bühler states it, is deceptively simple: "They enable us to understand sentences." He continued,

What then are grammatical rules? For the linguistic researcher they are something that can be abstracted from a given language. He notes them, perhaps pursues their changes, and is finished with them where the psychologist just begins. How are they actualized in real life? The associationist psychologist cannot allow them any real worth . . . the grammatical rules are, accordingly, laws of association. That this conclusion is incorrect is obvious, and still a strict associationist psychologist will hardly be able to avoid it. But the characteristics of grammatical rules, as opposed to laws of logic and those of association, are quite explicable through the particular events that occur between thoughts and utterances. They should be considered the agents of these events . . . we are first inwardly aware of a plan of operation, and this plan then masters the words. [For example] if we begin a sentence with "as soon as" and suddenly break off at the end of the phrase, we feel that we have expected something that is not merely a factual completion but also a grammatical one. We expect a main clause. In all these cases we consciously perceive as independent features that which otherwise mediates automatically between thoughts and words. Here we attain an awareness of the sentence structure and the relationships among the different parts of the sentence. This phenomenon is to be accepted as a direct manifestation of the grammatical rules that are alive within us.*

* K. Bühler, Tatsachen und Probleme zu einer Psychologie der Denkvor-

Shortly after Bühler's experiments Wilhelm Stählin studied and elaborated Bühler's introspection techniques. He gathered introspective reports from twenty-five subjects, again having them introspect on their experiences while comprehending complex sentences. The innovation in this test was that subjects were more numerous and were naïve regarding the object of the testing, which had not been the case in previous investigations. In the following excerpt Stählin summarizes his protocols and expresses some of the then prevalent viewpoints of *Sprachpsychologie*:

As for the question of cognitive representation of word-meanings, we meet an insurmountable obstacle. The question is put the wrong way to be relevant to our experiments or similar ones, for when a sentence rather than single words are presented a subject does not, under normal circumstances, arrive at a "word perception" (*Wortauffassung*) that is distinct and separate from sentence comprehension. Without exception, our protocols demonstrate Bühler's thesis of the primacy of sentence comprehension. That sentence comprehension is seldom reported as an individual conscious experience is simply a result of the fact that in most instances it occurs so naturally that one is not conscious of it. It can, however, be observed whenever there is any sort of interference with it. . . .

One finding for the psychology of sentence comprehension is the effort made by subjects to produce a complete thought as soon as possible to which they can add and incorporate everything that follows. This act is understandably unnoticed as long as it occurs effortlessly, but it becomes prominent when such a thought cannot be found or if the first parts of the sentence have led to a train of thought that turns out to be the wrong one. . . In an experimental set-up such as ours, word assimilation can be examined only in relation to sentence assimilation, for the manner in which the individual words are received and how they affect consciousness is significantly determined by the early anticipation of a thought to be expressed by the whole sentence. These alternating effects control attention to a greater extent than does the "representation of word meanings" which is essentially a labora-

---

gänge. III. Ueber Gedankenerinnerungen. *Arch. f. d. ges. Psychol.*, 1908, p. 85–86. Translated by A. L. Blumenthal.

tory concept inappropriate for understanding natural language. It hardly needs to be said that individual words must be understood before the sentence-thought can be comprehended. But the important fact is that the reverse relationship also exists: With the majority of words we do not at all arrive at a recognition and assimilation of word meaning separate from sentence comprehension. As soon as the sentence thought is assimilated in consciousness—and the tendency to do this as soon as possible is always there—then sentence comprehension determines the manner in which the individual words are assimilated as parts of sentence context. As long as the sentence-thought—whether right or wrong—remains unclear, word-understanding has the character of a tentative experience. It is possible to have understood all the words in a sentence and to know what they mean while having no idea what the sentence means, for sentence comprehension is something quite different and independent. Our protocols are not the best to demonstrate this fact, but they are in absolute agreement with the observations of Bühler and others who were the first to demonstrate it. . . .

One forgets that the meaning of the sentence is not simply a tying together of word meanings. The sentence thought itself must become clear, and specifically as soon as possible. A sentence that must be heard in great part before one can "see" what it is about is as good as lost. It is almost a prerequisite for effective speech that the principal idea be conveyed to listeners in a few initial words under which all subsequent expressions are arranged so to receive their direction from this idea and so to enrich it and give it finer shades of meaning.*

For those who had different views on the prerequisites for experimental research that had worried Wundt, this period seemed ripe for experimentation in psycholinguistics. Experimental studies with relevance to sentence structure perhaps began in 1894 when a former student of Wundt's, Victor Henri, collaborated with Binet in Paris on studies of the changes in syntactic structure of the recall reproductions of sentences. One of their findings, although of a preliminary nature, was that in sentence recall after a certain intervening period sentences may be reduced

---

* W. Stählin, Experimentelle Untersuchungen über Sprachpsychologie und Religionspsychologie. *Arch. f. Religionspsychol.*, 1914, p. 155–157. Translated by A. L. Blumenthal.

to more simple syntactic forms. In Germany and America other experiments followed that generally supported the primacy of the sentence in language comprehension and production.* But studies of word association (which were more amenable to experimentation) soon predominated over sentence studies. Word association research has a long history, which was frequently concerned more with the nature of memory or with something other than language per se. In founding the experimental study of memory Ebbinghaus (1885) had, in fact, taken great pains to avoid the effects of natural language by inventing the "nonsense syllable" for use as an experimental unit. We will return to this issue after examining further Bühler's views on language.

Bühler's first publication that directly concerned language was his review of Marty's *Untersuchungen* (1908), a book that may have had considerable influence on Bühler, judging from his later work. But it is obvious that Bühler reflected new trends in twentieth-century thought. Especially noticeable is the influence on Bühler of social psychology and animal studies. The following statement from Bühler illustrates these influences as well as his break with Wundt:

Through a study of all the material of actual observations on animals, I have arrived at the conclusion that the development and differentiation of semantic instruments is much more parallel to the level of organization of social life than to the level of mental development in the individual. It is on this important point that we have today surpassed Wundt.†

Bühler was apparently not strongly disposed to be an experimenter because after his 1907–1908 *Ausfrage* tests he undertook no further experimentation (a fact that seems to vindicate Wundt). As a theorist and commentator Bühler was prolific. The extent of his writings on the psychology of language is little known in America today.‡

---

* For a survey of these experiments see, Arthur L. Blumenthal, "Early Psycholinguistic Research: A Review." In T. G. Bever and W. Weksel (Eds.) *The structure and psychology of language* (Holt, Rinehart, and Winston, in press).

† K. Bühler, Les Lois Générales d'Évolution dans le Langage de l'Enfant. *J. de Psychol.*, 1926, **25**: 606.

‡ The following are Bühler's articles and books on language in chronolog-

Bühler was arrested in 1938 for his political opposition to the Nazis and for "philo-semitic behavior." Friends secured his release from prison and he came to the United States. But there he met with a disheartening indifference and was unable to find suitable employment. An expected appointment at a major American university failed to materialize. Although he was invited to the 1953 Indiana conference on psycholinguistics, he was too ill to attend at that time. Bühler died in 1963 in Los Angeles, never having had a major academic appointment in America, and having often been without employment congruent with his background. His productive career in psycholinguistics had ended in 1938.

Many of Bühler's ideas, such as the application of communication engineering models to psycholinguistics, were taken up enthusiastically by the subsequent generation of American psychologists, but with little awareness of Bühler's work.* Bühler was both a "functionalist" and a promoter of "field theory" in the study of language. Bühler incorporated many of the ideas of *Gestalt* and *Ganzheit* psychology, particularly principles of figure-ground relations, into the systematic study of language performance. With reference to the interpretation of the speech-using individual as a control system (a similar notion was later made popular in America in the study of "cybernetics") Bühler main-

---

ical order. Titles are translated from the German: A review of A. Marty's "Investigations into universal grammar and philosophy of language" (1909), Language comprehension from the standpoint of normal psychology (1909), A Critical Examination of modern sentence Theories (1918), The Nature of Syntax (1922), The Concept of Linguistic Representation (1923), General Laws of Evolution in the Language of Children (1926), The Concept of "Symbol" in Langauge (1927), The Symbolism of Language (1927), Sign Communication in Men and Animals (1931), Phonetics and Phonology (1931), Onomatopoeia and the Representational Function of Language (1933), Theory of Expression (1933), Axions of Linguistics (1933), Language Theory: The Representational Function of Language (1934), Collected Studies for the Theory of Language (1935), The Structure Model of Language (1936), The Psychology of Phonetics (1937), The Fourth Axiom of the Theory of Language (1937).

* Of the many texts on psychology of language that have appeared in America during the 1950s and the 1960s I am aware of only one that includes serious consideration of Bühler's work. It is H. Werner and B. Kaplan's *Symbol formation* (New York: John Wiley, 1963).

tained a distinction between language as a tool and man as the tool-user.

Bühler considered the setting outside of the individual to be as important a part of the performance structure as the mental events that accompany speech and thus he began with a "total performance field." An utterance occurs within a system of three covariants: the speaker, the hearer, and the facts or states represented by the utterance. These three points in the "language field" defined Bühler's three basic functions of language: the expressive function (symptoms of the speaker's disposition), the evocational function (signals for the listener to react), and the representational function (symbols that describe objects or facts). Later the Prague linguists added the aesthetic function, which is the capacity of a speech segment to attract attention to itself.

The field concept was most important. Given two speakers of the same language, no matter how well one of them structures a sentence his utterance will fail if both parties do not share the same field to some degree. For instance, if a person holds his hand up in front of another's face with fingers spread apart, that gesture would be meaningless unless the utterance, "How much is two plus three?" had just occurred. Misunderstandings at the phonetic, syntactic, or semantic level may occur to the degree that the field is not shared by listener and speaker. There are inner aspects of the field, such as an area of knowledge, or outer aspects, such as objects in the environment. Indeed, the field can be analyzed into many aspects. The total field (*Umfeld*) consists not only of the practical situation (*Zeigfeld*) in which an utterance occurs, but also the symbol field (*Symbolfeld*) which is the context of language segments preceding the segment under consideration. More specifically, the symbol field consists of those constituents that stand in *grammatical relation* to the utterance element under consideration. And thus the figure-ground concept is relevant to syntactic structure. Grammatical relations may be interpreted in the sense of sentence parts bearing various figure-ground relations to one another.

The structure of any particular language is largely field-independent, being determined by its own particular conventional rules, but the field determines how the rules are applied. For example, the formulation of connections between language rules and the performance field is a way of accounting for elliptical sentence constructions, that is, with a "rich" external field less needs to be specified in the sentence.

The communication act, in Bühler's description, has two control elements: speaker and listener. The listener is a control device in that he functions as a *selector* of cues (accurately or inaccurately) by which he constructs an interpretation. The speaker is also a control element in that he is a structuring station (*Formungstation*) for the "sending" of conventional cues. In cybernetic terms there are thus two covarying control factors always present in language performance, one in production and one in comprehension.

Through his later identification with the Prague Circle of "functional" linguistics* Bühler became the spokesman for functionalism in psychology of language. The following excerpt explains this approach. In this article, published in 1918, Bühler critically examines the current sentence theories, particularly that of Wundt. He says, "The processes of sentence formation are so numerous that it is impossible to formulate a satisfactory definition of sentence formation." Later a book by the German grammarian John Ries (*What is a sentence,* Prague, 1931) assembled no less than 140 different sentence definitions. By the 1930s the issue of the sentence was losing popularity, but not because of its complexity. Instead, it was because the earlier psycholinguistics had gone out of style and newer paradigms prevailed.

At the time the following article was written, Bühler had not fully developed his field theory, although its rudiments are present in the article. The full treatment came in his 1934 volume titled *Sprachtheorie* (Language theory).†

---

* For a description of the work of this group and its history, see J. Vachek, *The linguistic school of prague* (Bloomington: Indiana University Press, 1966).

† At the time of this writing the linguist Paul Garvin informs me that he is preparing a translation of Bühler's book which is to be published by Thomas Y. Crowell Co., New York.—A.L.B.

KARL BÜHLER · *The Functionalist Viewpoint*

1. Human language has a threefold function: *expression, evocation, and representation*. Words like *ow* or *Aha* indicate experiences of the speaker (pain, realization); this is expression.[*] An interjection such as *Hey you!* is intended to arouse the attention of the hearer; this is evocation. It is necessary to go back to earliest childhood and to the animal world to find the biological roots of these functions. The cry of pain, or anger, and the shout after triumph in battle are expression. The so-called warning cry of deer and the clucking of hens fulfill nature's purposes through evocation.

2. Wundt "has exhaustively treated the idea that language is expressive movement," says B. Delbrück.[1] That strikes the heart of the matter. Wundt placed language in the company of mimicry and of other gestures and expressive movements and thus for this view created a wide biological foundation. He employed everything that Darwin and others had already noticed.[2] Therein lies the strength and also the one-sidedness of the Wundtian theory of language. There is another completely different function of language that cannot be derived from expressive motions, that has no origin in the causal relation that joins speaker and hearer through sound, but rather is a relationship that mathematicians call coordination (*Zuordnung*).

SOURCE. Karl Bühler, Kritische Musterung der neuern Theorien des Satzes. *Indogermanisches Jahrbuch*, vol. 6, 1918, pp. 1–20. Translated by Inez Hedges and A. L. Blumenthal.

[*] The word Bühler used here was *Kundgabe* which is difficult to render accurately in English. As well as "expression" it also signifies "subjective interpretation." The reader should keep this in mind. The term *Kundgabe* was adopted and often used by later Gestalt psychologists.—A.L.B.

[1] *Grundfragen der Sprachforschung*, 1901, p. 84.

[2] Ch. Darwin, *Der Ausdruck von Gemütsbewegungen bei dem Menschen und den Tieren*.—This position of Wundt's on language is quite clearly expressed in the first sentences of his work: "Every language consists of sound utterances or of other sensorially understood signs, which brought about by muscular movements, announce inner conditions, concepts, feelings, and emotions to the outside." *Die Sprache*, 1904, 1: 37.

A name is coordinated with its object, the statement with content. For a conceptual illustration of this consider an arbitrary sentence from a scientific journal: *"The Alps rise steeply over the Po to considerable heights, whereas in the north they descend gradually."* We discover the real function of this sentence when we state its truth or falsity, and it is not true or false because of its relation to a speaker or hearer, but because of its relation to a geographic circumstance. This other function of the sentence is best rendered, I think, by the word *representation*.[3] For it is the same function that in certain circumstances is accomplished by pictures, or in others, by maps, curves, mathematical or chemical formulas, etc.; a person familiar with them can understand their content. And indeed, in this way our sentence appears in a geography book so that the reader can infer its content. In short, there are many means and methods of representation of which language is the most universal and the most important. Coordination, however, is a mental relation that can never be "derived" from external connections, so that all theories of language that recognize only exclamation and evocation fail to deal with the propositional sentence.

. . . .

3. So that nothing is missed, let us for a moment refer to the third and last of the possibly one-sided theories, the evocation theory. I do not know whether it has ever been represented uniquely by any particular scholar; but Marty comes close to it in some sections of his work. There is certainly good sense in explaining that sound utterances must also be heard if they are to fulfill their "proper" natural purpose, and I agree wholeheartedly with those who regard the communicative need as the most important impulse in the development of human speech. But one-sidedness is also a weakness here. The representational function can be "derived" as little from the imperative as it can from the exclamation, because such evocations do involve a causal relation. It would be going too far indeed if one regarded evocation as the only purpose of language under which expression and representation are subordinated as means to an end. Marty says of the propositional

---

[3] I have not found the word representation (*Darstellung*) as a technical term in any theory of language however relevant it is. I have used it for some years in my lectures and recommended it for the first time in a critical review [of Marty's Untersuchungen] in the *Göttingen Anzeigen,* 1909.

statement that it serves to "awaken in the hearer judgments of a particular kind," to "suggest" or at least to "insinuate" certain judgments to him.[4] This is certainly one function of the statement, but by no means the only one. What would Marty do with language in the solitary life of the mind where we do not think of communication? The explanation that this is the communication of the speaker with himself is only applicable to certain unusual cases. On the whole this would be a superfluous activity, whereas representation performs such important services for our thought that the existence of inner language can thereby be easily understood. We can dispense with an exact and complete criticism of the one-sided evocation theory in this short essay, especially because it has never been presented in any pure form, and Marty himself did not offer any comprehensive sentence theory.

4. H. Paul and Wundt have argued the question of whether the sentence is a synthetic or an analytic formation. Paul says, "The sentence is the linguistic expression, the symbol, for the fact that the connection of several ideas or groups of ideas has occurred in the mind of the speaker, and it is the means of creating the same connections in the mind of the hearer." Wundt, on the other hand, says the sentence is "the separating of a whole, present in the consciousness, into parts," it is "the linguistic expression for the voluntary sequential arrangement of a total impression into logically related parts."[5] After more than ten years' experience with the most varied psychological experiments we have found fairly determinate processes of sentence formation, according to the intent of certain experiments. This has convinced me that both definitions are at the same time right and wrong. Sentence production is a highly complicated process. Wundt's schema applies in a great many cases. The *thought* of the sentence is actually conceived as a whole and is converted subsequently into parts.[6] But in other cases the parts are primary; they exist unconnected

---

[4] *Untersuchungen zur Grundlegung der allgemeinen Grammatik und Sprachphilosophie,* 1908, 1: 280 ff.—The main value of this incredibly ponderous and circuitously written book is in the tireless and unsparing search for final clarity. It is noteworthy, that Marty did not think of representation as the third basic function of language; certain shortcomings in biological questions may be responsible for this. See also my extensive critical review in *Gött. Gel. Anz.* 1909.

[5] H. Paul, *Prinzipien der Sprachgeschicte,* p. 121; Wundt, *Die Sprache,* 2: 241, 145.

[6] B. Delbrück, incidentally, correctly notes that this is already very clear

in consciousness or appear as a sequence and become a unity only by combination. To consider all the possibilities one must include the processes of abstraction and discrimination, of primacy and subordination, and many other things that are just as important. My opinion is that the processes of sentence formation are so numerous that it is impossible to find a satisfactory definition of the sentence.

I am supported in this by the fact that Wundt's definition is accepted by many but has completely satisfied no one[7] and that Delbrück could claim, with justification, that it made no great difference for the linguistic scholar whether he chooses Herbart's psychology, which Steinthal and Paul represented, or the theories of Wundt: "The practitioner can live with both theories" (Delbrück, 1901, p. 42 ff.). This judgment of an experienced "practitioner" always appeared to me, as Wundt himself felt, to contain a powerful criticism. If it were only certain that every sentence contains more than one part, that some combination had to be present in it, then one could let this bear the weight of the definition. But not even this is certain. Delbrück has called attention to the fact that in their origins the Indo-germanic imperatives probably had no personal endings, thus no designation of the person, and thus no actor or agent—they were really one-member linguistic utterances just like the vocatives and interjections. The earliest sentences of a child's language are single-membered in this way. Nor is there any reason why there should be no single-member sentences. However, there is no complete unity in the logical interpretation of impersonals (*It is raining*). It is possible that those logicians who assume every content to be a formation of at least two members are right. But even if this is true, one can still not claim that an adequate linguistic representation of every content must be two-mem-

---

in Heyse's *Deutsche Grammatik*: "A statement, such as that which the sentence contains, arises when the mind structures a concrete (outer or inner) observation and connects this again to the totality of a thought. The direct unity of the point of view is resolved, and a higher unity created by the mind takes its place. The perceptual (*angeschaut*) unity is lifted to a conceptual one." (I. L. A. Heyse's extensive *Lehrbuch der deutchen Sprache*, new edition by K. W. L. Heyse, 1. 1838 p. 277).

[7] Even O. Dittrich, for instance, had all sorts of objections to Wundt's definition, among them that the processes of the hearer had to be considered in a psychological-conceptual interpretation of the sentence. See *Psychol. Stud.* 19: 93 ff. and *Grundzüge der Sprachpsychologie*, I: 87 ff.

bered. Why couldn't there be inadequate, but otherwise complete, unequivocal representations? Why shouldn't a single linguistic sign be attributed to a single content?

The genetic sentence definitions of Paul and Wundt are too restricted and too wide. Remaining for the moment with complex phonetic language, one need only think of any substantive with several attributive modifiers. For instance, I may begin by saying, *Munich with its towers of Our Lady and the monumental Ludwigstrasse, with its old streets and the green Isar*. Even if we consider the attributives as deriving from predicative specifications according to linguistic history, this is not a sentence in our language today, unless I conclude the sentence with an exclamation mark and mean it as an exclamation, a possibility that we shall exclude here. And still everything that Paul and Wundt tell us about the process of sentence formation, about the processes of consciousness from which this expression derives, is applicable here (a whole impression with division into its parts or structure). Furthermore, let someone draw a complicated figure, for instance the sketch of a human head, and describe the processes of drawing! He will inevitably come up with the same schema (a whole impression with subsequent division into its parts, or a synthetic process). But a picture is not a graphic sentence. No, we will not get a satisfactory sentence definition by these methods.

5. Sentences are formations with a purpose. They fulfill specific functions. The genetic conceptual definition in the case of purposeful formations is as a rule difficult, sometimes impossible. One can attempt it, for example, with the concept *Clock*. Whoever thinks first of a system of wheels with a clockface and hands will eventually also think of sandclocks, waterclocks, and sunclocks and he will quickly be convinced that a countless number of other arrangements can claim the name *clock*. On the other hand the definition of the term clock according to its function is quite simple, if we think of it in terms of "chronometer" or "chronoscope." In the same way, I think, sentence theory must start out from a functional analysis of language. According to the three main functions of language we expect three main types of sentence: expression, evocation, and representation sentences. The question remains as to what extent natural languages have formed pure types. This is the concern of linguistic science in which I do not trust myself to make an authoritative judgment.

. . . .

(Reading)

6. In 1887 a book by R. Dedekind appeared with the title, "What are, and what purpose have numbers?" (*Was sind und was sollen die Zahlen?*) Instead of "and" Dedekind could have written, "which means." In other words, he had determined the nature of numbers from their function. "If one examines exactly what we do in counting most things or a number of them, we are led to examine the capability of the mind to relate one thing to another, to let one thing correspond to another, or to fashion one thing in the likeness of another, without which thought is an impossibility. In my opinion the entire science of numbers . . . . must be built around this single and indispensable basis." (Dedekind, p. VIII.) Thus according to Dedekind, numbers are the tools of the ordering and representational activity of the mind and must be understood on the basis of this function. I think that a similar clarity of such basic concepts as has existed in the study of numbers since Dedekind, should also be introduced by a corresponding analysis of function as the basis of linguistics. The functions of numbers are less numerous than those of language; arithmetic has nothing to do with our "expression" or "evocation." If Bolzano is right, then all language could be handled like numbers as a part of logic, that is, as part of general representational science. That this is not so is shown by more than two generations of linguistics. But why it is not so has yet to be shown.

Vienna had become a center for the study of the psychology of language with Bühler there. In the 1930s he lectured in a large auditorium with an international audience, as Wundt had in Leipzig years before.* After Bühler's departure from Europe the interest in language at Vienna continued through the work of Friedrich Kainz with somewhat more emphasis on speech pathologies.

Philip Wegener, a German philologist at Magdeburg, was one nineteenth century intellectual who gave some inspiration to the

---

* For further contrastive comparisons of Bühler with Wundt, Paul, and Marty see: Hellmuth Dempe, *Was ist Sprache?* (Weimar: Hermann Böhlaus, 1930). For further summaries of his psychological theories see: J. F. T. Bugental (ed.) Symposium on Karl Bühler's contributions to psychology. *Journal of general psychology*, 1966, **75**: 181–219.

functionalist movement and who is little known today. In 1885 Wegener wrote *Die Grundfragen des Sprachlebens* (Basic questions of language life), a short book of only 208 pages containing no references, which is still a good presentation of the functionalist views that were later developed by Marty, Bühler, and by an English philologist, Allan H. Gardiner.* Gardiner, who had consulted extensively with Bühler, dedicated his book *The theory of speech and language* (1932) to Wegener.

In Europe and America during the 1920s there was an upsurge of books in the functionalist and quasi-behaviorist movement. Popular American examples of that day were Ogden and Richards' *The meaning of meaning* (1923), De Laguna's *Speech: Its function and development* (1927), and Pillsbury and Meader's *Psychology of language* (1928). The popular counterpart in France was Henri Delacroix's book *Le langage et la pensée* (1924); and in England there was Paget's *Human Speech* (1930). However, it appears today that Bühler's psycholinguistic writings were the most sophisticated and thorough of that era.

The American behaviorist movement did not come as a sudden revolution but rather as a continuation of trends that had received strong support from the American cultural milieu. Europeans who adopted strict behaviorist or empiricist views were warmly welcomed here. There were marked consequences for the study of language. James Baldwin's psychology, in his *Mental development in the child and the race* (1895), was framed in terms of reflexology and habit formation. Here the acquisition of complex skills was analyzed as the development of habit patterns. One fundamental principle was that the mere discovery of a skilled movement was sufficient reinforcement for its own recurrence. When Münsterberg was a student of Wundt's, he proposed a similar "motor psychology" and thereby fell into disfavor with the German master; he was forced to leave Germany and seek employment in America where he was enthusiastically received by James and given a position at Harvard.

The early behaviorist tendencies in Germany were confined

---

* A brief summary in English of Wegener's book may be found in Susan Langer, *Philosophy in a new key* (Harvard University Press, 1942), Chapter 5.

mostly to southern Germany or Austria. Other behaviorist notables were Solomon Stricker and Lazarus Geiger. Stricker worked in Vienna during the late nineteenth century and proposed a motor theory of speech perception.* Geiger was never affiliated with a university. However, his book *Ursprung der Sprache* (Origin of language) Stuttgart, 1869, was the major source of inspiration for the later German-American behaviorist Max Meyer. The writings of Wegener, Stricker, Geiger, and of men with similar views were critically discussed by Wundt in his *Die Sprache*.

In 1901 E. B. Holt began teaching at Harvard and promoted his own "objectivist" psychology, which was even more opposed to mentalism and more reliant on reflex analysis than others before. Prior to the turn of the century James M. Cattell proposed an intelligence measurement by recording sensory motor capacities. Cattell had studied with Wundt and then later with Galton in England. The latter obviously had more influence on Cattell's development of a "motor psychology." One of the early American attempts to consider language in terms of reflex chaining was the work of one of Titchener's students, M. F. Washburn (*Movement and mental imagery*, 1916). However, Washburn's approach still included the Titchenerian sequencing of mental images, but language was described here as the development of "successive movement systems."†

In America the functionalist viewpoint had its strongest representation at the University of Chicago under the influence of John Dewey. Among the psychology students at Chicago shortly after the turn of the century were John B. Watson and Jacob R. Kantor. They both went on to provide some of the most vocal American opposition to the German idealist tradition. Watson had very little to say about language. In his first book, *Behavior: An introduction to comparative psychology* (1914), he briefly argued that language represents no qualitative difference between men

---

* S. Stricker, *Studien über die Sprachvorstellung* (Wien: Braumüller, 1880).

† In this work Washburn considers language to be explainable as chains of stimulus-response sequences. Her analysis in those terms is one of the more explicit ones, although she favors nonsense syllables for her examples instead of natural language.

and animals and that it consists only of more complex combinations of the same responses that are more easily observed in animals. He claimed that if we teach a gibbon some primitive language (that is, "some simple language habits") that we would then find no difference between the behavior of gibbons and that of Australian aborigines. Of course, the remarkable complexity of the language of the native Australians was unknown at that time. Following such an experiment with the gibbon, claimed Watson, "we should lose the feeling at once that there is some qualitative difference between his (the gibbon's) behavior and our own." Watson was more often read and followed than other early behaviorists. The Watsonian movement received additional encouragement from studies of conditional reflexes by Ivan Pavlov in Russia. But the Americans did not follow Pavlov's belief that the existence of language in humans represented a qualitatively different capacity that separated human psychology from animal psychology. According to Pavlov, man was different from animal because he alone possessed this "second signal system."

The fountainhead of behaviorist linguistics in America was the fiery German professor Meyer who had the interests and training of an engineer. His psychological studies under Stumpf ended in a bitter quarrel and in Meyer's "banishment" to America. The argument concerned theories of hearing; Meyer's views were considered to be too mechanical. While at the University of Missouri, he wrote his first treatise on behaviorism *The fundamental laws of human behavior* (1911), which predates Watson's book by three years. Meyer differed from Watson in his heavy inclination toward neurologizing, with telephone switchboard models of the brain. But he was similar to Watson in that he almost never performed experiments nor made references to other works.

Meyer's strong influence on American linguistics was through his one doctoral student, Albert P. Weiss, who was destined to become the closest intellectual associate of America's leading linguist, Leonard Bloomfield. In his book, *Language* (1933), Bloomfield had adopted Meyer's and Weiss's psychology. This text was the greatest influence upon American linguistics for an entire generation, at least into the 1950s.

For most American psychologists and linguists in the 1920s it may have seemed that the two disciplines were beginning to lose touch with each other. Perhaps Delbrück's widely circulated dictum was taking effect. Weiss's student E. A. Esper laments this fact in a psychology of language review published as early as 1921.* With the rise of conditioning studies and the use of laboratory animals, attention to natural language declined. On the other hand, almost superhuman efforts were made to teach English to chimpanzees; or attempts were made to give elaborate linguistic descriptions for the "language" of chimps and various other primates. Examples are found in R. M. Yerkes's *Almost human* (1925) and in Yerkes's and W. B. Learned's *Chimpanzee intelligence and its vocal expression* (1925).†

The collaboration of linguist Albert Thumb with psychologist Karl Marbe in 1901‡ was the strongest impetus to the experimental study of word associations that sprang from psycholinguistic interests. In their work the *sentence* as a unit was of little relevance. Thumb and Marbe pursued the "analogy principle" that was of so much significance to Paul and the *Junggrammatiker* linguists. Their purpose was to demonstrate experimentally the "associative processes" underlying language evolution. As a definition of analogical change they simply referred to changes in the form or meaning of words or groups of words that were brought about through association with other words or groups of words. First, they found that word association responses tended to belong to the same word category as the stimulus words (noun responses followed noun stimuli, adjectives followed adjective stimuli). But this was already known from earlier nineteenth century research, although it had not been demonstrated as explicitly. Second, they found some quantitative relationships that could be expressed with appealing mathematical precision.

* E. A. Esper, The psychology of language. *Psychol. Bull.*, 1921, **18**: 490–496.

† For a summary of animal language research see Roger Brown, *Words and things* (Glencoe, Illinois: Free Press, 1957), chapter 5.

‡ Thumb and Marbe, *Experimentelle Untersuchungen über die psychologischen Grundlagen der sprachlichen Analogiebildung*. (Experimental investigations of the psychological basis of linguistic analogy formation) (Leipzig: Engelmann, 1901).

Namely, the more frequently a response is given by a group of subjects, the shorter the average reaction time for that response. Or, "$E = 1/T(T + 1)$," showing that the effectiveness (E) of an association increases as the average time (T) for the association to occur decreases. In the later associationist literature this became known as "Marbe's Law."

Many experimentalists (in the Ebbinghaus tradition) were inspired by Marbe's algebra. Yet in their research they drifted away from linguistics, and their allusions to linguistic structures became more and more superficial. The revival of psychologists' interest in linguistics in the 1950s has also renewed this earlier pursuit of the "associational basis" of language.* But here the original concern for Paul's principle of analogy has been largely missing. The analogy principle for Thumb and Marbe was explained by associative bonds between words or groups of words. Such bonds were effective in producing changes (that is, causing a word to change to resemble an associate) to the degree of the frequency of appearance of that association among the members of a speech community. The analogy principle was often used indiscriminately as an explanation of the evolution of language and of language acquisition in the child. Wundt's vitrolic opposition to this line of research must have cost him a considerable loss of esteem among a sizable number of psychologists because he considered this work to be naïve and referred to it as *Vulgärpsychologie*.

In addition to the word association studies, large accumulations of data on language acquisition and on reading skills also appeared, and these often supported the continuing work in theoretical *Sprachpsychologie*. We shall review some of these investigations in the following two chapters.

There was yet another new influence: the development of more sophisticated statistical procedures were especially applicable to the behaviorist's conception of language as an inventory of words. Word frequency counts began to appear in proliferation. We shall return to this issue later in Chapter Five. However, the

---

* See James Deese, *The structure of associations in language and thought* (Baltimore: Johns Hopkins Press, 1965).

experimental work known as "the verbal learning tradition" is not easily considered a part of the history of psycholinguistics because it typically had only superficial contact with linguistics, and interests in language were usually superseded by concerns about learning theories or associational processes.* Otherwise we should include mention of such voluminous investigations of verbal learning as those conducted by E. L. Thorndike at Columbia during the 1920s and the 1930s.†

One can see how estranged linguistics and psychology had become by reading the report of the 1953 Indiana conference on psycholinguistics (see Preface) where there was an atmosphere of near celebration over the discovery by linguists and psychologists of each other. Here were disciplines that relied on similar points of view about behavior. Esper, Weiss's student, was subsequently rediscovered by some members of that conference as "the original American psycholinguist." Esper, however, has rejected the use of that hybrid term.

In 1918‡ Esper had set out to introduce American psychologists to the word-association research of Thumb and Marbe. He performed a massive replication experiment to determine whether the results found in Germany would also appear in a test using the English language. And they did. Esper then continued his experimental research by constructing a technique that was frequently used later: experimentation with artificial (or miniature) languages. Esper devised a system of carefully constructed nonsense syllables for the study of language learning. The following is his statement of the premise underlying his experiments:

We can at least expect that the manner in which artificial linguistic material becomes organized into categories will bear a definite relationship to the tendencies inherent in the speech-habits of the subjects,

---

* For a summary of the results of work in this field see George Mandler, Verbal learning. In *New directions in psychology*, III (New York: Holt, Rinehart and Winston, 1967).

† Thorndike, E. L., Studies in the psychology of language. *Arch. Psychol.*, No. 23, Vol. 33, 1938.

‡ E. A. Esper, A contribution to the experimental study of analogy. *Psychol. Rev.*, 1918, 25: 468–487.

and that a comparison of the results gained from subjects of widely different language habits may reveal certain uniformities and general laws according to which the organization of language habits takes place.*

The artificial language in Esper's investigation involved eight nonsense syllables, four each associated with a different abstract figure and four each with a different color. Colored figures then constituted the semantic referents for the nonsense syllables. On seeing a colored figure, Esper's subject would respond with a two-syllable name, the first syllable designating color and the second designating shape. During recognition tests following the learning trials, subjects correctly gave the names of color-figure combinations that they had *not* been trained on previously. Esper explained this as the formation of *analogies* based on the familiar combinations. For Esper this result would not have indicated inventiveness on the part of his subjects. But the psycholinguists of the Wundtian school might have found that Esper's explanation of "analogy-formation" needed further discussion. Nor would it have seemed better to them to say that the learned categories in Esper's test were simply "generalized" to new instances. Rather, it may have been said that subjects had acquired a few simple rules for assigning names to colored figures; thus one would expect novel stimulus combinations to be named as easily as familiar ones. That was the earlier *Sprachpsychologie* viewpoint—that people are linguistically creative.

Esper's introduction of artificial linguistic systems illustrates a complete break from Wundt. To Wundt it certainly would have appeared that the manipulation of small sets of nonsense syllables, nonsense figures, or other miniature systems could in no way be considered natural language usage or be of relevance to natural language—and that Esper's experiment was a classical study of concept formation, or of more relevance to that topic than to language.

Shortly after Watson received his degree at Chicago, J. R. Kantor was a student there. When Kantor subsequently accepted

---

* E. A. Esper, A technique for the experimental investigation of associative interference in artificial linguistic material. *Language Monographs*, 1, 1925.

a position at the University of Indiana in 1920 he proceeded to develop a brand of behaviorism more radical than that of either Watson or Meyer. For Kantor, not only was the "mind" a product of the imaginations of old-fashioned psychologists, but so too were physiological explanations. Kantor was thorough in his restriction of psychology to input-output relations.

As seen throughout his career, the aspect of behavior of most interest to Kantor, was always language. His works reveal an acquaintance with the European philology literature that was uncommon among American psychologists. Perhaps for this reason Kantor remained somewhat outside of the mainstream of American psychology. Although his ideas have remained fairly isolated, he was one of the most devoted and polemical supporters of the behaviorist movement.

The main product of Kantor's psycholinguistic writings is the lengthy *Objective psychology of grammar* (1936). Many today would find the book to be mistitled since it refers to very little of what we might expect to find under the title of "Grammar."* However, he did mention Wundt, Paul, Bühler, and many others, and dismissed each one as if casting out demons. And in the 1936 book he used the term "psycholinguistics" in reference to the earlier *Sprachpsychologie* research. Kantor seemed preoccupied with the failures of his predecessors and contemporaries. Nevertheless, he effectively stated the popular American reactions to Wundt. Other behaviorist rejections of Wundt's psycholinguistics had become popular during the 1920s, such as those of de Laguna and of Ogden and Richards (cited above). But Kantor stands out because he devoted much more effort to this enterprise.

The basic effect of strict behaviorism on psycholinguistics was to deny authenticity to the view that language is the external expression of internal cognition. In contrast to the functionalist psychologists, these early behaviorists not only denied the existence of the mind, but in regard to language also denied the notion of "symbol," largely because it carried mentalistic implications. All these tendencies are quite clear in Kantor. The fol-

---

* The bulk of this work is an attempt to analyze parts of speech, person, gender, tense, mood, voice, case, and negation in terms of behavioral interactions between persons and persons, or between persons and objects.

lowing excerpt is from one of Kantor's articles on the relation between psychology and linguistics which appeared in 1928. At that date the estrangement of psychology from linguistics was of utmost concern to him and it had come about, he stated, because of mentalism.

JACOB ROBERT KANTOR · *Expression vs. Stimulus-Response Adjustment*

In the study of language the psychologist and the philologist must meet at some common point. There is no escaping this attitude. And yet an uncrossable chasm separates them.

Language, all the philologists agree, constitutes activity. Now is it not precisely the work of the psychologist to study action? And this includes language activity as well as every other type of psychological adjustment.[1] The great importance of language should make it stand out as a highwater mark in psychological study.

And yet it is not an unusual incident for the philologist to rule the psychologist out of the field of linguistics. Thus it is asserted that the conditions of cerebral activity, which are the main business of the psychologists, remain outside the field of the linguists.[2]

The expulsion of the psychologists from the linguistic garden is an old story. Recall the passage at arms between Delbrück and Wundt. The latter offers his two-volume work on the psychology of language as an improvement over the Herbartian psychology. Delbrück delivers the coup de grace in his declaration that, granting that Wundtian psychology is superior to the Herbartian, for the linguist it makes no difference.[3]

SOURCE. J. R. Kantor, Can psychology contribute to the study of linguistics? *The Monist*, 1928, 38: 630–648, LaSalle, Illinois with the permission of the publishers.

[1] As will appear in the sequel, two kinds of activity are referred to in this paragraph. The activities spoken of by the linguist are merely movements of the speech organs (including all anatomical parts relevant to speech).

[2] Vendreyes, *Language*, p. 66.

[3] "Man sieht, für den Praktiker lässt sich mit beiden Theorien Leben." See *Grundfragen der Sprachforschung*, 1901, p. 44.

(*Reading*)   *Expression vs. Adjustment*

Again, Jespersen, a philologist with a keen regard for psychological aids in linguistic scholarship, refers to the author of these two weighty tomes as "much less of a linguist than a psychologist and whose pages seem to me often richer in words than in fertilizing ideas."[4]

Now let it be clearly understood that if the philologist refuses psychological cooperation, it is the psychologist who is to blame. For what is the psychological procedure in linguistics? Nothing more than an attempted explanation of philological facts by the medium of psychic causes and psychic processes.

Now the secret is out. Why traditional psychology cannot contribute to linguistic scholarship is transparent. Language can in no fashion be regarded as an expression of ideas, desires, or feelings. Nor is it a physical medium for "psychic" processes. Language must be treated as in a genuine sense behavior. The matter has been exceedingly well put by Weiss. "As a form of behavior, language represents biological, physiological, and social conditions; as a medium of expression, it assumes the existence of non-physical forces or types of psychical energy whose existence has not been adequately demonstrated. Therefore, when the psychologist finds himself confronted with the request to make a "psychological" explanation, or a "psychological" interpretation of a careful and detailed linguistic investigation, he is unable to add anything and if anything is added it often only obscures the investigation.[5]

The philologist is quite right in ostracizing the psychologist. As long as psychology concerns itself with mentalities it can add nothing to linguistics. Worse still, it distorts the facts. Here is a typical example of how traditional psychology describes language.

Speech begins with a mental process, an idea, feeling, or desire in the mind of A. Somehow this psychic material is converted into or transmitted to the motor nerves that control A's organs of speech. The motor processes with their phonic products constitute the means of conveying the idea or desire to B. This communicating or conveying of the mental processes is, however, not completed until the sound is conveyed to B's mind where the auditory perceptions are translated into the appropriate and intended ideas.

What an unsavory mixture of "mental" and "physical." But this sort

---

[4] Jespersen, *Language*, p. 98.
[5] *Language*, 1925, I: 52.

of thing need no longer be regarded as psychology. To understand the psychological fundamentals of language it is only necessary to turn to scientific psychology. Only when we do so can the psychologist and philologist work shoulder to shoulder. We go further. We insist that there must be psychological and philological cooperation in order that some of the problems of language be solved at all.

What are some of these issues? Before attempting a statement of scientific psychology, which can really be employed in the linguistic field, or in any other for that matter, we might suggest some problems requiring cooperative study.

Let us turn first to fundamentals. Why do philological descriptions of language always fall far short of what persons actually do when they speak? Observe this enormous paradox. Philologists agree that language must be human activity. In fact they say too that it must be mutual activity on the part of at least two persons. But unfortunately it seems inevitable that they should immediately shift from activity to symbols, fixed forms. Jespersen puts this matter perfectly.[6] But he is mistaken in saying that it was only in former times that this fact was overlooked. It is just as true today as at any previous period that words and forms are treated as though they were things or natural objects with an existence of their own. Furthermore, this must be true just as long as language is regarded as expression and communication. Would it not be a contribution of psychology to indicate that speech is not merely the production of verbal-auditory symbols?

The first cooperative contact of the two sciences is therefore methodological. To understand the actual nature of language we must approach linguistics with adequate conceptual tools. When we arm ourselves with adequate psychological equipment it will be quite clear why grammar cannot cover actual language. For is it not a tribute paid to psychology when the philologist says that it is not unreasonable after all to claim that there are as many different languages as there are individuals.[7] Instead of regarding grammar as a vessel which

---

[6] "The essence of language is human activity—activity on the part of one individual to make himself understood by another, and activity on the part of that other to understand what was *in the mind of the first.*" *Philosophy of Grammar,* 1924, p. 17. We italicize the part of the statement that conceals the joker.

[7] Vendreyes, *Language,* 1922, p. 235.

spills over, it should rather be considered as a net which, in a very inadequate manner indicates the drift of the language at the time it passes through its meshes.[8]

Psychologists and philologists must jointly attack more intimate problems also. What is a word and what a sentence? Is it true that a word is an independent or indivisible unit? Or must it be regarded as a dependent element existing only in a condition of relativity with other elements? Can these questions be solved by the philologist without psychological aid? Let us dig a little deeper. Are words exclusively the elements of a sentence which define or carry separate ideas, concepts, or conceptual relations, while the sentence as a whole has no conceptual significance whatever? Or, is the sentence the carrier of meaning and thus the essential linguistic element?

Such questions of course lead to the problem of the relationship between ideas and the linguistic elements which express them. What is a semanteme really? And what a morpheme? Is there a principle relating them? Is it possible that morphemes are genuine phenomena if they range all the way from affixative formatives, to order of semantemes in a sentence? Are ideas always carried by roots or semantemes? Can affixative morphemes perform this function as well as whole words? Is it possible to order linguistic elements in a hierarchy using importance or fundamentalness as a criterion? Do only semantemes represent basic ideas as compared with linguistic elements which indicate number, gender, or person? Do these confining schematisms do justice to the dynamic or living character of language?

Let us turn now to still more concrete issues. Cannot the psychologist help the grammarian to seize hold of the vital and fleeting elements of speech? What is the relation of tense to time? Can there be or should there be a definite relationship between the temporal existence of an event, the idea of it in the mind, and the linguistic expression of the idea? How can we reconcile a spoken historical or unhistorical present with English grammar? Similar queries arise with respect to the parts of speech. One grammarian describes them one way, another gives them an entirely different description. Some philologists throw parts of speech entirely out of the linguistic field (Bru-

---

[8] As we shall see later, psychological cooperation can only be useful in part of the linguistic field.

not); others hesitate only at the noun and verb (Sapir). Somehow this all means that the psychology of speaking must have a place in the linguistic system. There is no alternative.

A final example: the problems of interjections. How can this persecuted member of the linguistic kingdom be properly treated? Very few grammarians wish to include interjections in the grammatical scheme of things. And yet, like the scriptural poor, they are forever to be reckoned with. Do we not have here another symptom of the need to replace the affinity of language for formal logic with a more serviceable liking for scientific psychology?

Now we are ready to suggest a reformulation of linguistic psychology. As we have already intimated, scientific psychology throws completely overboard the distinction of the mental and physical. Naturalistic psychology can find no merit in the division of mind and body. It can find no fact in nature describable as the translation of psychic states—ideas or what not—into the motions of lips and tongue. It is not within our province now to go into the origin of the misconceptions that lie at the basis of mind-body distinctions. Suffice it to say that they could only have arisen by misconceiving the psychological facts actually observed.

Psychology is the science of the reactions of individuals to stimuli. The two variables which the science demands as the minimal description of an event are persons and the objects to which they react. These objects may be persons or things. In many cases the reacting person is in direct contact with some object. Such is the situation when I withdraw my hand from a hot object or when I observe a ball or person moving toward me.

Another distinct type of psychological event occurs when the reacting person is not in direct contact with the stimulus object. The reaction may occur in the absence of the object. Now that I am at home I can only think of or remember the picture at the museum. The difference in the reaction here is owing to the fact that something other than the picture serves as a substitute stimulus to call out my response to it.

Now language actions are also adjustments or adaptations to objects. With this addition: In the case of language we have a triadic relationship. That is, there are three variables in the linguistic event. One is the reacting person, the second is the object to which I refer by verbal or gestural response, and the third, some other person to whom

I also react. The third variable may be the speaker himself. Language is the only type of psychological situation that involves such a triple situation.[9]

Mark this point well. Language is adjustment. It is activity. What is the nature of the adjustment? What happens when one speaks? In effect the speaker refers, and the hearer is referred, to some thing, person, or event. The event is the adjustmental stimulus which we have mentioned. For instance, A says to B, "the car is wrecked." What happens here is that A reacts to the event of the car-wrecking, and to B at the same time. The actions of A and B both constitute responses to the object. The interrelationship between the two persons and the event is made possible through a historical development which we may roughly sum up as learning to make language adjustments. Naturally there is involved here, besides the speaking reactions, responses of understanding, but these in no sense imply any ideas in the "mind" as we have already shown. Understanding the wrecking event is merely a more subtle form of reaction than actually participating in it. We may also say it is in a definite sense developed from it or from similar situations.

To assert that language is adjustmental action is to deny utterly two clearly related propositions. The first is that language is the expression of ideas. The fallacy of this conception has already been sufficiently revealed. No less false is the proposition that language consists of a set of symbols.

Scientific observation of language demands that we reject the belief that speech is primarily concerned with symbols. We must eschew both the conception that a linguistic fact is a symbol, and that it is a process of making symbols. We may well ask what is an act or a word the symbol of? The traditional answer is that it is a symbol of the idea that one has in "mind." If language is interpreted in this way it is incumbent upon those who accept this interpretation to show the existence of such ideas.

If such things do not exist, then the symbol theory must be rejected. We repeat once more then that A tells B of some event, he merely adjusts himself to two stimuli at once. His action may be facial or

---

[9] This we say because in the thinking reaction the response is made directly to, though not in direct contact with, the stimulus object. The substitute stimulus is an intermediary, standing on a lower level than a direct stimulus. Cf. Kantor, *Principles of psychology*, 1926, Vol. II, Chapter 23.

hand-gesture. He may point to the object or he may say what he has to say verbally. But if words are only some of the ways of responding we can hardly think of even the words as symbols. Once more, language is what persons do by way of acting to persons and things simultaneously.

Early behaviorist writings led many American psychologists (including Kantor) to believe that the Wundtian system required a spiritualistic principle—or that it invoked some theological notion of a "soul." Such an interpretation would have caused Wundt to take the proverbial roll in his grave. He was indeed a mentalist but he was also a vigorous opponent of Cartesian mind-body dualism.

In the Anglo-American and French psychology and linguistics of the 1930s a movement was underway that paralleled the *Junggrammatiker* movement of the late nineteenth century. We could call it the *Jungmethodiker* movement. It consisted of prescriptions for segmenting, classifying, and counting behaviors or speech elements.* And its influence has only recently been challenged. However, before we outline these shifting philosophies of social science we shall return, in the next two chapters, to the *Sprachpsychologie* period in order to examine two special interests of that field that merit more attention: research both on language acquisition and reading skills.

---

* For further accounts of the influences of early behaviorist psychology on American linguistics see M. Schlauch, Early behaviorist psychology and contemporary linguistics, *Word*, 2: 25–36; and E. A. Esper, *Mentalism and objectivism in linguistics: the sources of Leonard Bloomfield's psychology of language* (New York: Elsevier, 1968). For a further comparison of the basic points of view of Kantor, Bühler, Gardiner, and de Saussure see P. L. Garvin, Referential adjustments and linguistic structure. *Acta Linguistica*, 1944, 4: 52–60.

CHAPTER 3

LANGUAGE ACQUISITION
The Most Frequently Studied Problem

With the rise of modern psychology the acquisition of language by children has been the most frequently investigated subject. In this one aspect psychological investigation spreads across national, cultural, and geographical boundaries, as a brief survey of the field for the time roughly simultaneous with the early period of psycholinguistics would show.

"Scientific pedagogy" blossomed in Germany during the early 1900s. Institutes for the study of child development were founded and journals were devoted to developmental psychology. In France a tradition of child study from Rousseau to Taine to Binet formed a parallel movement culminating in the productive Jean Jacques Rousseau Institute in Geneva. In England there was the work of James Sully and the *Journal of experimental Pedagogy* (published at Edinburgh), in America G. Stanley Hall formally began a child study movement and edited the first major journal in the field there, *The pedagogical Seminary* (later the *Journal of genetic Psychology*); in late nineteenth century Russia the St. Petersburg Society for Experimental Pedagogy was productive, and several notable language development studies appeared in the Russian literature. Around the turn of the century the Hungarian Child Study Society became one of the most successful of these ventures owing to the patronage of Count Sandor Teleki and to the leadership of Ladislaus Nagy who also edited *A Gyermek* (The Child). In Italy the research on childhood by Paolo Lombroso became widely known and it stimulated language development studies; a "national museum for child study" had been founded in Spain at Madrid and for some years it published bulletins of research progress reports; Ivan Gheorgov directed child study at the University of Sophia in Bulgaria at the turn of the century, and his own studies of the acquisition of syntax in children brought him international recognition. In addition to the occidental scholars, many students came from the Orient to study in European universities, and then carried the new developmental psychology to the East (see *Transactions of the institute for child Study,* Tokyo, and the *Chung Hua educational Review,* Shanghai).

The investigations at the outset of the twentieth century were usually an extension of the psychology of Herbart, Wundt, or Binet. And everywhere language acquisition was a topic of major interest. In the literature of this earlier period one may read language acquisition studies of English, French, German, Dutch, Swedish, Danish, Russian, Hungarian, Polish, Bulgarian, Serbian, Greek, Estonian, Czech, Spanish, Italian, and Japanese children, as well as scattered observation on several children with more exotic languages. Many reports were largely anecdotal, but others were careful and reliable.* However, a thorough review is not possible in one chapter.

The modern era of child psychology is usually dated from the appearance of Rousseau's book *Émile* (1762), an informal but most influential account of child development. During the period of 1800–1875, biographical studies of child development appeared with increasing frequency and either included observations on language acquisition or were devoted entirely to that topic. The model for these studies was the research of a philosophy professor at Marburg, Dietrich Tiedemann (1787) which had represented a significant advance in rigor and detailed observation.† Tiedemann introduced the method of the systematic "baby biography," and in so doing he recorded observations on language acquisition. Interest in Tiedemann's procedure of keeping daily written records of an infant's activity

---

* For a starting point in this varied literature the reader should see Werner F. Leopold's *Bibliography of child language* (Northwestern University Press, 1952). This includes citations prior to 1949. Although the list is admittedly biased toward Western studies and is thus incomplete, it is 106 pages long! In addition, I have recently found several other early investigations not mentioned there.

† In 1927 Suzanne Langer and Carl Murchison translated Tiedemann's report and published it in the *Journal of genetic Psychology* (*Pedagogical Seminary*), 1927, 34: 205–230.

culminated during the nineteenth century in several widely read volumes that included influential descriptions of language acquisition. The best known were by the philosopher Taine (1876), the psychologists Steinthal (1871) and Lazarus (1857), pedagogues Strumpell (1880) and Perez (1879), the physicians Sigismund (1856) and Vierordt (1879), the linguist Egger (1879), and the naturalist Darwin (1877). There were, to be sure, many more.

Naturally, the first occurrence of language in a child is a very dramatic event for many parents, and this, in combination with other nineteenth-century trends that we shall examine below, may account in part for the profusion of published observations. In 1833 Heinrich Feldman tabulated the time of appearance of the first word in thirty-three infants. Countless similar tabulations appeared during the course of the next 100 years.

Most psychology historians divide the modern era of child study into early and late periods on the basis of the publication of one book: Wilhelm Preyer's *Die Seele des Kindes* (The mind of the child, 1881). It was soon translated into many languages with the English translation appearing in 1888–1889. Preyer's was the most thorough and systematic investigation up to that date.

Preyer was a physiologist at Jena where in the 1870s he had studied the development of the human embryo. He then set out with his newborn child to observe and record everything that the infant did and everything that occurred around the infant during its first 1,000 days of life. Observation sessions took place at least three times a day at regular intervals (morning, noon and evening) and the child "was kept away from all training as far as possible, as well as the frequent observations of other children. . . ." Preyer was able to maintain this schedule while missing only two days. (In Preyer's time the next most ambitious effort in this regard may have been Wundt's sixteen-month daily observations of two of his children, which was never published separately, but occasionally discussed in other writings.*)

---

* A detailed study of phonological development in child speech does

Preyer's data and its analysis formed the basis for his two-volume work that went through five editions. The book was a significant impetus behind what was later known as the late nineteenth-century "child study movement," which received immense popular and governmental support in several countries. Hall, who initiated the American child study movement, wrote the following in his introduction to the American edition of Preyer's book: "Among all the nearly fourscore studies of young children printed by careful empirical and often thoroughly scientific observers, this work of Preyer's is the fullest and on the whole the best."

Preyer's volumes were divided into three parts: the development of the senses, the development of volitional processes, and the development of the intellect, the latter receiving the most attention. Intellectual development was concerned first with the acquisition of language and second with the development of logical processes. Preyer's reason for this emphasis comes from his orientation toward comparative psychology and his consequent questioning of the difference between human and animal development. This naturally led him to a thorough consideration of language. In addition, his interests as a physiologist led him to make a detailed comparison of the progressive stages of language development with the regressive stages of aphasia and other language pathologies. This anticipated the highly fruitful study of such comparisons that was made by Roman Jakobson in 1942 in his monograph *Child language, aphasia, and phonological universals* (first English edition, 1968).

Does such a tedious empirical investigation as Preyer's with its thousands of detailed observations lead to any significant basic conclusions? In regard to language, Preyer concluded that it is impossible to account for acquisition solely on the basis of learning, and that human language acquisition is pos-

---

appear in Wundt's *Die Sprache*, Part I. However, Wundt apparently did not share the popular enthusiasm for studying child-language development. He felt that it was more important to first understand the fully developed language ability in the adult and to have a description of language before one could profitably study language acquisition.

sible only if we assume that the child inherits some fundamental "ideas or concepts or judgments or inferences." Preyer was thus forced to adopt the nativist position.

Later generations thoroughly criticized, analyzed, corrected, vindicated, or rejected Preyer's work, and immediately following him the child study movement reached its "golden age."

At the turn of the century, child development research had grown so large that it was evolving into an independent discipline with its own professional associations, journals, and other formal arrangements. Pedagogical institutes and at least one child development journal had been established in each country where researchers were active. Then, too, the established nineteenth-century philology journals were frequently carrying articles on child language. One concise early review of the field appeared in Ament's *Sprechen und Denken beim Kinde* (Speech and thought in children, 1899). And one of Wundt's students, Ernst Meumann, presented in *Die Sprache des Kindes* (The language of children, 1903) a brief review of the theoretical issues and research methods of that day. Meumann was then the leading figure in German "scientific pedagogy."

The twenty-five years of research on language acquisition that followed Preyer's book culminated in Clara and William Stern's *Die Kindersprache* (Child language, 1907) which in turn was the most influential text for the next generation of developmental psycholinguists. In comparing the Sterns' work with Preyer's, we see that language development studies had improved in at least one important respect: they were becoming more linguistically sophisticated. However, the Sterns' book still left much to be desired concerning phonological aspects of development.

William Stern began his graduate studies in philology at Berlin. But the two occasions of hearing Lazarus lecture on the psychology of language and hearing Ebbinghaus lecture on experimental psychology caused him to change his course. He finished at Berlin as a psychologist under Ebbinghaus and Carl Stumpf. Stumpf himself published an influential language acquisition investigation in 1901. This background may have placed Stern somewhat outside the influence of Wundtian psychology which in Germany at that time had met its greatest opposition from the Berlin school, particularly from Stumpf (like Marty, Stumpf had been a student of Brentano's).

Stern later followed Ebbinghaus to Breslau where the language development work began. Daily observations were made on two of the Sterns' children for the first six years (records were kept in a daily diary—this was the primary contribution of Clara Stern), and less extensive observations were made on a third child. Analysis of data concerning the three children (Hilde, Gunther, and Eva) occupied the first quarter of their book; the rest treats the general psychology of language acquisition and includes discussions and comparisons of the work of other investigators including work in other languages. There are descriptions of expressive gestures, one-word sentences, syntactic structures (for example, the development of negation, clauses, interrogatives), and the development of word-forms and categories. A final section covered special linguistic problems of child language such as phonetic distortions, sound development, elliptical constructions, and original creations.

Many early writers on acquisition are easily categorized as arguing either for an *imitation* theory or for a *spontaneity* theory of language acquisition.* The Sterns show how each position when taken alone is too simplistic. William Stern's critique of Wundt's theory of the sentence might also be considered one of the major commentaries on Wundtian psycholinguistics. (This critique appears below as a long footnote in Stern's discussion.)

Stern viewed the development of languages as an unfolding process similar to the development of an embryonic cell into a complex organism—an analogy widely used at that time. This school of thought, known as "genetic psychology," extends from Wundt to Heinz Werner (see Werner's *The comparative psychology of mental development*, 1948). Genetic psychology was well described by the British psychologist James Ward in his article on Psychology for the *Encyclopedia Britannica* in 1911, Vol. XXII, p. 555:

---

* For a review of writings on language acquisition from Aristotle to Stern, see Friedrich Richter, *Die Entwicklung der psychologischen Kindersprachforschung* (Münster, 1927).

Psychologists have usually represented mental advance as consisting fundamentally in the combination and recombination of various elementary units, the so-called sensations and primitive movements: in other words, as consisting in a species of "mental chemistry." If we are to resort to physical analogies at all—a matter of very doubtful propriety—we shall find in the growth of a seed or an embryo far better illustrations of the unfolding of the contents of consciousness than in the building up of molecules: the process seems much more a segmentation of what is originally continuous than an aggregation of elements at first independent and distinct.

E. G. Boring in his *History* (1950) wrote that Ward, who was trained in Germany, had not been popular as a psychologist in England.

In Stern's opinion the *sentence* is the fundamental unit of language, and even some rudiments of syntax are inherent properties of the embryonic language "cell" at the outset of development. The reason for this lies in Stern's definition of the sentence as the reflection of a "disposition" (*Stellungnahme*) instead of merely a unified "whole impression" (*Gesamtvorstellung*). The influence of the Würzburg school of psychology is evident in this position.

Again, the notion of "analogical formation," reappears as one of the processes of language acquisition in Stern's writings. But Stern was also impressed with the "egocentric" nature of the initial language patterns in children. He argued that we must not force these language beginnings into the forms of the adult's elaborated syntax and categories. Rather, he stressed the productivity of children's attempts at language. The phenomena of a child's word-orderings provided Stern with fruitful observations on the unfolding of the mature surface structure of language.

Stern postulated the notion of a "speech-need" (*Sprachnot*) to account for many of the child's creative productions. When the child has developed a wealth of experiences that run far ahead of language development it is forced to be productive or inventive to the utmost to make use of its limited language means. According to Humboldt, this is after all the essence of language—to make "infinite use of finite means" (see Chapter

One). All the themes found in the Sterns' book reappeared in later prominent works on developmental psycholinguistics.

CLARA AND WILLIAM STERN · *The Language of Children*

External and Internal Causes. As with all mental development,[1] the main issue concerning language acquisition can be formulated as follows: what part of the developmental process is accounted for by external factors and what part by internal factors? This question was posed ages ago concerning the origins of speech itself. And just as two extreme viewpoints evolved whereby speech was conceived as arising either through *nature* or through *convention,* so it is with the modern discussion of the appearance of speech in children.

It might be assumed, of course, that there is an observable correlation between a child's speech and its environment, and that consequently the process of language acquisition by a child would be considered simply as the mechanical acceptance of external speech forms and meanings through imitation. In contrast, those who emphasized the internal contributions a child makes to its own speech looked for productions having nothing to do with imitation. They sought so-called "word inventions" or early manifestations of self-produced logical activity. Both views are capable of obscuring the real situation.

The fact that children imitate does not permit us to deny their spontaneity. For spontaneity by no means need be opposed to imitation, but can appear through the material acquired by imitation.[2] The real problem therefore is not one of imitation vs. spontaneity

SOURCE. Clara and William Stern, *Die Kindersprache* (Leipzig: Barth, 1907). Excerpts from chapters 10, 12, and 13. Translated by Jim Lyon and A. L. Blumenthal.

[1] See W. Stern, Tatsachen und Ursachen der seelischen Entwicklung, *Zeitschrift f. angew. Psychol.* I: 1, where the psychogenetic causal question in its general principles is discussed.

[2] See W. Stern in: *Bericht über den I. Kongr. f. exp. Psychol. in Giessen,* p. 108.

but rather concerns the extent that internal tendencies and forces are at work during assimilation, selection, and internal processing of externally presented forms.

Spokesmen for spontaneity have also gone too far, but in the opposite direction. Some who have hunted down "word inventions", that is, the child's neologisms for which there are no precedents in sound gestures and sound imitations or in words of conventional speech, got far off the track. Others have construed spontaneity too intellectually as a logical formation of concepts, thus contradicting the primitive makeup of children's speech.

We believe that the proper position is a synthesis of these two opinions. In his form of speech a child learning to speak is neither a phonograph reproducing external sounds nor a sovereign creator of language. In terms of the contents of his speech, he is neither a pure associative machine nor a sovereign constructor of concepts. Rather, his speech is based on the continuing interaction of external impressions with internal systems which usually function unconsciously; it is thus the result of a constant "convergence." The detailed investigations pertaining to the development of speech and thought should determine the relative participation of both forces and also show how they accommodate each other.

First, however, an overview of the various ways in which external and internal factors converge in the origin of child speech is necessary here.

In the words of Lazarus,[3] one can teach a child speech but not speaking. Speech consists of externally presented material; speaking, however, presupposes the impulse and the capability to express and communicate internal experiences in the form of symbols. If the child's speech-impulse is not fed something it can process, then the child remains on the creature level. But regardless of the means, if the child has the opportunity to form any material into symbols of expression and communication, he seizes upon this with an intensity, autonomy, and adroitness that vividly illustrate the internal productivity awaiting release.

. . . .

The Production of Speech Forms. Not everything an adult says

[3] M. Lazarus, *Leben der Seele,* 2nd ed., p. 166.

aloud to a child is imitated by the child; but the child says much that the adult has never said aloud to him. Here we mean neither the distorted words that the child produces through awkwardness in speech, nor babbled words, nor onomatopoeia, but rather spontaneous productions that the child makes using the material acquired from imitating.

The motivating factor in these derivations is primarily a deficit (or a need) that may be designated as a "speech need" (*Sprachnot*). Normally a wealth of experiences, and commensurately the need-for-utterance, develop more quickly than vocabulary acquisition. Yet the child makes a virtue of adversity. From his limited vocabulary he forms new language material. Certainly neither the "adversity" nor the means of eliminating it are conscious. Cases in which subjective inhibitions are added to the objective need are exceptions. And only intentional efforts to overcome this can lead to language formation.

In the great majority of cases this effort at internal production shows in analogy formations.[4] Certain partial impressions gained from familiar material become firmly associated with corresponding parts of sound images. Now when analogous parts occur in other situations the sound symbol will be reproduced and annexed as a new association. One should not interpret this to mean that in analogic speech the child sees a definite form something like a paradigm before him on which he patterns a new construction. When the child says "gived" (*gegebt*) instead of "given" (*gegeben*), the words "lived" (*gelebt*) and "strived" (*bestrebt*) do not necessarily have any influence—perhaps he does not even know these words. Instead we must assume that the weak conjugation generally produces a more rapid and definite association with the various concepts of time, number, etc., because of its stereotyped inflections subject to little change. Thus it creates the general tendency to form additional verbs according to the same system. Often there is absolutely no special similarity that might have produced the analogy. For example, consider the children's comparatives, "gooder" and "mucher."

[4] On analogy as a general speech and psychological phenomenon, cf. Wundt, *Die Sprache*, II (in the index under "Analogie und Analogiebildung"); Paul, *Prinzipien der Sprachgeschichte*, p. 96 ff.; W. Stern, *Die Analogie im volkstümlichen Denken*, Berlin, 1893, p. 140 ff.

Here, too, one can only speak of an indirect effect from the regular familiar comparatives.

Analogy formations render a tremendous savings in the enrichment of speech, since maximum productivity is attained with a minimum of consumed language. A small number of inflected, derived, compounded, and other forms learned by the child is enough for him to create a wealth of new constructions by analogy. This wealth must be much greater than we can prove, since formation by analogy is only recognizable beyond question when it results in incorrect or unusual forms of speech. But it surely must be active in forming correct constructions, though it is then not possible to decide whether these arose through imitation or analogy.[5]

. . . .

There are also syntactical productions with imitated material. Of course in most cases of a child's syntax the etiological decision as to whether a specific phrase or sentence structure is imitated or formed independently cannot be made. As with analogy formations, the role of the child's autonomy is clear only where the product deviates markedly from normal usage. This deviation is most apparent in three forms. Frequently a child's word order takes the strangest departures without concern for the conventional "normal order," for example, "don't big get dolly, little one yes." Further, two opposing deviations become evident in attempts to find a corresponding phrase for a thought content; one expresses the thought more succinctly while the other does so in a more involved way than convention would allow. Both have the character of a stop-gap measure, for

---

[5] The above is valid not only for child speech, but for all speech. Paul says (ibid., p. 99), "It was a basic error of earlier linguistic science that as long as speech did not deviate from existing usage it was treated as something which was reproduced from memory." He believes that in speech, analogy has "approximately the same impact" on related words and syntactical relationships that it has on speech reproduced from memory (p. 100). On the influence of a child's analogy formations in the general development of speech he says (p. 105), "Generally the deviations of child speech in this area have no consequences for the general development of later speech; nevertheless, traces are left here and there. Especially in cases where adults are prone to coin new constructions is a similar tendency shown in children, and they will succumb to this tendency as soon as the inhibition of adult speech is absent."

the child uses them in cases of speech-need. Yet he is not necessarily aware of this. In certain frames of mind (haste, or excitement) a child compresses into a "laconicism" what conventional speech expresses with many words and complicated sentences, for example, "dolly looks too bad" = the damaged dolly looks so terrible, that's too bad; or "I have button undone, please" = I have a button undone, please button it. In other cases the opposite occurs when a missing expression is circumlocuted more or less originally but always intelligibly, for example "the box where the lights are" = match box. [Other examples of laconicisms and circumlocutions are found in Stern, pp. 113–114.—A.L.B.]

. . . .

Consider now the internal factors of this process of convergence, to see more clearly what takes place in the child's mental process. It is clear that an explanation of children's linguistic meanings had been sought using the classifications and categories that were used successfully in grammar, logic, and even psychology to explain adult speech. But precisely this approach has for a long time obscured the true situation, especially for the early stages of language acquisition. Here the meanings are still in part so undifferentiated that it is erroneous even to question whether they belong in certain categories. To apply to the embryonic condition of child language the sharp distinctions that logic makes between abstract and concrete or individual and general concepts, between comparison and differentiation, or those that grammar makes between words and sentences or different word classes, or those that psychology makes between subjective-affective and objective-intellectual contents would constitute a distortion. Just as the primeval cell of an organism does not yet show a division of separate organs or functions, so too the primeval symbols of speech do not yet have a definite special character. Thus the development of the child's language meanings represents a progressive process of differentiation. When in the following genetic analysis we attempt to postulate certain orders of succession of the logical, grammatical, and psychological categories, this does not imply a clear division between them existing from the outset. But rather, there are definite forms that gradually emerge in a certain sequence from an undifferentiated, unimaginably primitive condition.

. . . .

The Beginnings of Language in Syntactical Constructions: One-Word Sentences . . . It is quite difficult to describe language acquisition in terms of internal structure; here there are many disputed questions, and great effort has gone into this problem of the first language meanings. The fact that these meanings reveal variations that appear to defy classification in the conventional categories causes consternation. A solution can only be found in the above-mentioned idea of gradual differentiation.

Thus the question of what word class a child's first utterances fall into is incorrectly formulated. The division made between interjections and nouns is only valid for consideration of the external grammatical form. Psychologically it is not justifiable. A child's language units belong to no word class at all, since they are not individual words, but sentences. A word is an expression of a unified content of consciousness. A sentence, however, is the expression of a unified position either taken, or about to be taken concerning a content of consciousness.[6]

---

[6] On defining the sentence: The above definition does not agree with any of the numerous definitions given up to now which all seem to miss the essence of the matter (see Wundt *Die Sprache,* II, p. 222 ff.).

The older "synthetic" definitions that regard the sentence as a combination of words or concepts or ideas fail, because the sentence does not arise through the combination of primary elements, but is a primary element itself. For approximately one-half year the child learning to speak uses sentences consisting of only a single word.

In contrast to earlier definitions, Wundt presents an "analytical" definition that has been acclaimed by many contemporaries. The sentence is "the articulation in speech of the voluntary structuring of a whole impression into its constituents according to their logical relations to one another." The improvement with this definition lies in its recognition of the principle that "the whole precedes the parts"; but it fails to grasp the decisive difference between a word and a sentence (or word-complex). Whenever I read aloud with understanding some sign on the street, for example, "German Monthly" or "Tavern at the Sign of the Lion," or whenever I recite a poem and announce the title, for example, "The fight with the dragon," in each case it is the expression of a total idea that is structured out of components brought together in logical relationship to each other. But these are still not sentences. The mere expression of ideas leads only to words, word sequences, and word complexes. It is another matter if upon seeing the tavern sign I *exclaim* "Tavern at the Sign of the Lion" in the sense of "There's the Tavern at the Sign of the Lion," or if I answer the question as to which ballad I like best by saying "The fight with the dragon." I express the same ideas, but this time as objects of my expressed

Thus in recent times linguistic science has generally come to assume that language development begins with sentence units and not word units, an assumption confirmed as true by scholars of child language. The speech novice does not speak in order to utter isolated ideas, but rather to take a *position* on them or to demand a position from others (interrogative sentences). This is the only explanation for the fact that one unit of speech can be used within such a wide range. The child's *mama* cannot be translated into adult speech as the word unit "mother," but only as sentence units "Mother, come here,"

---

opinion (or comment); thus my utterances have become elliptical sentences.

In order to explain terms that are not widely used in psychology such as *comment, assertion,* or *disposition* (*Stellungnahme*), or even *self-disposition* (*Selbststellung*) as Münsterberg says, and in order to contrast these with the concept of mental representation (*Vorstellung*), note that "representation" means the indifferent existence of a content of consciousness having the nature of an object. Comment or attitude (*Stellungnahme*), however, means an alternate type of behavior of a unified subject, a recognition or rejection, approval or disapproval, wishing or denying, praising or blaming.

By incorporating attitudinal comment into the definition we dispose of a series of difficulties. With a child's one-word sentences it would be possible only with great artificiality to prove that the total articulated impression is ordered into its component parts and that these are related to each other. Dittrich, who essentially accepts Wundt's definition for his own analysis of one-word sentences (not from children, of course), is often compelled to call the result of his ordering an "impression" plus "feeling" instead of several partial impressions. Thus he does not call his point of departure for the process a "whole impression" (*Gesamtvorstellung*), but the "state of meaning" (*Bedeutungstatbestand*) in a more general sense. See O. Dittrich, *The linguistic definition of the concepts "sentence" and "syntax,"* in Wundt's *Philos. Studien,* 19, 1908, pp. 93 ff., especially p. 124.

The concept of "structuring" (or "ordering") is by no means universally valid. When a one-year-old child utters the one word sentence "bottle," the content of consciousness is neither analyzed nor joined with anything. But as an undivided, unified content it becomes the point of attack for the comment or disposition.

Our definition further unequivocally delimits the sentence unit in a way not done in the other definitions. Often it is questionable as to what can be considered one whole impression. Is the sentence, "From the streaming brow the sweat must flow," really only the unfolding of a single total idea? Certainly, however, the articulated content of consciousness, regardless of how many ideas comprise it, is the object of a unified disposition, namely of a demand (summons, or claim). This makes the utterance become a sentence.

"Mother, give me something," "Mother, put me on the chair," "Mother, help me," etc. For these reasons the first stages of children's language have been designated as the stages of the "sentence-word." The name "one-word sentence" would be more precise.

The stage in children's language when the sentence consists of only one word is a rather long period. The following figures show that this is usually around a half year in length, though a few are shorter and some considerably longer. A long period is less a sign of slowness in language development than of the efficiency of one-word sentences.

The one-word sentence stage lasted:[7]

5 months in Günther Stern and Tögel's son.
5-1/2 months in Gheorgov's son I.
6 months in Gheorgov's son II.
7 months in Hilde Stern and Idelberger's son.
7-1/2 months in Ament's niece and Eva Stern.
8-1/2 months in Lindner's son.
12 months in Preyer's son.

. . . .

Development of the Sentence

Simple Sentence Stage. . . On the average the child begins around the middle of the second year of life to speak multiple-word sentences. Table 1 shows samples of such early sentences. Their orthographic representation, however, does not adequately portray a peculiarity usually seen, namely, the jerky manner of punctuating the spoken words with pauses. This occurs in various kinds of sentences, usually vocative sentences. When the child says *ata-puppe* [have-doll], each word actually has sentence value. To be absolutely accurate, one would have to speak of a chain of primitive sentences. But at the same time real sentences like Hilde's *da ist brbr* [there's an animal] or Ament's *babedd dschidschi* [Babett rode on the train] occur.

In their grammatical structures these sentences are very different. In the earliest stage, the prevailing type is where one part is formed by a vocative or an interjection and the other part represents the actual central matter to be communicated. But sentences with related parts soon take over, for example,

---

[7] The times shown here were determined by subtracting the dates when the child began to speak from the dates when the first sentences of more than one word were spoken.

subject + object: *danna kuha* [Auntie, give me some cake],
verb + adverbial designation: *mama ada* [I was walking with mama],
subject with predicate nominative: *kind kalt* [the child is cold].

The combination of verb and object appears very frequent, as the examples in Table 1 show.

As Table 1 shows, the first multiple-word sentences consist of only

TABLE 1
Initial Multiple-Word Sentences (Reduced list from Clara and William Stern, 1907)

Child	Sentence	Age Years, Months	Explanation (Translation)
Eva Stern	hildä—kakao!	1, 4⅔	Hilde, come for cocoa!
	ätä—puppe	1, 4⅔	Father, I have a doll.
	mama komma	1, 6	Mama, come here.
	mama—hilda	1, 6	Mama, carry me to hilde.
Axel Preyer	haim mimi	1, 11	I want to go home and drink milk.
	danna kuha	2, ½	Auntie gave me cake.
	kaffee nein	2, ½	There's no coffee there.
	mama ětse	2, ½	Mama should sit down.
Ament's niece	babedd dschidschi	1, 7	Babett rode on the train.
	lulu dai	1, 8	Lulu's here.
	lili alden	1, 9	Willi should hold (it).
Lindner's son	a, bennt	1, 9½	Oh, it's burning.
	mama geben	1, 9½	Mama should give.
Idelberger's son	mama obba-obba	1, 3	Mama, get up.
	mama ada	1, 4	I was walking with Mama.
Tögel's son	baba bisch-bisch	1, 7	Papa is sleeping.
Major's child *R*	gash faw	1, 11½	The glass falls.
	aga baw	1, 11½	Ball is gone.
	wead moom	2, 0	Read the story about the moon.
Tracy's Boy *C*	papa cacker	1, 6½	Papa has firecrackers.
Sully's Child *M*	mama tie	1, 6½	Mama, button it.
Taine's Girl	abûle coucou	1, 6	The burning (ça brule) is hiding: the sun sets.
Gheorgov's first son	daj chieb	1, 7	Give bread.
	ela nana	1, 8	Come, brother.
Deville's daughter	i pa	1, 1½	Eugene's gone.

(*Reading*) *The Language of Children*

two parts each. But as soon as the child acquires the ability to synthesize, he has no basic difficulty in forming more complex combinations, and they appear quickly. With the first synthesis of three or more words something similar to what happened during the transition from the one-word sentences to two-part sentences occurs. The new element is not integrated into the grammatical structure of the sentence but is appended as an independent word instead. Through a sentence chain the child thus acquires a sentence structuring that becomes increasingly complex. At 1 year, 10 months Hilde, could already express the main components of such thoughts as "Mama should get me the pictures from the back room," but only by making a chain of six primitive short sentences: *Mama. Bildä hamele. Zimmä. Hamele bildä. Hinten. Dada mana eholn.* ["Mama—Pictures want—Room—Back—Dada, mama bring."]

Just as the last sentence in this chain has three words, other sentences of more than two words appear, and they begin to approach the conventional sentence form, for example, *Hier liegt er doch* ["He's lying here"] or *mama, zeig doch de bildä* ["Mama, show me the pictures"]. The more the number of words increases, the more difficulty the child has putting them in the correct, or the conventional, order. The result of this is a dominant word-order to which we devote a special section of this chapter.

It appears that toward the end of the second year the child leaves the stage of the simple sentence by means of the increasingly complex sentence. As examples of early complex sentences Hilde (1,11) says *hommit die mama und der papa auch* ["Mama is coming and Papa, too"]; Tögel's son (1,11 1/2) says *buwi supe esn waisch* ["Bubi's eating soup and meat."].

The contents of the first multiple-word sentences have one thing in common: they are all positive in nature. Our list shows only one negation example out of 40 (Preyer's *Kaffee nein*), and it occurs at a fairly late age. When negating sentences do appear after some time, they almost always have the nature of a primitive sentence chain. Negation is not part of the sentence but an independent expression of attitude that usually does not occur until after the positive part of the sentence has been spoken. Thus the first negating word is "no" rather than "not," a phenomenon that has analogies throughout the development of language. [The Sterns give extensive examples of this principle with other structures.—A.L.B.]

. . . .

Word Order. Word position as used in children's sentences deserves special discussion. It too is a product of both imitation and spontaneity. Several sentences will have absolutely conventional word order and then there comes an apparently whimsical and irregular word sequence. The departure from colloquial language is especially noticeable in the first two years of speech. Individual differences are especially strong. Some children quickly acquire the essential features of conventional word order; others resist for prolonged periods with unusual tenacity. Our daughter Hilde and Tögel's child belong to the first type; our son Günther and Stumpf's son belong to the second type.[8]

. . . .

Even disregarding seemingly spontaneous creations of the child, there are countless instances where we can in fact speak of free word placement. Their variety and arbitrariness defies final classification into a series of grammatical-linguistic laws. What might appear as a rule can be refuted by the opposite structure of the next word sequence. On the other hand, with some care it is permissible to consider certain psychological factors whereby peculiarities of children's word orders are at least in part intelligible.

Every person who utters a sentence—be he adult or child—must anticipate in consciousness, however vaguely, the essential content of what he wants to say. Whether we talk about a whole impression (*Gesamtvorstellung*) as does Wundt, or whether the anticipation is more of a sensory or volitional nature is not relevant for this study. With more simple contents of consciousness, a relaxed mental state, and a ready mastery of language, this anticipation easily achieves articulation. Through long practice a conventional unified word-sequence appears for each thought constituent. This is not so for distinctly different mental states, that is, in different conceptual

---

[8] A corresponding distinction exists, moreover, among various natural languages. For example, in many modern languages a rather fixed and firmly rule-governed word order obtains, as opposed to Latin where almost completely arbitrary orderings are possible resembling the freedom at times observed in children's word orderings. Wundt in *Die Sprache* (II, p. 349) presented the example of the sentence, "Romulus founded Rome," which in Latin may occur as either of six permutations of the three words *Romulus condidit Romam.*

processes, in highly emotional states, and where there is limited mastery of language. Under these conditions there is a barrier between the anticipation and its articulation. Whatever was experienced as a whole must be developed arduously into a succession of constituents and, correspondingly, be expressed as a succession of words. For example, anyone who has done scholarly work has experienced the process of intuitively sensing a thought without being immediately able to articulate it in words. He then experiences how it crosses the speech threshold in individual parts. In an emotional state speakers commonly say "Words fail me" which is indeed the description of the corresponding psychological process. Here, too, the experience is gradually refined into sequences of thoughts and words that often run counter to conventional sequences. Finally, in a foreign language that a speaker has not fully mastered we also see the breach between anticipation and ultimate articulation. Not until one has learned "to think" in that language do inhibitions disappear.

These mental pre-requisites apply even more strongly to a child who often attempts to master contents of consciousness that are difficult for him. He is subject to highly emotional states more often than adults, and further, his mastery of speech is still incomplete. Thus we see the phenomenon of "accelerated attention" which plays an important role in language formation generally. From a disorganized general impression or an unstable feeling, a child must gradually work out the individual constituents. Language functions as a transcribing apparatus that should accurately reproduce this succession of mental constituents.

Why the sequence in which thoughts are converted into speech should proceed in one way or another usually escapes our grasp; perhaps very fine impulses or such very small differences of value among the elements are so decisive that psychological analysis breaks down. Take for example our son Günther's statement that was used three different ways within a few minutes: *freude machen ä muttsen* (*ich will der Mutter Freude machen*) = "I want to make mother happy"; *muttsen freude emacht a günther* (*Der Mutter hat Günther eine Freude gemacht*) = "Günther made mother happy"; and *freude günther emacht ä muttsen* (*Eine Freude hat Günther gemacht der Mutter*) = "Günther made his mother happy." It would be splitting hairs here to explain the special nuance of the thought sequence on the basis of the word order. Major reports an analogous example:[9] The boy *R* normally did not depart from conventional word order. "But when a strong emotional state prevailed, then convention, example, and habit lost their influence completely, and he mixed up the sentence parts in every possible way." Thus at age two he demanded food for his brother's doll to eat: *Budda doi betie* ["brother's doll food"]. When he did not get it right away he became angry and cried: *Doi betie—etie buddah doi—Doi buddah*. Stumpf also presents an analysis of his son's unusual word-sequences.[10] "Felix was (in regard to word order) totally unconcerned. It apparently did not concern him how all the words necessary for expression of his thought were ordered in the sentence. But he always used all the words even though they appeared in colorful disorder." For example, *Ich olo hoto wapa* = "My Rudy horse tipped over," that is, "Rudy tipped over my horse."

Wundt[11] compares the active process of word placement with that of visual perception in which a total view is perceived (for example a landscape) and after that the successive apperception of parts takes place. Just as it is difficult to say why in viewing a landscape a certain church tower or a grove of trees is noticed before other things, it is often difficult to establish the chronology of the linguistic analysis of the mental state.

In rare cases we encounter phenomena of a child's word arrangements in which clearly determinable psychological *motifs* are at work. Through a survey of different children's languages we were able to determine only two really unmistakable factors: the tendency to place the visual before the non-visual, and the tendency to place what is interesting before what is not.

1. Priority Placement of that Emphasized by Feeling. The words of a sentence do not have equal value for the speaker. We adults sometimes allow for this difference in values by our word order: "The *knife* is what I want" (when someone passes me the fork). More often, however, we let ourselves be bound by conventional word order and only emphasize feeling through sound stress: "I want the *knife*" (not the fork). The child also employs stress, but to a greater extent he

---

[9] D. R. Major, *First steps in mental growth* (New York, 1906), pp. 278–333.

[10] C. Stumpf, Eigenartige spachliche Entwicklung eines Kindes. *Ztsch f. päd. Psychol.*, 1900, p. 15.

[11] Wundt, *Die Sprache,* II: 351.

uses word order for emphasis. Those constituents having the greatest emotional value are the first to work their way out of the total complex, and their appearance in speech follows the same order. Thus word order becomes a natural symbolism for the order of values.

The fact that words of strongest interest occur in primary positions has often been observed. Wundt formulated the principle for general linguistics in the following manner: "Wherever word order is free and is not bound by conventional norms or other conditions, the words are ordered according to the degree of emphasis of the constituents."[12] Various observers of children have pointed out the special role that this principle plays...[13]

2. *Priority Placement of the More Visual.* The second thing that influences word placement is the degree of concreteness or abstraction that attends various mental contents. As soon as an integrated complex of any substantive impression with its inherent qualities (conditions, characteristics, activities, relationships) is released as a series of mental constituents, there is a strong receptiveness for that element which can be conceptualized alone, which is the concrete visual object. The concepts that follow are then only those needed for the dependent substratum—the abstract components.

This sequential principle is especially strong in sign language, since here the ordering of individual symbols is slower than in spoken language. Thus the sign-language sentence of a deaf-mute or of a primitive tribesman always has the adjective follow the noun, the verb follow the object, the negation follow that which is to be negated, and the interrogative word follows whatever it asks about. The sentence, "The large man shoots the bear," would come out in sign language as, "Man large bear shot." And an American Indian expressed the thought "Where is your mother?" with the sign-sequence "Mother yours see not where."[14] Wundt explains this as follows, "It is a prerequisite for clarity that those impressions take

---

[12] *Ibid.*, Wundt also traces this phenomenon to the psychological law of "successive apperception of parts of a whole according to the proportion of impression on consciousness."

[13] See W. Ament, *Die Entwicklung von Sprechen*, etc. 1899, p. 164; G. Lindner, *Aus dem Naturgarten der Kindersprache* (Leipzig, 1898), p. 57; and H. Tögel, 16 Monate Kindersprache. *Beiträge zur Kinderforschg. u. Heilerziehung*, Vol. 13, 1905. p. 30.

[14] Wundt, *Die Sprache*, I: 211.

priority that can be thought of separately from any others. The impressions that follow are those that have need of the other ones in the structure of thought."[15] In child language this tendency is not nearly so strong, but it is present. Just as the gesturing Indian put the "where" at the end, we occasionally heard Hilde say *apfe wo?* ["apple where?"] and *natz wo?* ["scissors where?"]. . .

The Stern's book is now little known in America. In Europe, however, it has continued as a popular text up to the present day. Two later editions appeared, the final one in 1928. It has been reprinted in Germany as recently as 1965. One effect of the 1907 appearance of this book was a renewed general interest in child language during the early twentieth century. The strong incentive for the earlier child language investigations had come, perhaps, from Darwinian evolution theory. A blend of evolutionism and nineteenth-century romanticism stands out in the proposal that the appearance of language in the child is a recapitulation of the evolution of language in primitive man. Paul, for instance, encouraged the examination of child language development as a means for testing principles of historical language change. Carl Franke seems to have been the linguist who took Paul's suggestion most seriously. Franke made a detailed comparison of the development of language in children with the development of language in societies (see his "Sprachentwicklung der Kinder und der Menschheit,"* in *Encyclopädisches Handbuch der Pädagogik*, 1899).

In publications of about 1900 one finds again and again Herodotus' account of the attempt by the ancient Egyptian king Psammeticus (or Psamtik I, 663–609 B.C.) to isolate children and thereby discover the first human language.† But even more obvious in these publications is the proliferation of theories about the historical origin of human language (see Chapter One).

---

[15] Wundt, *Die Sprache*, I: 217.

* "Language development in the child and in mankind."

† This experiment was performed again by later monarchs in Germany and Scotland, but the traditional folklore descriptions never clearly revealed their results.

Speculation on the subject had become so intense that in the 1880s the French Academy voted that it would refuse to hear any further papers concerning language origin.

The early theories of how men first came to use language were similar in that they all assumed the problem to be one of the origin of single words. The three more prominent views were the "onomatopoeic," the "interjectional," and the "natural response" theories. Each received a derogatory name assigned by opponents holding other viewpoints. Thus there were respectively (1) the "bow-wow" theory that explains the origin of language through the imitation of sounds made by animals and objects in man's immediate environment, (2) the "pooh-pooh" theory where the first words were held to be emotional exclamations provoked by environmental events, and (3) the "ding-dong" theory that first words were naturally fixed responses forced out directly by environmental stimuli, just as automatic and mechancial as the occurrence of sound that follows when a bell is struck.

One of the most active participants in these discussions was Müller at Oxford (see Chapter One), and who was identified with the "ding-dong" theory. Needless to say, these explanations were of little interest to most of the new psychologists—Their greatest objection was to the limited power of the explanations. If taken literally, each "theory" explained far too few words or utterances to be of any value. Nor was it feasible to derive the rest of language by complications or generalizations from such beginnings. And when the theories were interpreted loosely or programmatically they lost all specific meaning. Another objection was to the assumption that the *word* developed in isolation as the unit of communication; it was believed that *sentences* probably developed first and that words came to be recognized only after language had been committed to writing.

Wundt had directed strong criticisms at the simplistic theories of language origin. However, Wundt then went on to propose his own theory based on innate gestures; although his theory was worked out in greater detail than the others, it generated no more enthusiasm. The issue of the historical origin of language is a relatively quiet one today, so we will not pursue it further here.

Nevertheless, related to these discussions of origins are many descriptions of unique or original languages invented by children, and these discussions formed an issue that prompted strong debates among developmental psycholinguists. An American ethnologist, Horatio Hale, presented several cases of invented child-language before the American Association for the Advancement of Science in 1886 and before the Canadian Institute in 1888. Occasional records of unique child-languages have continued to appear, sometimes written by psychologists or linguists. Certain anthropologists (see Romanes, *Mental evolution in man*, 1888) had seriously considered the inventive capacity of children as an explanation for linguistic change. This was especially useful for explaining American Indian languages with their troublesome diversity because it seemed plausible that children of wandering nomadic tribes might have become isolated through adversities of the environment being thus forced to invent their own and new aboriginal language.

At the end of the 1900s numerous authorities believed that if an infant were left alone from birth it would develop its own language as rich as that of its parents (for example, George Romanes, 1888, Frederick Tracy, 1896, James Sully, 1896, Wilhelm Preyer, 1898, Wilhelm Ament, 1899, Alexander Chamberlain, 1900, Carl Stumpf, 1901, and Amy Tanner, 1904. Wundt was influential in turning back this excessive tide of romanticism in child study.

As a strict adherent to careful research methodology, Wundt intended to separate romantic myth from psychological possibility, particularly concerning the hope of discovering mankind's original language in a one-year-old child. There is much in the early literature that speaks of the child as "creating language out of nothing." In the early twentieth century the reaction to this careless writing was one of extreme caution whenever approaching the subject of language creativity.

It was often said that Wundt gave no credit to the child for language learning, and Wundt was frequently quoted superficially and out of context as saying that speech is a "product of the child's environment, something in which the child in essence only participates passively," or that Wundt relied on *imitation* as the device of language acquisition. But that does not adequately describe his position. He also wrote that "language is re-developed anew in each child under the influence of its environment." Wundt considered imitation and habit to play a *secondary* role in language acquisition (see *Die Sprache*, 1900, I:361; or 1911, I:385). Habit and imitation may be active, but according to Wundt they were not the forces that made acquisition of human language possible. Wundt argued that the form of language among isolated children remained an open question because of the lack of adequate observations; but he agreed that such children could develop a language of some type. His views on the whole matter were summarized in *Outlines of psychology* translated by C. H. Judd, 1907, p. 339.

We obtain no information in regard to the *general development of speech* from the individual development of the child, because in the case of the child the larger part of the process depends on those about him rather than on the child himself. Yet, the fact that the child learns to speak at all, shows that he has psychical and physical traits favorable to the reception of language when it is communicated. In fact, it may be assumed that these traits would, even if there were no communications from without, lead to the development of some kind of expressive movements accompanied by sounds, which sounds would form an incomplete language. This supposition is justified by the observation of the deaf and dumb children who have grown up without any systematic education.

Wundt's support for these views came from his own investigations of the elaborate sign languages that arose spontaneously among untutored deaf-mutes, who were certainly in a situation of isolation from the usual language environment.*

Despite a declining interest in the phenomenon, most reports of children's invented languages are found in publications since 1900. In 1903 the Danish linguist Otto Jespersen made such an investigation. He found two boys, identical twins five years old, formerly under the care of a deaf, elderly woman who had been found guilty of neglect. Authorities had placed the children in

---

* The first institute in Germany for the scientific study of deaf-mutes was organized at the University of Leipzig in 1876 shortly before Wundt founded the psychological laboratory there.

an orphanage (at age four and one-half) where they first began to speak Danish. Although they comprehended simple spoken Danish, they spoke very little. Jespersen analyzed what was apparently their own unique language. Phonetically, this language differed from Danish in a marked but regular way. Jespersen claimed that the syntactic structure was unlike Danish. The following are several sentences he recorded plus his description:

Nina enaj una haena mad enaj, "we shall not fetch food for the young rabbits." nina = rabbit (Kanin), *enaj* = negation (nej, no) repeated several times in each negative sentence, as in Old English and in Bantu languages, *una*=young (unge). *Bap ep dop,* "Mandse has broken the hobbyhorse," literally, "Mandse horse piece." *Hos ia bov Ihalh,* "brother's trousers are wet, Maria," literally "trousers Maria brother water." The words are put together without any flexions, and the word order is totally different from that of Danish. . . But then it must be remembered that they spoke a good deal that neither I nor any of the people about them could make anything of.*

These children had been isolated and obviously developed their language through interacting with each other. A distinctly different situation is that of the child who develops a "language" alone that no sibling or other person understands or uses. Stumpf's own son was reported as such a case. In 1901 Stumpf presented one of the most elaborate analyses of a child's unique (*eigenartige*) language. But for the reader's convenience we shall discuss a case reported in the English language literature.

America quickly assumed leadership in developmental psychology owing to the efforts of one of the great leaders in child study, Hall, a popular innovator who introduced Freud to America. In the late 1870s in Leipzig, Hall became Wundt's first American student, but the two men differed strongly and Hall soon returned to America. Later at Clark University he was influential in establishing the most productive laboratory, training center, and the major journal for child psychology. Such qualities per-

* O. Jespersen, *Language, its nature, development, and origin* (New York: Holt, 1921), pp. 185–186.

haps compensated for Hall's lack of concern for careful methodology that has plagued his reputation.*

Of the many students from Hall's "shop," perhaps the one who wrote most on language development was Margaret Morse Nice. At the University of Oklahoma between 1915 and 1925, Nice published a dozen studies on acquisition. One of Nice's own children, identified only as R, did not talk until sixteen months of age, and then proceeded to develop in a bizarre way. Nice describes the progressive development of some of R's words and concludes that the child's utterances are an exaggerated form of baby talk. The viewpoint of the description is that the child showed a form of "retarded speech." This is a sample of R's vocabulary:

nya = long, far, big, thick
co = outdoors
cut = broken, injured
choo = go
fu = blow
ner = have, want
hun or her = they, that, this, it
har = thing
ha = there, what
gia = two (or indefinite number)
er = yes
un = not
na = no
da = (1) don't; (2) dear
ah = me, my, mine
cuggan = sister, other
ker = (1) with, at, to; (2) cold, bare
va = (1) other, more, again; (2) very well; (3) good
on = in, off

A very large portion of the other words designated objects or creatures and were derived from imitations of the sounds they

* For more of this history see William Kessen, *The child* (New York: John Wiley, 1966); also A. A. Roback, *A history of american psychology* (New York: Collier, 1964).

made, for example, Wawa = dog. R had many words that were exactly alike in pronunciation, but different in derivation and meaning. The child stretched the capacities of her small vocabulary to the utmost, avoiding the use of new words: with terms such as "va" for *other*, "un" for *not*, and "ker" for *cold*, she could then say "va mama" instead of *papa*, and "un Ker" for *warm*. Very few sample sentences were reported. Nice professed some difficulty in understanding the longer constructions.

During *R*'s fourth year understandable English began to replace the child-dialect. The acquisition rate for English words was amazingly rapid, increasing by eight words a day—much faster than commonly observed. Just prior to this change Nice made the following observation:

It was at this time that her needs at last outstripped her means of expression; she began to imagine things and wished to tell stories. She liked to relate exciting tales after she had gone to bed, shouting "Mama" in indignant tones every tenth or twelfth word for fear I might entertain notions of leaving. These stories were evidently amusing for she laughed over them, but unfortunately I could not understand them at all, having no clue as to what they were about.

As long as her communication needs included only expression of emotions and simple wants, *R* could get along with this "original language," relying on gestures, tone of voice, and the intelligence of others. Then Nice wrote, "It was only when she herself had reached the stage where she wished to communicate intellectual experiences that she found herself seriously hampered." Nice concluded that for this child, speech was not primarily for purposes of communication but was largely a matter of self-expression, and she was critical of linguists for not making that distinction clearer. The following is an excerpt from the concluding sections of her report.

MARGARET MORSE NICE · *The Child as a Language Creator*

Only one previous study of a child's "peculiar" (*eigenartige*) speech appears to have been published—that of the psychologist Stumpf on his son (1901).[*] Enough data has, however, been given to afford us some idea of the nature of the retarded speech of four children: Buckman's daughter at three years, Major's son at three, and two boys described by Town—one of five (Town, 1921) and the other of twelve (Town, 1907). The case of another three year old boy was reported to me by his mother, Mrs. M. H. Allee (Nice, 1918). Five children, besides R, who were unusually slow in talking and who ranged from the ages of three to six years, have come under my personal observation: a little girl in a Montessori Nature Study School (Nice, 1915), three of my nieces, and a nephew.

The chief characteristic of Felix Stumpf seemed to be stubborn insistence on his own pronunciation and his own "words"; he had a small vocabulary but larger than R's and like her he extended the meanings of many of his words. Although his language seemed as far from German as R's from English, his father was able to trace the origin of every word but one—either from *Lallwörter* (babblings) or from the language he heard. Several of his *Lallwörter* developed into definite words: for instance, he had a general term of approbation "aja" meaning "good, pleasant, lovely" coming from a baby expression of joy used especially over new foods; R used "va" in the same way. Felix used "ä"—an imitative sound of disgust to mean "bad, ugly, black, dirty"; the last two uses remind us of R's "coal" for black and dirty. Felix employed "ich" from his 26th month for all cases of the first personal pronoun, just as R used "ah" beginning two months later. Again he used his brother's name "Olul" somewhat as R employed "Cuggan," for he designated a boy cousin who

SOURCE. Margaret Morse Nice, A child who would not talk. The pedagogical Seminary (Journal of genetic Psychology), 1925, 32: 105–142, with permission of the publisher.

[*] References appear at the end of this excerpt.

was about his brother's age as "Tap-Olul" (Tap was his word for Scheere—the last name of the cousin).

When he was 39 months old he suddenly one day became willing to repeat German: *"War es doch wirklich, als ob der heilige Geist über ihn gekommen wäre und ihm die Gabe der Sprache eingegossen hatte"*. He learned conventional speech rapidly after this and in two months his first complete spontaneous sentence appeared. Stumpf considered that the chief motive for the peculiar speech of his son was his pleasure in new forms (*Neubildungen*); but the surprising thing was the constancy with which he clung to these expressions long after they had ceased to be new. His sudden change was explicable on the ground that he had become tired of his play. R's change to conventional speech was a much more gradual matter than was this German boy's.

One of my nieces, A, evidently had something of a language making genius akin to R's ability. As a baby she had digestive troubles for some months after she was weaned; she was nearly two years old before she walked although she was not a heavy child. She worked out many original expressions and showed great unwillingness to adopt ordinary speech until after she was four. Like R she devised special terms for "yes" ("ah") and "no" ("er-er") and used "ah-ah" to designate crying. Again, with her as with Felix and R several *Lallwörter* apparently developed into words as "her-her" meant "want" and "hin-hin," "lost" or "gone." Although she gradually dropped her peculiar expressions, at the age of six and a half she is still talking with a marked infantile stammer.

. . . .

Theories as to the Cause of R's Delay in Speech

I have no satisfactory theory as to why my third daughter should have followed such an atypical course of speech development. She is of normal intelligence and she has suffered from no defects of the auditory or vocal apparatus. I cannot feel that she was a "victim of rearing" for she was not pampered nor her "slightest wish anticipated" (Blanton, 1919). The Sterns (1907) suggested that peculiar speech development may be due to stubborness (*Hartnäckigkeit*) or originality of the children concerned, but R has not shown these characteristics in any special degree. On the other hand she has been the most sociable of all our children, a fact that does not seem consistent with her refusal to adopt conventional means of communication. There does not seem to have been any relation with handedness, as she became definitely righthanded at the age of 26 months.[1]

The Blantons (1919) state that "slowness of speech may be due to serious illness in infancy. A large number of children who suffer from digestive disorders incident to the first taking of food other than mother's milk are often in this class." It may be that this was the disturbing factor in R's case. A exhibited a somewhat similar history. On the other hand, A's twin brother and sister, my niece G, my pupil, and Mrs. Allee's son all enjoyed continuous good health.

As to the method of dealing with a child who will not talk, the Blantons say that "where full intelligence is present" he "should be required to make an attempt at repeating the names of things before they are given to him. Even such vital things as food and water may have to be withheld until necessity forces the child to concede to these new demands and repeat or attempt to repeat the word that the giver says." We did not try anything so drastic with our child and our practice of trusting to the force of good example was justified by the outcome. But if her refusal to talk had continued much longer, more direct methods of encouraging correct speech would have been necessary.

Invention of Words and Languages

The statement is often met that little children invent words and occasionally whole languages. Indeed, on the strength of the report of four "original languages" having been "invented" by small children, Hale (1887, 1888) based a theory of the origin of linguistic diversity on the "language making instinct of very young children," i.e., that families of children might become separated from their parents and thereafter develop among themselves a new language.

A great controversy has been waged upon this matter of invention of words—some writers citing instances of such words, while others deny possibilities of such a thing in the true language learning

[1] With Major's son and my pupil, the child's handedness had been interfered with; Town's five-year-old boy was left-handed, while Mrs. Allee's son was ambidextrous until the age of two and a half and G until after she was three (Nice, 1918). The matter of handedness does not seem to have been involved with A or the Twins.

period. Inventions (*Erfindungen*) have been defined as "deliberate creations for which no source shall exist in sound habits nor onomatopoeia nor in words of the environment."[2]

Onomatopoeic words are clearly not "inventions" for in their very essence they are imitations of sounds. Babblings or *Lallwörter* may take on the dignity of words in two ways: either they are adopted by the child's associates and taught to him, or occasionally they gradually develop a definite meaning with no help from outsiders (as in the case of R, or A and of Stumpf's son). Such words might truly be called "original" but they probably were not intentionally created, so would not come under the definition of inventions. Other supposedly invented words are probably attempts to imitate the speech of the environment. It seems improbable that a baby would ever "invent" a word which would meet the criteria of the above definitions.[3]

. . . .

Some Conclusions

Several conclusions may be drawn from this study of an unusual course of speech development.

First, it is impossible to take a cross-section of a child's individual language and hope to be able to solve the question of the derivation of the words; such a matter takes most careful study and voluminous note taking throughout the whole previous speech history of the child.

Second, most children learn through imitation to speak earlier than they really need to. On this point I emphatically disagree with the Blantons when they say that "Speech will not be acquired until there is a necessity for it" (1919).

Finally, with this child, speech was not primarily for purposes of communication but was largely a matter of self-expression.

[2] "Absichtliche Neuschöpfungen, für die weder in Lautgebärden und Schallmalerein, noch in Worten der Konventionellen Sprache eine Voraussetzung existiert." Stern, 1907, p. 337.

[3] Buckman says of his three-year-old daughter: "Isabel would at first be thought to invent *enher* for *pencil*, *ongun* for *children*, and so on. Yet these and all her words follow definite rules, and they are no more inventions than Irish *ibim* for Sanskrit *pibami* or French *âge* for Latin *aestaticum*" (1897, p. 806).

(Reading)   *The Child as a Language Creator*

As to this last matter, philologists tell us that, "It is beyond all doubt, in the first place, that the desire of communication was the only force directly impelling men to the production of language" (Whitney, 1910). I think, however, that they have been led astray by too intellectual a viewpoint and that the desire for self expression was the main impelling force. Whitney (1904) says again, "Man speaks, primarily, not in order to think, but in order to impart his thoughts." I would change the last phrase to *express his emotions*. All people feel, while few think.

A baby's babblings are self-expression, his first words are largely emotional and volitional,[4] most of the continuous chatter of the little child is self-expression, not communication. Even the conversation of adults is often not so much to inform their listeners as to satisfy themselves. Letter writing is an important outlet for some people—they do not feel content until they have told someone their small experiences. Diaries are even more striking illustrations of this need.

To the baby, self-expression is enough in itself, but with most adults some response must be evoked from other people in order that self-expression should be truly satisfying. This is true with all creative activities. However, in the case of speech, this desire for influencing others obscures the self-expressive instinct; talking is made to appear to be wholly a matter of communication.

Most of us have too little of this spirit of art in speech activities; with the majority of adults speech is not an art at all, it is merely a tool, a convenience, a method of bare interchange of information or opinion. We would do well if we kept more of the child's creative impulse in this matter of expressing our thoughts.

[4] Miss Shinn (1900) says, "The baby begins slowly to turn some of his commonest chattering sounds to special uses—not to carry thought to other people but as mere exclamations to relieve his own mind."

References

Blanton, M. and S. *Speech Training for Children.* New York: Century, 1919.

Buckman, S. S. The Speech of Children. *Nineteenth Century*, 1897, **LXI**: 792–807.

Hale, H. The Origin of Language and the Antiquity of Speaking Man. *Trans. Am. Ass. Adv. Sci.*, 1887, **XXXV**: 279–323.

——— Development of Language. *Proc. Canadian Ins.*, 3rd series, 1888, **VI**: 92–134.

Major, D. R. *First Steps in Mental Growth.* New York: Macmillan, 1906.

Nice, M. M. The Speech of a Left-handed Child. *Psych. Clinic,* 1915, IX: 115–117.

———— Ambidexterity and Delayed Speech Development. *Ped. Sem.,* 1918, XXV: 141–162.

Shinn, M. *Biography of a Baby.* New York: Houghton, 1900.

Stern, C. and W. *Die Kindesprache.* Leipzig, 1907. 2nd ed., 1920.

Stumpf, C. Eigenartige Sprachliche Entwicklung eines Kindes. *Ztshft. für päd. Psychol.,* 1901, III, 6: 420–447.

Town, C. H. An Infantile Stammer in a Boy of Twelve Years. *Psych. Clinic,* 1907, 1: 10–20.

———— Analytic Study of a Group of Five and Six-Year-Old Children. Univ. of Iowa Studies. *Studies in Child Welfare,* 1921, I, No. 4.

Whitney, W. D. *Language and the Study of Language.* New York: Scribners, 1904.

———— Philology. *Encyclopedia Britannica.* 1910, 414–430.

Nice did not suggest that unique child-language is anything but the reflection of unusual environmental circumstances or some health problem. Stumpf (1901), on the other hand, felt that the motive for the unique speech of his son was pleasure in new forms; but then his child retained the unique utterances long after they ceased to be new. The creative ability of these children is interesting. Exposure to the parents' language sets off language acquisition. In these cases, however, development seemed to move off on its own course fairly independent of the parent language until necessity of communication eventually realigned it with the parental dialect. It is the same situation to a lesser degree with the normally developing child who uses "baby talk" before mastering parental speech. Forchhammer (1939)* has given further descriptions of other cases of unique child language.

It is a commonplace that children comprehend adult speech long before they can reproduce it. Thus it may be that the major task in language acquisition is mastery of phonetic skills or "surface structure" aspects of language. The child gradually improves this production skill over a longer time than seems

---

* E. Forchhammer, Ueber einige Fälle von eigentümlichen Sprachbildungen bei Kindern. *Arch. f. d. ges. Psychol.,* 1939, 104: 395–438.

necessary for mastery of comprehension. Also, children have been seen to acquire comprehension of several languages with no increase in the length of time for learning. J. W. Tomb wrote in the *British Journal of Psychology* (1925) about the "intuitive capacity of children to understand spoken language," comparing the ability of Englishmen in India with that of their children to learn several Indian languages. Children at the initial language-learning age easily acquired comprehension of as much as Bengali, Santali, Hindustani, Tamil, and also their English mother tongue. Their parents, meanwhile, could not match this achievement in the least and came to rely on the children as interpreters. There may be a critical stage that fosters language learning in young children.

Developmental psychology has flourished in the French-speaking world. Thus it is not surprising to find numerous volumes in French on developmental psycholinguistics. In France itself this research appeared in profusion during the 1920s. Previously the *Bulletin de la société libre pour l'étude psychologique de l'Enfant* had reported several investigations. (That journal was later renamed *Bulletin de la société Alfred Binet*.) In 1921 and 1932 the *Journal de Psychologie*, under the influence of Henri Delacroix, published special issues devoted to psycholinguistics, and in 1924 it devoted an issue to language and mental development in children. Delacroix studied in Germany (Berlin and Heidelberg) before he went to the University of Paris in 1900. His writings were heavily flavored with German *Sprachpsychologie*, which was in sharp contrast to his predecessor, Alfred Binet, who did not read German. Delacroix's best known works were *L'activité linguistique de l'enfant* (1924) and *Le langage et la pensée* (1924), later revised and expanded. Delacroix had influence as a polemicist and a proponent of collaboration between psychologists and linguists. This is strikingly exemplified in a statement from *Le langage et la pensée* (p. 7):

There can be no psychology of language without recourse to linguistics. Without it one could, of course, study certain aspects of the speech of one individual. There are numerous psychologists, above all in France, who believe it is possible only by psychological observation to determine the nature of language acquisition, of inner language, of external forms of expression, and of language pathologies. But a reading of their works reveals their incompleteness. They give general viewpoints and schemes, while quite obviously neglecting considerable facts that condition what they attempt to explain. They are led inevitably to ask useless questions, to forget essential questions, to misformulate the necessary questions, to create non-existent facts, to misconstrue the actual facts, and to misinterpret established facts. The history of the doctrines concerning aphasia furnishes a striking illustration of this pessimistic observation. If they had ignored the structure of language less, physicians and psychologists would not have misconceived the conditions of speech for such a long time.

In the 1920s the University of Paris became an established center for psychology of language. One of the most psychologically oriented linguists of that day, Brunot, was then Dean of the Faculty. His lengthy volume, *La pensée et la langue* (1922), was a source book for many French psycholinguists. We shall just mention a few prominent names of this sphere of influence. Ovide Decroly in Belgium had made several investigations of child-language.* But more important, Decroly was to Belgium what John Dewey was to America. He inspired a tradition of child research there that, among other advances, culminated in Antoine Grégoire's *L'apprentisage du langage* (1937), one of the most exact and thorough studies of language acquisition to date, particularly concerning phonological development.

Oscar Bloch, of Paris, wrote a series of articles from 1913 to 1924 on the development of language in his three children. His emphasis was on the syntactic aspects of language development, and the work is distinguished by the quantity of supporting observations. Later, Marcel Cohen published a series of insightful reports (1925–1933) that also emphasized grammatical phenomena in child-language. These articles are interesting because they view child-language as a series of overlapping sublanguages. Cohen explained it this way:

* See Decroly's Le développement du langage parlé chez l'enfant. *Cahiers de la centrale du P.E.S. de Belgique,* Vol. II; Comment l'enfant arrive à parler. *ibid.* Vol. VIII; *Épreuves de comprehension, d'imitation, et d'expression* (Bruges: Beyaert, 1935).

These [child] languages constitute small systems, the first of very reduced dimensions and the final ones of considerable breadth. As in the evolution of language, any given system is encumbered by the remnants of the preceding system; the beginnings of the system that will follow can also be found.*

Cohen claimed that the beginnings of the sentence, which serve to "declare" and "relate," occur much earlier than generally realized (that is, in the form of gestures), and he asserted that the infant's successive languages thus begin with gestures and facial expressions in the preverbal period.

Jean Piaget in his first book, *The language and thought of the child* (1923—first French edition), had dichotomized child language into early "egocentric" speech and later "socialized" speech; this is similar to the phenomenon reviewed in Nice's article. It is the notion that a child first talks only for himself or for his own pleasure. Subsequently, when the child becomes more concerned with influencing hearers, his speech changes and becomes "socialized." This viewpoint touched off a wide debate on an international scale that carried through the 1930s.† Most of these discussions were arguments about methodologies for categorizing child speech forms. One of the first to become an active investigator of the issue was the Russian L. S. Vygotsky, see his *Thought and language* (1934—first Russian edition). However, both Piaget and Vygotsky were more interested in the child's thought processes than in language acquisition.

Further influential French work in developmental psycholinguistics during the 1920s was that of Paul Guillaume. Guillaume later became well known as the writer who effectively introduced Gestalt psychology into France with a highly popular book, *La psychologie de la forme* (1937) and with the translation of Wolfgang Köhler's *Mentality of apes*. Guillaume began his study of language development with his doctoral dissertation at Paris (*L'imitation chez l'enfant*, 1925). This was followed in 1927 by two continuations of the same study: *Les débuts de la*

---

* Cohen, M. Sur les langages successifs de l'enfant. *Collection Linguistiques*, Vol. 17 (Paris: Librairie Ancienne Edouard Champion, 1925), p. 109–110.

† For a summary of this literature see McCarthy's review in L. Carmichael (Ed.) *Manual of child psychology* (New York: Wiley, 1954).

phrase dans le langage de l'enfant (The emergence of the sentence in the language of the child) and *Le développement des éléments formels dans le langage de l'enfant* (The development of formal elements in the language of the child).

Guillaume had a keen interest in the emergence of primitive sentences, that is, those utterances that consist of the first separable but grammatically related parts developing out of the "undifferentiated verbal protoplasm" of the child's first expressions. He had observed his own preschool children for several years, and then made additional observations on children, ages two to five, in a nursery school. As many had before him, Guillaume criticized the division of children's words into conventional grammatical categories. At age one and one-half or two, the child's "verbal unities do not belong to any class of words, because they are not words, but sentence." Guillaume discovered that there are two kinds of elements that first emerge from the autonomous word-sentences. These are the names of people, and expressions of volition. The structure of early sentences turns the dissection of experience into one part that is concrete and represented, and another part that is lived, acted or felt. This follows an argument made earlier by Alfred Binet that the most primary division of mental life is into objects and acts. The same notion had been the basis of Brentano's psychology in the mid-nineteenth century (see Chapter Two).

But Guillaume's analysis also seems to share in the Wundtian approach that language production depends on the dismembering of a mental complex. And in this way he proceeds to describe and explain the unfolding of language up to the age of five. Guillaume's articles illustrate a blending of twentieth-century functionalism with Wundtian psycholinguistics. His definition of the *sentence*, near the end of the article that follows below, is obviously taken directly from Wundt.

There is never any scarcity of observations or illustrations but they are not as neatly organized nor as extensive as were those of the Sterns. The following is a translation of part of his second article which concerned the first appearance of the sentence in child-language. Guillaume begins with the argument that we must escape our subservience to the written mode of language because this distorts our analysis of child-language. Then he continues to show how the elements, recognized in adult language as sentence constituents, gradually detach themselves from the child's primitive unstructured utterances. In this way we see the surface structure of sentences unfold during the course of only a few months.

PAUL GUILLAUME · *The Emergence of the Sentence*

Words in Spoken and Written Language. It is common nowadays to say that among children sentences, whether comprehended or spoken, are prior to words, or even that for children there are neither words nor true sentences. The child develops a "word awareness" later. But when? Certain facts lead one to believe that this development is very slow and appears only with school education. There is a confusion concerning language that we must now dispel.

It is said that the writing of semi-literate people reveals no awareness of the individuality of words. I have made a small collection of written letters corresponding to different levels of education on the part of the correspondents. There are three sorts of alterations of words, such as severings, linkings, and confusions of homonyms[1] that arise from the same cause.

To interpret these facts accurately we must observe that people who write so poorly still speak their language fluently. Their language is not a simple mosaic of ready-made expressions applicable to every situation. They knew how to *construct* sentences conforming the rules of the language with the resources of their vocabulary. In a certain sense, the words bear witness to isolation and differentiation by the very manner in which they are combined. There is no doubt that the person who writes *l'ettre* (for *lettre*) can say, "I wrote a letter," "letters," or "I sent my letter." *Letter* acts in the spoken language like a single indivisible word. If someone writes *sans* for *s'en*, that doesn't keep him from saying, "Je *m'en* vais." In

SOURCE. Paul Guillaume, Les débuts de la phrase dans le langage de l'enfant. *Journal de Psychologie*, 1927, **24**: 1–25. Translated by A. L. Blumenthal and Judith Goodman.

[1] See A. Lalande, La conscience des mots dans le langage. *J. de Psychol.*, January, 1905.

spite of linkings and arbitrary graphic severings, the spoken sentence obeys rules that give it well defined points of articulation. It is constructed with elements as substantial as the subject knows how to manage. Similarly, grammatical differentiation of words exists, in a sense, in spoken language, although the graphic forms of a noun can be confused with those of a verb, that of a possessive with that of a demonstrative, that of a participle with that of an infinitive, etc. . . .*

The expression "word awareness" thus does not have a precise descriptive value and can lead only to ambiguities. The isolation and differentiation of words correspond to a superposed stratum of convention, and these terms take on a new sense when one passes from spoken to written language, and from the latter to explicit logical and grammatical analysis. These functions have become closely interdependent for educated adults; they pass easily from one to the other, the graphic form becoming symbolic to all. However, this graphic form was added after the spoken form. It may be surprising that the graphic division of the sentence into words doesn't result from a simple graphic transposition of the words of the spoken sentence with the one being imitated or deduced from the other. There is no perfect correspondence between the two systems of articulation in all their details (for example, the endings of inflected words could logically be written separately from their roots, etc.). In fact, we have seen that graphic parsing reveals, above all, the influence of the written mode, and does not directly reflect the inherent organization of speech.

The Understood, Undifferentiated Sentence. To describe this speech structure we must return to the first two years of childhood. Consider a child of eight or nine months who already understands a series of sentences. . . . It is perhaps the general form of the verbal melody which is recognized rather than its elements. However, we believe that all the sounds do not have the same value, that certain words are detached, and that others are only accessory embellishment, flourishes, or notes in passing. When addressing a child a speaker doesn't restrict himself to rigorously uniform and concise expressions; there are variations, as well as essential words, stress,

---

* In the original text Guillaume gives many further French examples of these phenomena.—A.L.B.

(Reading) **The Emergence of the Sentence**

and repetitions. This does not much impede the child who, quite the contrary, recognizes the same sentences from the mouths of other people despite differences in tonality. It is thus possible that certain words acquire an early distinctness.

On the other hand, it is impossible to group them into grammatical categories. This seems true even for the names of people (papa, mama, Marie, Suzanne). They are named on the occasion of certain acts. The names are imperatives or signals; it is necessary to turn toward the person, look at him, smile at him, give him a kiss, lean toward him to be taken in his arms. There is no need to separate the name of the person from that of the act in this signal of complex experiences. It is the same for the child's personal name. To ask at what age a child understands his name is to pose a completely ambiguous question; it would be necessary to describe in detail the succession of reactions that the name provokes. First of all, it is a common call. It is the attitude or expression of the speaking person that arouses the child's personal interest. It is a synonym for utterances like, *Attention! Look over here!* It is the signal for interesting experiences, or for an action in which the child is being invited to participate. It is an interjection and an imperative, as well as a name. The same observations would apply to the names of things; the qualities of objects are inseparable from the acts that are related to them and that make them interesting.

The period of the first comprehended sentences is distinguished by irregular results of certain tests. If I say to P (12 months, 8 days), "Give to papa" (a candy that he has in his hand), he gives it to me. If I say to him, "Give to mamma," he gives it to me again. I repeat the order, and he puts it in his mouth. There is an indifference or lack of attention to the particular form of speech, a habit of guessing according to the totality of the situation rather than according to precise analytic perception of the content of the sentence. The child answers at random all sorts of questions (whether Who? What? or How?). He counts more on intuition than on language to make distinctions. This situation could be compared to that of a child who is beginning to read and who always tries to guess rather than spelling out rigorously. When there are several means of comprehension, there is always a special laziness regarding the least familiar which in this case is surely language. Even correct comprehension reveals the relation of each word more with the intuitive situation than with the structure of the sentence. From 9 months 17 days, *P* seems to understand sentences like: "Give papa a little hug! Give mamma a little hug!" He passes his hand across the cheek of the person named, even if this person is not pointed out by gestures. Yet it is necessary to repeat the sentence insistently. The first time he gets his bearings for the act but hesitates about the person. At this point one repeats, "Mamma! Mamma!" In a way this is a second expression being juxtaposed to the first rather than subordinated to it. The second term is interpreted by its occurrence in the concrete situation created by the first and not by its function in the sentence of which it is a member. According to the terms of a linguist who has made a good study of the origins of the sentence,[2] the words here are *predicates of the situation*. Actually, there are the same number of sentences as there are significant words. If the whole has a psychological unity, since it concerns aspects of a single act, then this unity is still not that of a grammatical form obeying the rules of a definite language. The whole has the structure no more of a French sentence than of a foreign sentence, no more of the elite dialect than of pidgin French, or of a telegram than of a formal announcement. Even these comparisons are insufficient since for us words are the differentiated parts of speech that appear as members of possible sentences; they are considered as grammatical parts not only in the material sense, but also because of their constantly sensed formal value.

The Undifferentiated Word-Sentence. Spoken language confirms the absence of word differentiation. We know that a child's imitation is a simplification. The same acts that reduce a word to a syllable and even to a vowel result in the child's condensing of one of our sentences to a word (the easiest to pronounce, the best known, or the most accentuated). Somewhat later, the child includes in his utterances the sounds that correspond to the accessory words. This advance, which substitutes *Je n'en ai plus*, for *A plus*, is of the same order as that which transforms *colat* into *chocolat*, and *ti* into *parti*. But besides the phonetic aspect, there is a semantic and grammatical aspect, and that is what concerns us.

The first words are used in a variety of circumstances thus making their definition difficult. *Papa* (*P*, 12 months) is said in the presence

[2] P. Wegener. *Grundfragen des Sprachlebens*, 1885.

(*Reading*) *The Emergence of the Sentence*

of any object belonging to me, or when the child takes a paper, a card, a pen, when he enters my empty office, when he wants to write, to come near me, to see me, or when he recognizes me after an absence. He says, *Maman*, when he wants to suckle, to be taken in someone's arms (even when he turns to me), to attract his mother's attention to an object that he wants to show, or to his physiological needs. *Nénin* is used to ask for the breast, but also to ask for a biscuit. Seeing the latter only as a kind of verb meaning *Eat!* would give us little understanding of how the child comes to say it while showing the red button of a piece of clothing, the point of a bare elbow, an eye in a picture, or his mother's face in a photograph. *Tata* is said when he wants to to go potty or to urinate, or when he has done it, when he sees a stain on a cloth or a napkin, when he puts a pencil, a copper cup, a piece of fruit, or a potato into his mouth, when he sees dish water, coffee grounds, or someone who displeases him. *Blablab* . . . designates successively the act of making his lips vibrate with his finger, then a mouth (especially in a child's picture) then any picture, drawing, or the illustrated cards that I sent during an absence, every written or printed manuscript, a newspaper, or a book; but it expresses also the act of "reading" or the wish to read. Almost all these meanings coexisted at 11 months, 15 days.

. . . .

The Beginnings of Sentences. Names of People. Let us look first for the beginnings of sentences in the comprehension of speech. At the beginning of his second year it seems that the child understands phrases like, *Brosse papa* ("Brush papa"). . . . Also there are common games such as *coui-coui* (pinching the nose), *dida-dida* (pulling the ear), *blab-blab* (a vibration produced by intermittently covering the mouth with a hand), etc. The words are associated with the name of a person present ("Make *coui-coui* to papa"), and the child performs the game on this person. He immediately adapts his action to a series of people, and the new combination is understood right away. A word like *papa* is here no longer a sentence, but a member of a sentence. In the beginning, such expressions had to be scanned word by word so that the effect of the second word was exercised in context of the intuitive situation already defined by the first. Doubtless the advancement here consists of reducing the immediate effect of the first perceived words to an activity that is preparatory to a definite response, and it leaves them in suspension until the completion of the sentence by the expected "complements."

What are the first words affected by this progress? I was struck by the role played by the *names of people* in the first sentences understood by the children whom I was able to observe. Their sentence function varies; they are subjects, direct or indirect complements, etc. Associated words are still undifferentiated signs of total experience. This phenomenon seemed much less clear to me for combinations of other familiar words at this point in time. We have seen that P (12 months, 13 days) would move a brush through the hair of one or another person when it was asked of him, and even over the head of his doll (which he had never witnessed). Then I said to him, "Brush the hat," *Brosse le chapeau*. (This word *chapeau* is known in the sense that he knows how to find the object and to put it on his head when someone says to him, "Where is the hat? Put on your hat.") But the sentence wasn't understood. He abandoned the brush and took the hat wanting to put it on his head. When I repeated the order he returned to the brush and wanted to polish my shoes. Each of the two words by itself tended to release habitual reactions. The utterance was not (effectively) structured. Notice that a structure of this type is always implied to some degree by knowledge of sentences. If the child has never seen the prescribed action, then the sentence, when he has understood it, exerts a constraint on his imagination that makes the object appear in a new light where it can undergo the action expressed by the verb. If the action is familiar to him, the form of the verb at least orients his mind toward one of the uses of the object which is perhaps not the one he would spontaneously think of. But at the time of this observation, "hat" is still not a real name of an object; it suggests certain experiences with a hat too special to combine with the experience of the brush. On the other hand, at this stage the names of *people* associate with these beings a whole variety of acts without by themselves specifying any acts, the thought being completed only by the context. These then are truly differentiated names.

. . . .

Volitional Speech. At the same early time that personal names appear, another element of free combination appears in sentences.

These are expressions of volition, that is, the verbal elements of negative reactions (refusals of objects of aversion), and then of positive reactions of desire (desire for an object, or an action, or for its continuation or renewal). Moreover, these words quickly come to reflect attitudes—assent or dissent—toward an expected event. Thus volitional language takes on intellectual value.

Words are borrowed from quite varied categories of the imitated language. Such are *A plus* ("I don't want any more," or, "There aren't any more"), or *Pas, A pas, Non*,[3] to which it is necessary to compare *Caca*, an expression of aversion whose sense is as much willful as affective. At first the object of these negations remains unexpressed. They are word-sentences, predicates of intuitive situations; but already the variety of unexpressed objects or phenomena to which these words apply anticipates their use in the combinations of the subsequent stage. In these combinations the object of the negation still has no definite grammatical nature. *Pas momo* (P, 14 months) can be indifferently interpreted as: "I don't want to sleep," or, "I don't want the bed."

. . . .

Thus, from the autonomous word-sentences, we have seen two kinds of words emerge: the names of people and the expressions of volition. Both are used primarily in combination with nouns that are undifferentiated relative to a total experience. But these two types of words are two opposite poles of language. People are objects of perception and individual thought, concrete and stable, and are strikingly detached from the subject who speaks and from his interests and functions. They seem to exist "in and for themselves." The words that relate to them are easily detached from those that relate to the total experience to become "names." On the other hand, words of volition are first of all the attitudes of the subject with regard to his experiences. They are the verbal part of his reactions. They are so little detached from him that at first they are not represented. The structure of sentences dissects primitive experience into a part that is represented and thought, and a part that is lived and acted.

Names of Things. There is no profound difference among things,

---

[3] We have no examples of *Non* in combinations. But the German children often use *Nein* in this case instead of *Nicht*.

animals, and people, especially for children. They pass easily from the combinations that we have studied to sentences like these: *Sien, tape* ("I hit the dog") (*P*, 17 months, 18 days), or to that of *L* (12 months, 19 days) who seeing water run out of a gutter (which she calls by a "generic" name, *Dada*) says, *Pipi dada*.

Names of things do not in a strict sense constitute a grammatical category. For us the category of nouns in the final analysis takes in semantic equivalents of all words (names of quality, actions, states, and relations) and gives them a particular mode of grammatical construction. But the child's first nouns, as people's names, are names of *things* in a very narrow sense as is shown by vocabularies of the first half of the second year. There are names of foods, of objects relating to the games and needs of the child, and especially of objects easily handled at his level and for his uses. Often preceding specific names one observes very broad generic nouns. Thus *P* (13 months, 27 days) uses *ato* (which seems to stem from *marteau*, "hammer") and until 14 months, 22 days, extends it to cover the following uses: buttonhook, hand mirror, comb, lady's handbag, saucepan, hair pin, wooden shovel, key, gun, box, belt, purse, ruler, diapers, basin, safety pin, candle holder, coffee grinder, plate, and spoon. This master-key name never designates men, animals, or food. It is the equivalent of *machine*, and *thing*.

. . . .

Verbs. . . . As a law of all imitation, each new usage naturally tends to supplant the preceding one in the production of verb forms, and it does not necessarily keep exactly the same value that it had in its earlier simple use. It is therefore unnecessary to attach much importance to these forms, the distinctions of person, tense, or mood, are purely transparent; a child does not know how to use them to express the corresponding nuances. But further, these forms are not even verbs, if one calls the verb a word which in the total experience refers particularly to actions or states, because here verbs still refer to the whole of the experience. The child indifferently uses verbal and non-verbal forms *in the same sense*. *P* (18 months, 2 days) says, *Cour* or *Zouzoute* ("to run," and "plaything"), *Mémir* or *Tasiet* ("to sleep," and "the nap") . . . Action is separated in language only when the agent and object of the action are separated at the same time.

However, before a sentence of several words is composed, there has already been a preparatory stage of verb function when word-sentences refer to different situations whose common aspect is essentially their action, while actors, objects and circumstances are allowed to vary. Every expression has its unique origin. For some time certain verbs are used by the child only in reference to himself, but he does not expressly designate himself. Now he is the subject, now the direct or indirect object of the action. *Habir* (16 months, 26 days) is applied to *his* toilette, *Mémir* to *his* sleep, *Néné* to *his* walk. *Lever* signified "I want to get out of my *bed*." *Descendre* signifies "I want to get down from my *chair*."

. . . .

Finally, the dissociation of action, person, and object becomes apparent in the speech itself, in sentences of two or several words containing a verb. The verb is combined with a person's name, most often the name of the child himself. ("Give *P*." "*P* working." "*P* wants them." "*P* gets them." (20 months, 4 days).)

. . . .

The sentence is now definite in its structure regarding the order of the words. It is no longer a question of two or several juxtaposed word-sentences representing two moments of thought. The construction is imposed by the rules of the language. It no longer undergoes capricious variations in the course of the thought. Sometimes, when words still come in successive jumps, there is a tendency to put them together again later in normal order. We must not misunderstand certain apparent inversions like "It is closed, the window." If he says, "To look for doctor," we must understand that *P* is going to look for . . . or wants to look for . . . etc. Infinitives used in an imperative sense preceding their complements are elliptical reproductions of subordinate propositions that are regulated by verbs like *vouloir* (to want) or by prepositions. For the same reasons the German child, in the same conditions, will in contrast place the complement before the infinitive, conforming to the rules of the German language. And he will also place a participle at the end as well as the separable verb particles often expressed alone (see Stern, 1907).

The development that first isolated special symbols for people from the undifferentiated word-sentence has continued by isolating a symbol for things. In overall experience, people and things correspond to what is furthest from the subject and the most independent from his affective and active life, although things are less autonomous beings than people and are more likely to be instruments of the subject's needs and passive objects of his acts. At the other pole of experience, the attitude of the subject that is acted-out rather than thought is likewise isolated as the verbal function. . . .

To follow the progress of the sentence further it would be necessary to study the differentiation of other parts of speech (adjectives, pronouns, prepositions, conjunctions) and to show how inflexions are established, etc. This would be the subject matter for another study.* Let us now consider what conclusions emerge from the facts we have studied.

Child language surely results from slow and continuous impregnation whereby forms similar to the vocabulary of the mother tongue progressively emerge but this happens gradually without abrupt or drammatic changes. No imitation is completely passive. First, there is selection. The child does not indifferently repeat everything he hears; rather, he above all begins to *construct* with the resources of his vocabulary on the model of the expressions that he knows how to reproduce. It is the acquisition of this behavior that we wanted to describe.

The child does not invent grammatical categories, he finds these tools ready-made, but he must learn to handle them by making a direct correspondence between the sentence and the concrete situation. Thus, expression of thought in a language like ours involves an arbitrary dismembering of a total experience into different parts corresponding to certain abstractions, either subjective or objective. The system in its mature form is difficult to assimilate having developed to express more complex ideas in analogous ways that variously extend and modify syntactic categories.

To master abstractions we have to find images and symbols in concrete things. At the same time, it is necessary that a practical or an emotional interest correspond to this dissection of reality. The human being, his attitudes and their relations to varied experiences, his new dissections of experience, his objects, and his actions all form the centers of perspective and interest for the child at the age we have

---

* For this further study see Paul Guillaume, Le développement des éléments formels dans le langage de l'enfant. *J. de Psychol.*, 1927.—A.L.B.

considered. It is the expression of these aspects of reality that he assimilates into language. Thus anthropocentrism is precisely the key to the system of abstractions in language, because this surely was its origin. The structure of the sentence and the functions of its parts cease to seem artificial when one recalls that language first serves to speak about men and later about all of nature in terms made for men.

Guillaume and other early psycholinguists criticized the investigators who analyzed the initial utterances of infants into parts of speech and then used frequency counts in studies of the vocabulary growth in each category (noun, verb, adjective, pronoun, and so forth). This taxonomic approach was a form of linguistic phrenology that had a strong following among functionalists in France. In America in the early 1900s such frequency counts appeared in a great wave of investigations.* But for a time during the late 1800s American views had been much closer to holistic German views. The pedagogical psychologist Herman Lukens wrote a report on language acquisition for Hall's *Pedagogical Seminary* in 1896 in which he argued convincingly against parts-of-speech studies of child-language. His analysis dealt with the arbitrariness (and hence impossibility) of classifying a child's utterances into conventional categories until the child uses all the "parts" of adult language.

Dewey in reviewing a vocabulary development report by Frederick Tracy (1893) described the difficulty of word classifications:

Mr. Tracy, I take it, has classified his words according to the sense which they have to an adult, and I have followed that principle in my own table. In a sense, however, this is as artificial as to put knife under *K* instead of under *N* because we spell it with a *K*. The psychological classification is to class the word according to what it means to a child, not to an adult with his grammatical forms all differentiated.

---

* See D. McCarthy, Language Development in C. Murchison (Ed.), *Handbook of child psychology* (Worcester: Clark University Press, 1931); also the last edition in L. Carmichael (Ed.), *Manual of child psychology* (New York: John Wiley, 1954).

Such a classification would in all probability increase immensely the percentage of verbs. It is true that such a method demands much care in observation, and opens the way to the very variable error of interpretation; but the greater certainty of the method followed above is after all only seeming—it does not express the *child's* vocabulary, but our interpretation of it according to a fixed but highly conventional standard. . . . [Dewey then lists many examples]. . .

What I would suggest, then, along the line of a study of the distribution of vocabulary into parts of speech is such observation and recording as would note carefully the original sense to the child of his words, and the gradual *differentiation* of the original protoplasmic verbal-nominal-interjectional form (as it seems to me), until words assume their present rigidity.*

The first sophisticated, though brief, observation on sentence development reported in America came from Kathleen Moore: "The mental development of a child" (*Psychological Monographs*, 1896). Her discussion was just a portion of a larger report on mental development in children. She listed sequences of expanding expressions (noted at regular intervals of development) which she reasoned as being synonymous with one another because each utterance was an expansion of the previous one. For example,

Developmental stages
1. Book.
2. Mama book.
3. Mama sit down, a book.
4. Mama sit down, read a book.
5. Mama is sitting down, reading a book.

All these utterances had the same function and represented the same situation. In effect, they were all subject-predicate representations. Thus in Dewey's terms Moore's data illustrated the "gradual differentiation of the original protoplasmic expression." And in the later thinking of Cohen, Bloch, and Guillaume this indicates a series of subdialects that succeed each other while approaching adult speech.

* John Dewey, The psychology of infant language. *Psychological Review*, 1894, p. 64.

The issue here is akin to the classic debate between Paul and Wundt concerning sentence production. There is a parallel opposition of views in developmental psycholinguistics: (1) acquisition is considered as a building-up process starting from isolated speech elements (Paul), and (2) acquisition is seen as a progressive differentiation of a primitive whole or of mass-units (Wundt).

The spirit of the times in America changed radically and became almost completely isolated from pre-twentieth-century thought and research as well as from most European research. On the particular issue of vocabulary frequency studies the Lukens, Dewey, and Moore viewpoint had little influence later.

In America behaviorism, objectivism, and "biological naturalism" (see Chapter One) commanded the study of language acquisition in the early 1900s. The new trend typically yielded data showing relations between language and some other measurable physiological function. An example is the language acquisition research of Clark and Bertha Hull (1919)* who plotted parallel learning curves of an infant for vocabulary growth and for voluntary bladder control. The bladder control curve revealed a familiar learning curve for skills or "simpler mental processes." It rose rapidly at first and then tapered off as the score approached the "limit of perfection." But there was the exception of a marked plateau in the bladder-control curve of Hull's graph. It showed little improvement during the nine months that were contiguous with the rise of language in the infant. The plateau spanned a period from the first word to simple but adult-like sentences (see Figure 1). As well as the Hulls could determine, no other developmental events or health changes were exactly contiguous with that nine-month span.

Thus the effect on certain body functions of learning to talk may be dramatic. We might also note that the form of this vocabulary curve is in sharp contrast to the familiar learning curve that would be similar to the curve for bladder control. Vocabulary growth starts off slowly and then assumes a rapid

---

* C. L. Hull and B. I. Hull. Parallel learning curves of an infant in vocabulary and in voluntary control of the bladder. *Pedagogical Seminary*, 1919, **26**: 272–283.

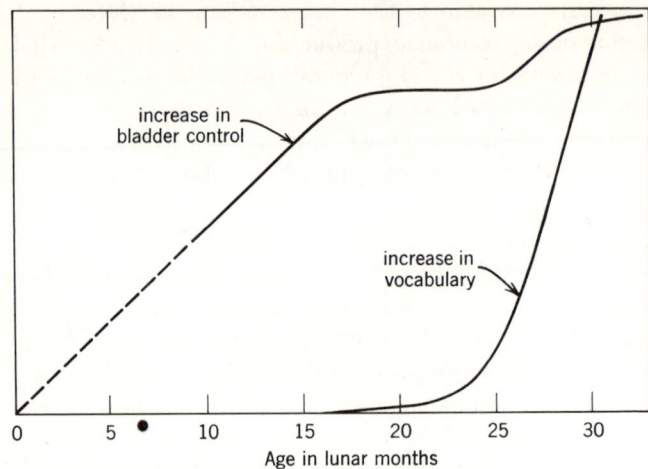

FIG. 1. Effect of language acquisition on bladder control. Results of observations on one infant (abstracted from Hull and Hull, 1919).

rate through the end of the investigation (thirty months). In his studies of the development of intelligence, Terman reported in 1916 that the rate slowed down at age seven but still continued upward at an even rate for eleven more years.

The new generation of American psychologists apparently had little interest in linguistics. There was only a requirement of convenient units of verbal behavior (namely words) and little concern for the discussions among theoretical linguists about what were linguistically valid units of language. It was assumed that it was sufficient to characterize language as an inventory of words.

In the name of objectivity the American orientation fell along various points from pure physiology to pure behaviorism, while classical cognitive psychology declined. The study of animal behavior made rapid gains. Attempts to study language in a laboratory animal indeed led to a very different conception of "psycholinguistics." There were no longer any "subjects and predicates" nor "apperceptions" to worry about because these notions were of little value in generalizing the animal data to human beings.

The most influential writing on language acquisition by an

early behaviorist came from Floyd Henry Allport in his chapters on "social stimulation," in his book *Social psychology* (1924). His remarks on social psychology are now seldom remembered, but his description of language learning is still frequently cited in handbooks and texts.

Allport elaborated in more detail the views that had been strong in the native American functionalist psychology. (See above pp. 64-66.) His views on language acquisition may be traced back at least to Baldwin whose book *Mental development* (1895) contained a description of the acquisition of habits and discussed especially the acquisition of complex skills, with the principle that the mere discovery of a skilled movement is sufficient reinforcement for its own recurrence. This principle applies in the early vocalizations of infants in providing the child with practice in speech sounds that are later used for communication.

Allport had been a student of Harvard's early behaviorist (or "objectivist") Holt who taught and wrote about the psychology of reflex action while at Harvard from 1901 to 1918. At Harvard the *Sprachpsychologie* definition of language as the expression of ideas had been replaced with a thorough acoustical and physiological description of vocal responses and their contiguous environmental events. Immediately prior to World War I, Holt and Hugo Munsterberg were major contributors and proponents of this definition. Holt was later known for his discussions of the "circular reflex hypothesis" and for his opinion that consciousness is associated more directly with the muscles than with the brain. The circular reflex notion is essentially what Baldwin had described for the acquisition of skills. It is also what Allport offered in 1924 as the basis of language acquisition. In the first section of his book Allport outlined the principles of his approach to language.

Reflexes may be joined into functional patterns at the end as well as in the middle of their course. It often happens in a series of responses that one movement affords a kinaesthetic or cutaneous stimulation which evokes the next movement. In walking, the pressure on the foot and the strain on muscles, tendons, and joints resulting from one step become the stimuli for the response of taking the next step. . . .

The circular reflex is a special type of chain reflex in which the afferent impulse, originating from the effector response passes back to the brain or cord and out again through the same efferent pathway previously used. The effect of this circuit is to maintain and reinforce, or to repeat, the muscular response. The holding of an object in the closed hand, and the repetition of syllables in the "talk" of the infant, probably involve this type of compound reflex. . . . The circular reflex is an indispensable aid in the infant's acquisition of speech.*

Allport emphasized the notion of *practice*, and stated that the truly lasting elements in a young speaker's repertoire were verbalizations followed by advantageous environmental events. He reasoned that speech developed through the child's attempts to control the behavior of others and to avoid aversive stimuli. At first, word habits would appear that only amounted to "parroting." Then language comprehension followed by means of conditioning and social stimulation. Concerning the common and contradicting observation that comprehension *preceded* speech habits, Allport stated that at that early stage children were only responding to the emotional tones of speech, for example, pitch and intensity; and that these reactions were the same as animal responses to growls and cries.

This trend in American thought independently paralleled other lines of thought reviewed thus far in this chapter. It is instructive now to read Allport's behaviorist statement (including his schematic neurology) on language acquisition in order to contrast it with the other writings on acquisition at that time and because Allport's chapter has been so influential in the United States. Also, it illustrates the absence in the mainstream of early twentieth-century American psychology of certain issues, such as the priority of the *sentence* to the *word*, that were of major concern to many linguistically and cognitively oriented psychologists elsewhere.

---

* F. H. Allport, *Social psychology* (Boston: Houghton Mifflin, 1924), p. 39.

FLOYD HENRY ALLPORT · *Control of the Verbal Response*

The Development of Language

Stage 1. Random Articulation with Fixation of Circular Responses. The marvelously intricate and versatile speech mechanism . . . is at birth, like other motor mechanisms, simply a crude possibility. Further growth of the nerves and muscles must combine with *practice* to produce a repertory of sounds adequate for language. With such development as a basis the social environment furnishes the stimuli necessary for the acquisition of perfected speech habits. The earliest used consonants, which according to Miss Blanton, occur during the first month of life, are chiefly nasals and gutturals, such as *m, n, ng, g,* and *k* (also *h, w,* and *y*). These represent easy mouth positions adopted probably as random movements. They are articulated with various long and broad vowel sounds, and with some diphthongs (double vowels), as in "*gow*" (writer's son at two months).

. . . . .

With random articulation we enter upon a new phase contrasting somewhat with that of pure laryngeal utterance. The latter is imperative in mode. It arises with some strong, unpleasant emotion due to thwarting or discomfort; and it rapidly assumes the function of social control. "Baby talk" on the other hand is spontaneous and indicative of a pleasant mood. It is a form of play, a part of the diffuse outflow of energy, rather than an effort at the control of others. If stronger emotions enter the field, bringing in the functions of the sympathetic nervous system, the pleasant prattle at once gives place to the inarticulate cries of the earlier period.[1]

Too much attention has been paid to the acquisition of vocabularies,

SOURCE. F. H. Allport, *Social psychology* (Boston: Houghton Mifflin, 1924), Chap. 8, Social stimulation. Reprinted by permission of the publisher.

[1] Cf. the theory of antagonistic emotions explained in Chapter IV [of Allport].

and too little to the study of the pre-verbal stage of random articulation in infants. This stage not only affords the material for language but gives the practice necessary for the control through the ear of the muscles of speech. The chief significance of the vocal play of babies seems to be in establishing circular reflexes between the sound of the syllable and the response of speaking it. Let us suppose, for example, that the baby utters the syllable *da*. By so doing he stimulates himself through two channels. He receives certain kinaesthetic sensations from the movement of the vocal organs, and certain auditory sensations from the sound which he produced. It is with the auditory stimulation that we shall be chiefly concerned. Returning to the brain centers these afferent impulses are, or tend to be, redischarged through the same motor pathways as those used in speaking the syllable itself. There are two possible methods of explaining this. We may suppose that the synapses connecting the afferent impulse with the motor outlet of speaking *da*, having been recently used, are in a state of relatively lowered resistance, and are therefore readily put into operation again. Or we may infer that, in some cases at least, the return stimulations are received while the speaking response is still going on (as in a prolonged vowel sound), and the motor synaptic resistances for *da* are completely overcome because discharge through those synapses is actually taking place. We have here the exact situation for the formation of a *conditioned response*. The response *da* becomes circularly conditioned by the sound *da*; and this sound when later heard will tend of itself to evoke the response of speaking it. This latter explanation is probably the true one.[2] While the babe is practicing the syllabic elements of his future vocabulary he is therefore also fixating ear-vocal reflexes through which a spoken sound may directly evoke its enunciation. Articulation has now advanced to a stage where it is capable of being controlled through the auditory

---

[2] Direct proof of this process is, of course, difficult to obtain. There are, however, a number of exact analogies, of which the micturition reflex is perhaps the most convincing. When the bladder is partially filled, the mere *sound* of running water is a sufficient stimulus to cause either an increase in bladder tonus (desire to urinate), or the act of voiding itself. Here, as in the vocal reflexes, the sound produced by the act performed in the past by the individual himself has acquired, by conditioning, a stimulus value for evoking the act itself. Feeling impelled to cough when we hear others cough is a similar example.

receptor. The process just described is illustrated diagrammatically in Figure 1, A.

Stage 2. Evoking of the Articulate Elements by the Speech of Others (so-called "Imitation"). At this point the social influence enters the process of language development. If the ear-vocal reflexes have been sufficiently established for the sound of a word to call forth the response of articulating it, it is no longer necessary that the child himself should speak the stimulating word. It may be spoken to another. The effect will then be that of the child repeating the sounds which he hears others utter. This stage is suggested in Figure 1, B. It is, of course, assumed that only such speech responses as have been acquired through growth and practice will be evoked in this manner. The child does not imitate or duplicate the speech of his elders. There is evoked simply the nearest similar ear-vocal reflex which, with his present limitations of pronouncing, he has been able to fixate. The word "doll," spoken by the parent, would probably be repeated *da* (*a* as in father). In this manner whole phrases far beyond the learner's comprehension may be reiterated in rote fashion with as fair accuracy as the speech habits already acquired permit. It is essentially a parrot stage. In popular parlance it is known as "learning by imitation." The term "imitation" is however both inexact and misleading, for it suggests that the process is one of learning the speech reactions of others by voluntarily copying them; whereas it is really the touching off of *previously acquired* speech habits by their conditioning auditory stimuli.[3]

Discussion of the Theory Involved in Stages 1 and 2. The reader should bear in mind that the process thus far described is largely hypothetical. Precise physiological data are wanting; but in their absence we may review certain lines of evidence in support of the hypothesis.

1. If vocal responses are circularly fixated, with the sound of speaking them serving as stimulus, we should expect that reiteration of the same syllable over and over would be a necessary result. The baby would learn to mimic himself as a prerequisite for repeating sounds

---

[3] Although the theory thus far discussed was developed independently by the writer, he does not claim to be the first one to have advanced it. A concise statement of the principle involved may be found in Smith and Guthrie, *General psychology in terms of behavior,* p. 132.

FIG. 1. The development of language habits in the infant.

A, Stage 1—Random articulation of syllables with fixation of circular responses. Chance articulation of the syllable *da* causes the baby to hear himself say it. The auditory impulse is conveyed to the brain centers where it discharges into the efferent neurons to muscle groups used in pronouncing the same syllable. An ear-vocal habit for *da* is thus established.

B, Stage 2—Evoking the same articulate elements by the speech sounds of others. An adult speaking the word "doll," which is closely similar to *da*, causes the auditory excitation again to discharge into the response *da*.

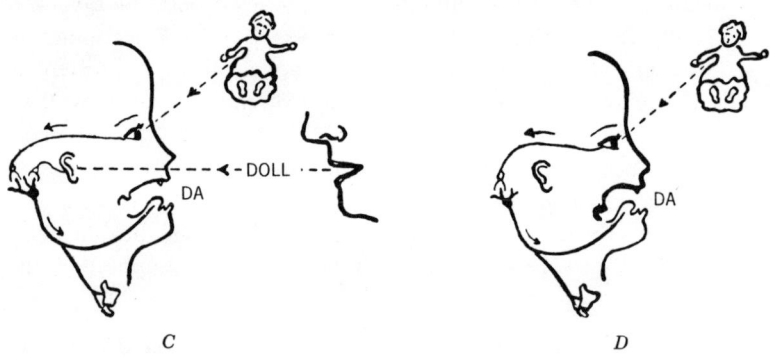

C and D, Stage 3—Conditioning of the articulate elements (evoked by others) by objects. In C the process shown in B is repeated. A doll shown at the same time stimulates the baby's eye, and forms a visual connection with the motor neurons being used in pronouncing the syllable. There is thus established a conditioned response between the sight of the doll and the speaking of *da*. The sight of the doll alone (D) is now sufficient to evoke its name (*da* being as close as the baby can come to the pronunciation of "doll").

made by others. The facts support this supposition. Reduplication of syllables (*da-da-da*, etc.) in a tireless manner is a common phenomenon of baby talk. Later many objects are named with doubling of syllables (for example, *wah-wah* for water), and longer phrases are reiterated as a kind of play.

2. Only sounds which have been already pronounced in random articulation can be evoked by the speech sounds of others. That is, only those sounds can be evoked which have had a chance to become circularly fixated as ear-vocal reflexes. The spoken word "pencil" was repeated by the writer's son as *punka* (*c* and *l* sounds not yet acquired). The phrase "What is that?" involving difficult consonants, was reproduced as *uh i ă*. The words "down," "doll," and "clock," when spoken to him, were all repeated as *da*. *Ba*, similarly, was his reproduction of "box," "bath," "bottle," "block," and "bye."[4]

3. There exist in the central nervous system mechanisms adequate for the circular fixation of vocal habits. Leaving out of account the cortex, relatively undeveloped in infancy, there are adequate connections between the auditory nuclei of the brain stem and motor fibers controlling the organs of speech. Neither high intelligence nor conscious imitation are necessary for the use of this apparatus. The ear-vocal connection is direct and immediate. The evidence for this is at hand in cases of *echolalia* in idiots and asphasic patients.[5] These "human parrots" accurately reiterate whole phrases spoken in their hearing without the slightest comprehension of their meaning. We are probably dealing here with sub-cortical mechanisms representing early formed and circularly fixed responses comparable to those of the baby.

4. It is well known that congenital or early deafness is usually accompanied by mutism. Deaf-mutes are able to articulate in the manner of the random infantile period (baby talk); but they cannot, without special methods, learn the use of spoken language. Since the ear-vocal reflexes were not and cannot be acquired, some other form, such as eye-vocal reflexes, must be substituted if the knack of speaking words is to be imparted to them. The lack of the usual, early formed, circular vocal reactions is responsible for their mutism.

Without pursuing this question further we may tentatively accept

[4] Cf. E. L. Thorndike, *Educational psychology, briefer course*, p. 43.
[5] L. S. Hollingsworth: Echolalia in Idiots. *Journal of educational Psychology*, 1917, **VIII**: 212–219.

the foregoing explanation of the so-called "imitative stage" of language development.[6] Word habits have been formed which are capable of being put into effect by the sound of the same words spoken within hearing. The next step is to convert these parrot-like reactions into true language. This step like the preceding is achieved through social agencies.

Stage 3. Conditioning of the Articulate Elements (evoked by others) by Objects and Situations. As soon as the stage is reached in which the parent can evoke repetitions of words from the infant at will, the process of teaching him to name objects begins. It does not suffice to say "doll" and hear the child repeat *da*. The doll itself is held up for inspection while the learner repeats the word pronounced by the parent or nurse. A conditioned response is thus formed; the afferent visual impulse from the doll discharges its energy through the motor pathways of the speech pattern of pronouncing the word. The object itself thus becomes a stimulus adequate for evoking the response of speaking its name. Figure 1, C and D, illustrate schematically this conditioning process. Stages two and three are practically synchronous in the actual development of the child. We have separated them in the description only for the sake of clearness.

Progress from this point is rapid. A child may learn in this manner to speak the approximate names of several hundred objects while he is still laboring over the exact pronunciation of difficult consonants. The naming, or vocabulary-acquiring, process begins early in the second year and increases by ever-lengthening strides up to six years, at which age the average child has a vocabulary of about three thousand words.

---

[6] A rival theory asserts that every vocal response pattern is connected *innately* with the sensory pattern produced by the sound of the word in question. Special instinctive mechanisms of imitation supply the ear-vocal connections which we have assumed to be developed through a conditioned circular response within the experience of the individual. The four points in the discussion above might all be construed to fit this theory. (Cf. Professor Hollingsworth's article, *loc. cit.*, in regard to echolalia.) It would be necessary, however, to meet the criticisms in regard to maturation theories and inheritance of "perceptual dispositions" . . . . The maturation theory is particularly awkward, compared with the circular reflex theory, in connection with the second point of the discussion. Instinctive imitation is at best a speculative hypothesis, while cases of circularly fixated, ear-motor reflexes are clearly established.

Our explanation thus far has involved only the control of the speech reactions of the child by the adult. Social control, however, soon operates in the reverse direction. The child learns to use his naming habits as *demanding* habits. Suppose he sees a new and interesting doll out of reach on a shelf. Manipulative tendencies cause him to reach for it. Failing in this, the usual law of trial and error brings into play all possible movements. One of the readiest and easiest of these movements is the pronunciation of the word "doll"—a reaction which is moreover elicited by its recent association (conditioning) with the sight of an object of that general sort. The word is therefore spoken, and the pleased parent presents the doll as a reward. The manipulative drive now proceeds unhampered, and the arcs involved in this solution of the problem are fixated for future use. By simple vocal expression the child thus learns to control others. He increases vicariously his own stature, his power, and his sagacity by enlisting these attributes of adults in the service of his needs. Little wonder that his linguistic progress is rapid!

The naming reaction can be conditioned not only by the sight of an object but by other stimuli inherent in the *general situation*. The word "doll" may have been evoked at a time when the child was handling the toy, "talking" to it, or even running to get it. The proprioceptive stimulations arising from these acts therefore become adequate conditioning stimuli for producing the response of speaking the word. In all relations in which the doll itself was formerly experienced the word "doll" may now be called up in consciousness and evoked as an audible or a "thought" response. At any future time therefore when the child may recall or have the tendency to manipulate such an object through habit, he will be likely to say "doll." The attendant again produces the object; and the arcs involved in this solution are fixated as before. The learner has now reached the advanced stage of demanding objects *desired but not seen*. Verbs, adverbs, and particles, such as "give," "down," "again," "move," and "no," are acquired and used in the same fashion. Having been learned through social agents in connection with attitudes, postures, and situations, they are now used to control these agents with respect to the situations they represent.

In the learning of language then, as in the stages of laryngeal and gestural expression, we find that social control is a cogent factor. With increasing development, however, other considerations enter. In addition to naming and demanding objects the child begins to talk *about* them. He discourses to his toys and about them. He verbally reviews bits of the day's experience as he lies in his crib in the evening, and in so doing substitutes word responses for the overt movements he originally employed in living them. In other words, language becomes for him a vehicle of *thought*.

Development of Response to Language

A few words may be added concerning the understanding of language by the infant, a function which precedes its actual use by some weeks or months. Speech sounds of others stimulate the child in many ways beside the eliciting of ear-vocal reflexes. They control his behavior in consoling him, diverting his attention, and offering signs by which he knows that he is to be tended in various ways. Language serves to condition the prepotent activities of the baby in the same way that the incidental growls or sex sounds condition the withdrawing or approaching responses of the lower animals. Experiments show that dogs respond very little to words as articulated symbols, but chiefly to the pitch, intensity, and quality of the voice. The earliest effect of vocal stimuli upon the baby is through these same laryngeal components. An infant will cry at a scolding tone of the parent long before the words themselves are understood. By the end of the first year the response to commands, or to the direction of attention, that is, to some part of the child's body, indicate that he is beginning to understand the meaning of articulate word symbols.[7]

The final achievement of linguistic development is the response to language by the use of language, as in answering a question. This occurs late, usually after a fair mastery of speech has been obtained. Aside from the intellectual difficulty involved, there appears to be a kind of inertia: the child is loath to quit the placid, irresponsible haven of ear-vocal reflexes for the uncharted sea of interrogation.

The contrast between the early American behaviorist's view of language acquisition and that of many writers in other

[7] Romanes states the case as follows: "While the understanding of certain tones of the human voice extends at least through the entire vertebrated series and occurs in infants only a few weeks old, the understanding of words without the assistance of tones appears to occur only in a few of the higher mammalia, and first dawns in the growing child during the second year." (*Mental evolution in man,* p. 124.)

countries at the same time is a striking one. There is practically no overlap of references or citations in Allport's chapter with those in the Stern or Guillaume monographs. Among many continental psychologists the reaction to Allport's and to similar writings was apparently the same as it had been to the earlier "pooh-pooh," "ding-dong," and "bow-wow," theories of language origin. Although behaviorism was descended from the older functionalism in the United States, the European functionalists retained aspects of mentalism in their psychology and continued on a course that had little contact with the American behaviorists.

Data on language acquisition continued to accumulate in even more massive amounts in the United States during the 1930s. However, in America there was less interest in language *per se* and more energy expended for relating infant speech to sensory, motor, social, and emotional development. The taxonomic approach prevailed. By 1949 Edgar Dale was able to assemble a bibliography of 1,855 vocabulary development investigations.*
There was evident progress in the development of statistical procedure and experimental methodology. Although this improved the techniques for data gathering and analysis, psychologists in the United States were largely untutored in linguistics, so there were few "psycholinguists" to benefit from the technological innovations.

Several other painstaking and extensive biographical studies of infant language were published during this period. Most notable was the Russian Gvozdev's (1929 and later) Grégoire's (1937–1938) in France, and Leopold's (1939 and later) in the United States. Research on language acquisition has never really declined other than as research in general was slowed by the two World Wars. Only the approach and emphasis may have shifted in the 1930s. It was during this decade that the best studies on phonological aspects of language acquisition were performed; and this had in part been made possible by advances in linguistic theory at that level. There are too many large investigations and momentous works to list them all here. Grégoire's work was one of these land marks. Another, now little known,

---

* E. Dale, *Bibliography of vocabulary studies* (Bureau of Educational Research, Ohio State University, 1949).

was that of the French physician Jeanne-Andrée Feyeux working at the University of Lyons: *L'acquisition du langage et ses retards* (The acquisition of language and its retardation) 1932. In England M. M. Lewis wrote first of a series of books on the topic: *Infant Speech,* 1936. Another was Jakobson's *Kindersprache, Aphasie und allgemeine Lautgesetze,* 1942 (English translation, 1968: *Child language, aphasia, and phonological universals*). The recent translation and reprinting of Jakobson's monograph, which has been largely unknown in the United States, is indeed fortunate in that it constitutes a historical survey of research on the phonological development of child speech and includes much Slavic and Scandinavian literature. Grégoire later wrote a short history of the 1930s period in European child language study terming the movement a "renaissance" in language acquisition research.* Remarkably, these investigations arrived independently at similar conclusions, namely, that the pattern of appearance of rudimentary sound systems follows the same schedule regardless of language or culture. A review of phonological investigations in the history of psycholinguistics would require another volume. But Jackobson's now widely available monograph helps to fill that need.†

Before turning to the mid-twentieth-century revival of psycholinguistics, there is another topic that deserves attention because of its relevance to early psycholinguistics—investigations of the *psychology of reading*.

---

* A. Grégoire, La renaissance scientifique de la linguistique enfantine. *Lingua,* 1950, **2**: 255–398.

† There is a noteworthy tradition of developmental psycholinguistics and "Sprachpsychologie" research in the Soviet Union, known there as *psikhologiya rechi*. However, lack of availability of relevant sources has prevented an analysis of that tradition here. Dan Slobin of the University of California at Berkeley has argued that the Russian "Gvozdev's two books on the phonological and grammatical development of his son far surpass in detail and linguistic sophistication anything done in Western Europe." (Personal communication, 1968.) For Slobin's review of that work see his "Early grammatical development in several languages, with special attention to Soviet research." In T. Bever and W. Weksel (Eds.) *The structure and psychology of language,* Vol. II (New York: Holt, Rinehart and Winston, in press).

CHAPTER 4

THE PSYCHOLOGY OF READING
Early Contributions to Psycholinguistics

In those societies that have a written form for their language and have adopted an alphabetic instead of ideographic writing system there has frequently been one hotly debated issue. This is whether one should begin instruction in reading with linguistic units that have meaning (words, phrases) or with smaller units that do not carry meaning (letters, sounds). Different ideas about the nature of perception and of language are often implied in the two views. The latter approach often holds that the reader decodes written symbols into sounds and then to meaning (or reference). The former approach assumes a different sequence, that is, that the reader proceeds from written symbol directly to meaning and then, optionally, to sound. Pedagogues have referred to instructional techniques based on the former as "whole" methods and those based on the latter as "part" methods. More recently they have been called the analytic and the synthetic approach, respectively.*

Reading research was once a more prominent topic in experimental psychology than it is today. By the 1920s researchers in this field began to separate from the mainstream of psychology and to form their own professional associations and technical journals. Thus the "reading field" became specialized with its own laboratories usually centered in schools of education. One can judge psychology's shift away from reading research by comparing the 1938 edition of Woodworth's *Experimental psychology* with the later 1954 edition. In the former volume, "Reading" constituted one of the longer chapters. In the latter, it

---

* The cyclical fluctuation of opinion between the two aproaches is reviewed in M. M. Mathews, *Teaching to read, historically considered* (Chicago: University of Chicago Press, 1966).

was completely omitted, with only a few references to reading research reported in another section.

Earlier, in the late 1800s, a number of psychological experiments threw the ancient issue of learning to read and reading perception into a whirl of new debate and confusion. In part this was a result of the activity in psycholinguistics during the late nineteenth century. An explanation of the early strong interest of psychologists in reading appears in an often quoted remark by the American psychologist Edmund Huey:

And so to completely analyze what we do when we read would almost be the acme of a psychologist's acievements, for it would be to describe very many of the most intricate workings of the human mind, as well as to unravel the tangled story of the most remarkable specific performance that civilization has learned in all its history.*

Judging from this quotation, an explanation of reading was a major goal of cognitive psychology.

Early reading research was almost synonymous with studies of attention, a field that Wundt had cultivated. An 1897 experiment by J. O. Quantz revealed that the eye's position *vis-à-vis* the written line usually precedes that of the voice by a few words when reading aloud. This *eye-voice span* is a maximum of seven words with an average span of five. Such a finding confirmed Wundt's conclusion that the limit on the scope of apperception is six or seven items. Some of the questions that psychologists then pursued were these: Why does the attention span vary as the presentations change from numbers, to letters, to words, or to sentences? Can the focus of attention move backward as well as forward during the sequential perceptions, and can it move independently of eye-movements? What are the effects of context and set on attention, and through what mechanism do these operate in reading? Early experimental studies of reading often developed directly out of issues concerning the fundamental nature of attention.

It was soon discovered that there was a low correlation of reading ability with abilities in other visual tasks, and that sheer

---

* E. B. Huey, *The psychology and pedagogy of reading* (New York: Macmillan, 1908), p. 6.

reading skill did not depend on intelligence but depended instead on a special linguistic factor. Such results led investigators toward psycholinguistics because the vital difference between reading and other visual perception was found to be in the nature of human language.

Early experimental psychology had an unintentionally profound effect on reading instruction. During the founding years of the new psychology apparently the "part" or synthetic methods were dominant. Children learned to read by spelling out words (the "ABC" method) or by sounding them out (the "phonic" method). By popular consensus it was assumed that the perception of written language required that the eye fixate each letter while moving from left to right. Indeed, physiologists and ophthalmologists commonly held that reading is mediated by letters or dominant letter-groups that must be perceived individually. Then in 1878–1879 Émile Javal, a French oculist, reported some simple contrary observations: the movement of a reader's eye across the written page is never continuous, as if letter by letter, but is erratic and sometimes advances by long jumps. That year, 1879, is also the date of the opening of the psychology laboratory in Leipzig. And Cattell, the first American student to write a dissertation under Wundt, undertook investigations of the reading skill.

Cattell's work came amidst the excitement generated by Javal's discovery. Using the newly devised tachistoscope, Cattell claimed to have found that the units of perception in adult readers are words or even phrases, when using items that are meaningful as opposed to unknown languages or nonsense syllables. At extremely brief exposures, subjects were able to read words and even short sentences although the presentation of the written material was too brief to permit the eye's scanning of the line of letters.

During the 1890s there followed a proliferation of attempts to record and measure eye movement. Plaster cups were attached to the cornea with threads running to recorders; microphones were fixed to eyelids; and systems of lenses, mirrors, headrests, and bite-boards were concocted for viewing the actions of the eye. In 1898 at the University of Halle, Benno Erdmann and Raymond Dodge computed the speed of the eye's movement from one reading fixation to the next and found it to be so rapid that no perception could take place during those movements. In other tests they showed that words could be perceived at distances from the eye too great to permit perception of isolated letters. And at a yet farther distance, sentences could be read while isolated words were not readable.

In 1897 Pillsbury, an American interpreter of Wundtian psychology, employed the reading skill in an experimental study of Wundt's theory of apperception. He found the apperceptive faculty to be "creative" as Wundt proposed. In one test, distorted words or words with missing letters were shown for brief intervals. Subjects typically reported seeing them as normal and not distorted. An apperceptive process had apparently made a correction or had filled in the missing letters. Edmund Huey (1900) later extended this experiment using sentences with deleted words. With similar results, subjects reported seeing complete sentences.

It should be no surprise that one of the next great movements among educators concerned the technique of reading instruction. In the wake of the above findings the popular conclusion proclaimed that the smaller elements, the letters, when taken alone are only of minor importance in the act of reading and, therefore, in learning to read. The "whole" method soon appeared in full force in many classrooms. Later we shall discuss how the eagerness of educators in applying early experimental findings led to some misinterpretations. The psychologists had described the behavior of mature readers, not the nature of reading acquisition.

One classic book summarizes the early period of reading research: Huey's *Psychology and pedagogy of reading* (1908). Edmund Burke Huey's career in psychology might have been better known if it had not been cut short by his early death. Nevertheless, he did write a text on the psychology of reading that remains as the best work from the turn of the century period. (At the time of writing this chapter the M.I.T. press reissued Huey's book with special introductions by psychologists John Carroll and Paul Kolers.)

Huey was a protégé of Hall and of the pedagogical psychologists at Clark University. His dissertation in 1899 concerned the psychology and physiology of reading. He then went to Europe to study with Javal at Paris and with Erdmann in Germany. Huey's 1908 text shows the influence of Wundtian psycholinguistics and of the early research on attention, and further, he believed that language should not be described merely as a means of communication but also as a means of directing the attention. The following excerpts are taken from chapters where Huey draws his conclusions from the accumulated early research. They show the concern with "automatization of function" which was frequently studied in that day. Also, Huey compares Wundt's notions of language with the comments on language made by James.

EDMUND BURKE HUEY · *Language, Perception, and Reading*

Goldscheider and Müller[1] were profoundly right when they said that readers perceive in various ways as their purpose can be best attained. We must allow for considerable variety, not merely of individuals but of occasions. The manner of perceiving words must depend, for the child, very largely on how he is *taught* to perceive them in learning to read, and here, as we know, the methods are most diverse. To take a simple example, the writer still finds himself hesitant in naming or recognizing several capital letters of the Greek alphabet, perhaps even incapable of recognizing one or two of them when seen in isolation. Yet Greek was a favorite study with him through years of college and secondary school. The reason for his persistent inattention to the letters is evident enough. He began Greek with the sentence method, and his attention was seldom called to the particular letters in reading. . . .

However, there are general features of the perceptual process which appear as we survey the collected data from all the experi-

SOURCE. Edmund Burke Huey, *The Psychology and pedagogy of reading* (New York: Macmillan, 1908), excerpts from Chapters 5, 6, and 7.

[1] Goldscheider, A. and Müller, R. Zur Physiologie und Pathologie des Lesens. *Zeitschrift f. Klin. Med.*, Vol. 23, 1890.

ments on reading. In the first place, perceiving is an *act*, a thing that we *do*, always and everywhere, never a mere passive sensing of a group of passing sensations or impressions. It probably always involves actual innervation of muscles, and indeed coordinated and organized, we may say unitized, innervation of muscles. Certainly on the psychic side there is an active and more or less unitized movement of mind, a sense of inner activity.

Perceiving being an act, it is, like all other things that we do, performed more easily with each repetition of the act. To perceive an entirely new word or other combination of strokes requires considerable time, close attention, and is likely to be imperfectly done, just as when we attempt some new combination of movements, some new trick in the gymnasium or new "serve" at tennis. In either case, repetition progressively frees the mind from attention to details, makes facile the total act, shortens the time, and reduces the extent to which consciousness must concern itself with the process. One may say that the "memory image" helps in the later perception of the word; but it may well be that, as Goldscheider and Müller put it, the memory is but an exercise or habit of the apperceptive activity (*Uebung der Apperceptionsthätigkeit*)—that we perceive better at the later trial just as we shoot better or skate better with practice.

Again, as in the performance of any act, a perception may involve more and more complex constituent acts as these are progressively welded together by practice, and especially as they become synthesized to a total performance which may be set off from a single consciousness cue. It comes about, therefore, that just as the complicated but associatively concatenated and organized movements of hitting a target with a ball may be touched off by the mere sight of the target, in one attention-act, so the various activities involved in apperceiving a phrase or other word-group may become one complex but unitary act, and this act may be set off very simply by this or that cue or set of cues given from the page, and may be done with a minimum of consciousness concerning details.

Again, perception is always a projection or localization outward of a consciousness which is aroused or suggested by the stimulations that have come inward, but which is conditioned strongly, also, from within. We have seen how, when some dominant parts of a word or sentence were exposed without the other parts, the reader would project the absent letters upon the page and would "see" them as distinctly as when they were actually before him. We have seen, too, how in every moment of our reading we project letters and parts of letters to fill up the gaps that are always left in the peripheral parts of our retinal image. We know how we project a consciousness content to serve for what should be imaged on the "blind spot." Such projection is as certain and as common as is any mental phenomenon. The simple fact is that the words and all the other objects that we ever see are thus thrown outward, projected upon a page in the case of reading, somewhat as a lantern might throw them outward upon a screen. In the case of perception it might be said that the mind furnishes the screen as well. It must be remembered that consciousness does not dwell in the retina or in retinal images. Objects may be pictured very well without any retina or optic nerve. For our purposes here consciousness may best be thought of as in the brain, totally in the dark as to physical environment, constructing even its light as well as its forms and meanings according to the excitations that come in to it and their relations with those that have previously come in. I raise here no question of idealism, and there need be no discussion of metaphysics.[2]

When we consider that the arrangement on the page, of the words and of their parts, is a construction within from cues which are probably given in non-spatial order, we are prepared for the statement of Zeitler[3] that in the first awareness of the dominating letters of a word they are not seen in any very fixed spatial arrangement, and are only put in place and "anchored" there as the recognition completes itself with the coming of the associative contribution from within. The wonder is that the cues to the arrangement of the letters are not more often fallacious, and that misreadings like *Krone* for *Korne*, *aneotic* for *anoetic*, *Larabee* for *Labaree*, actual cases which I have noticed recently, are so infrequent with most readers. In this view of perception one is inclined to accept what the experiments of Zeitler, Messmer,[4] and others seem to show, that the first factors of

---

[2] Of course the whole matter could be stated equally in terms of James' radical empiricism, without affecting the argument here. I have come to consider the doctrine of James to be nearer the truth. However, my thought about perception in reading is doubtless more intelligible as stated in terms of my working hypothesis of plain dualism.

[3] Zeitler, Julius, Tachistoskopische Versuche über das Lesen. Wundt's *Philosoph. Studien,* Vol. 16, No. 3, 1900.

[4] Messmer, Oskar, Zur Psychologie des Lesens bei Kindern und Erwachsenen. *Archiv für die gesamte Psychologie,* December, 1903.

perception in reading are not usually the total form, word-length, etc., but certain striking "dominant" parts, the appreciation of total word-form and word-length coming a little later as the recognition is completed at the suggestion of these dominant cues.

However, while the experiments of these investigators indicate the special part which the dominant letters and letter-groups play in setting off the word-recognitions, we need by no means suppose that the former are always or usually apperceived as distinct letters in performing this function of special signs. Through their being the most obvious parts optically, and through habit, they have come to be most quickly operative in unlocking the word-recognitions; but in ordinary reading they would seem to have but a minimum of attention, performing their function automatically and without any apperceptive act that is distinct from that for the larger whole in which their recognition is subsumed. When that total recognition completes itself, however, we are apt to be conscious of these dominant forms as the most prominent parts of the word.

. . . .

The constant practice of writing words letter after letter, and the use of the letters in abbreviations, etc., tends to increase the consciousness of single letters as they appear in words, and thus to break up the consciousness of total word-form. Of course, too, the school practice in spelling and the synthetic methods of learning to read contribute strongly to the dominance of letter-units in the perception of words. Even in the more pronounced cases of letter consciousness, however, it is perfectly certain that words are not perceived by a successive recognition of letter after letter, or even by any simultaneous recognition of all the letters *as such*. By whatever cues the recognition may be set off, it is certainly a recognition of word-wholes, except when even these recognition units are subsumed under the recognition of a still larger unit. The only question is as to what parts are especially operative as cues in setting off this recognition.

. . . .

The visual recognition of a familiar phrase, *as* a phrase, is . . . the recognitions of constituent words as well as of letters in this case being partially inhibited in favor of the total recognition of the larger unit. Total visual form seems to be a less important factor in mediating the recognitions as the unit grows larger. Unitary recognition of phrases is very common in reading, or mentally the words do not stand entirely apart. The exigencies of printing have brought about the division on the page of much that belongs together in speech, and again many of our words are logically phrases and might be printed as separated words. The psychological process of apperceiving these words or phrases would not change very greatly if they were printed differently. Very many compounds are written sometimes as separate words, sometimes as two words with a hyphen, again as a single word. Indeed, as we shall see elsewhere, the usual separation even of words upon the page, in Latin and Greek, came very late. In partial disregard, therefore, of the printer's divisions, there is naturally a gradual progress, with practice, toward recognition in larger units, for those who learn first the recognition of letters and words. Larger and larger unitary reactions are set off as familiarity makes this possible, the same excitations coming to serve as cues for the larger recognitions instead of for the smaller, while the earlier processes or recognition habits, even when they do not atrophy, are performed automatically, consciousness ever tending to leave them for higher levels.

We must remember, however, that there are continual reversions to older habits, cnsciousness descending to even the level of letter-recognitions, on occasion, and very often taking account of particular words. Here there seem to be very great individual differences, and these depend partly, although never wholly, on the methods by which the reader has learned to read. We are brought back to the conclusion of Goldscheider and Müller that we read by phrases, words, or letters as we may serve our purpose best. But we see, too, that the reader's acquirement of ease and power in reading comes through increasing ability to read in larger units.

We cannot complete our account of visual perception in reading until we have first taken account of the part played by inner speech and by the consciousness of meaning. These have an important function in conditioning recognitions in reading. Meaning, indeed, dominates and unitizes the perception of words and phrases, as indeed, according to such writers as Stout[5] at least, it dominates all perceptions. Zeitler's remark will be remembered, that the word's form first gets anchored or established as the sense is filled into it. This appears in perceiving phrases in which words are "seen" which are not there, but which make sense. The excitations from the page act here as cues to a meaning which reacts in the projection of an equivalent expression.

. . . .

Language begins with the sentence, and this is the unit of language everywhere. A sentence is a unitary expression of a thought. A thought may be expressed in a word sometimes, and this is then a sentence-word, as when Preyer's child put his milk cup down quickly and said "Hot!" This single word was to signify, "This drink is too hot." It was "a whole proposition in a syllable," as Preyer says.[6] The *meaning* that might have suggested "This drink is too hot" and that would have bathed every part of it as spoken, suggested only "Hot" as its expression, with this child who yet knew but little of language. But there was more than the articulated word. The pitch, accent, modulation of voice, which characterize a sentence-word's pronunciation, are important factors in expressing the particular unitary meaning that is felt. "Papa" may mean "Come here, papa," "Look out, papa," "Please do, papa," according to variations in the tone, etc., and according to the situation context. Often the modulation, accent, or rhythm are more expressive of the speaker's meaning than are the words as such, and the former factors belong to the sentence *as a whole*.

The child, the primitive man, and indeed any speaker, when he would form a sentence, begins with a *meaning*, a total idea, as Wundt calls it, which he would express. This total idea is at first little differentiated and may find expression in a gesture, a tone, or a word, as when the earnestly spoken "Hot" was all that came. With more experience this total idea or consciousness situation, of being burned with milk, falls apart somewhat into the subnotions milk—this—hot —drink, and gets a correspondingly analyzed expression in these

---

[5] Stout, G. F., *Analytical psychology* (London: Macmillan, 1896).
[6] Preyer, W. *Development of the intellect* (New York: Appleton, 1898).

several words, these expressing still, however, one unitary meaning. The part of the total idea that is most prominent in consciousness is apt to be expressed first, and in child speech, as with many primitive tribes, the words may come in any order according as the various aspects of the total idea successively become prominent in the speaker's mind.

The child's language, however, is not an invention, but is learned by imitation; and he accepts, in English, certain fixed habits of breaking up the total ideas into parts that are expressed in parts of speech, such as nouns, verbs, adjectives, etc. Certain habitual sequences of these parts are also learned by imitation and his words come to fall into this habitual order. Thus, beginning with a total meaning and a total intention of expressing this meaning, the development is toward a more and more particular division of it into aspects or parts, and toward the expression of these parts in words that are arranged in grammatical sequence, this arranging and indeed the whole development being largely automatic, the result of associative habits learned gradually by experience and by imitation. But *meaning leads*, and the idea of the whole dominates the parts. The sentence is *not* naturally composed of words which originally existed independently, just as we shall find that the word is not a mere collection of syllables and letters.

In the ancient languages a single expression would often be word and sentence together. Wundt says in his "Völker-Psychologie:"[7] "The Latin *amavi* is both word and sentence. The Romance languages resolve this thought into three words, *ego habeo amatum, j'ai aimé*. Accordingly, if we compare, on the one hand, languages of an evidently more primitive development with those that are more developed, and if on the other hand we compare the earlier with the later stages of one and the same language, the differentiation of the parts of speech everywhere shows itself as the process of gradually resolving the word out of the whole to which it belongs; namely, the sentence—the process which lends the word a relatively greater independence and fixes its grammatical form at the same time with its independent significance." There exist today languages in which the sentences are spoken without differentiation of either words or parts of speech, in a continuum of syllable sounds, or it might be

[7] Vol. I, p. 561.

said that the sentence is one long word. Our English and the kindred languages have made the analysis into parts of speech, words, etc., and our fashion of printing has made us very conscious of the results of this analysis. But in the living speech of conversation and thought these parts still inhere organically in the original sentence-wholes, and the actual structure is very different from the written or printed expression, as we shall presently see.

Genetically, then, as we might go on to show, the growth of living speech both in the race and in the child has been from the protoplasm of total meanings expressed in sentence-wholes, through a progressive analysis to parts of speech and words, then to syllables and to elementary sounds. We shall later trace the analogous development of the written and printed characters from primitive picture-wholes to characters representative of word-meanings, word-sounds, and finally to symbols for syllables and for elementary sounds. Let us now look more nearly at the processes that go on as we speak our English sentences today.

In the first place it is certain that in ordinary speech some thought of the whole sentence pervades every part as the part is spoken, and the part is felt in a perspective of the whole. This is true of the sentence's beginning as well as of its other parts, and some consciousness of the whole usually precedes even the initial utterance. Says Wundt in the volume mentioned (p. 563): "At the moment in which I begin a sentence the whole of it stands already in my consciousness as a total idea." Wundt adds, however, that the sentence is then felt only in its main outlines, its constituent parts being at first dark, but coming out as the speaking goes on. "The process," he says, "is something like the sudden lighting of a complex picture, where one at first has only a general impression of the whole, and then successively of the particular parts, always seen in their relations to the whole." Only thus, Wundt thinks, can we explain the fact of a speaker going correctly through with a complex sentence without having reflected on it before.

The total idea of what is to be said thus exists in consciousness precedent to the utterance, and dominates the utterance throughout. This total idea is not a mere sum of associations, but is an apperceptive unity. This unity becomes differentiated in the manner and in the direction indicated in its sentence expression, and the sentence is, according to Wundt, "the analysis into its parts of a whole that is present in consciousness." Accordingly, he says, sentence formation is analytical, as it is a separation of the parts of a whole, but it is also synthetic in that it is an appearance of part after part in the focus of consciousness. "Above all, however," he adds, "it is an analytical process."[8]

Again, Wundt considers the sentence to be a "voluntary act," willed as a whole. True, it is a complex act, but the constituent movements of articulation, etc., go off automatically like the constituent movements of any other unitary performance. We "give the direction to the thought" and "the requisite words stream to us of themselves"; that is, "they are awakened associatively from the first-excited word-ideas under the influence of the total idea that is present. . . ."

Professor James[9] bases his psychology of the sentence on his view of consciousness as a continuous stream of processes in which "breaks are produced by sudden contrasts in the quality of the successive segments." Consciousness makes us aware of things, and things, being discrete and discontinuous, "pass before us in a train or chain, making often explosive appearances and rending each other in twain." But these do not break the *flow of the thought that thinks them*, with its continuum of feelings, bodily sensations, etc. There are, however, the apparent breaks, which are really "transitive places," places of rapid flow, of flight from the perch of one substantive resting-place to that of another—to a conclusion perhaps or to a place in which the thought may bask in sensorial imagery. The consciousness life is like a bird's life, made up of an alternation of flights and perchings. "The rhythm of language expresses this, where every thought is expressed in a sentence and every sentence closed by a period."

. . . .

That the *general* meaning dawns upon the reader precedent to the full sentence-utterance is evidenced by the many cases in which variant words of equivalent meanings are read, and also by the comparative ease with which a reader may paraphrase the thought of what he reads. This is especially noticeable in the case of a person reading a foreign language which he does not pronounce easily but which he comprehends rather rapidly. Here the visual word and

---

[8] "Völkerpsychologie," Vol. II, 1900, p. 236.
[9] James, William, *Principles of psychology*, Vol. 2, 1890, Chap. 9.

phrase percepts touch off total meanings which clothe themselves, as the meanings become articulate, in English sentences, and we have as a result the mongrel reading which passes for French or German in so many modern language classes.

It is of the greatest service to the reader or listener that at each moment a considerable amount of what is being read should hang suspended in the primary memory of the inner speech. It is doubtless true that without something of this there could be no comprehension of speech at all. When a considerable amount is thus suspended, the attention may wander backward and forward to get a fuller meaning where this is needed, with no fear of losing the minor parts, which are taken care of physiologically and may be taken into the focus of consciousness at will. Any careful introspection of actual reading will show that the main focus of attention is often far behind the eye, concerned perhaps with the sound of some word or phrase that is giving difficulty; and we know that the entire process of visually perceiving and inwardly pronouncing may go on, for even an entire paragraph sometimes, with but very little of even marginal consciousness, the attention being absorbed in some thought suggested earlier, or perhaps in some irrelevant imagery. Indeed, any part of the reading process or the whole of it may proceed automatically with but a minimum of consciousness, just as in walking, dancing, or other complex motor activity requiring adaptive reactions to stimuli. The attention, the concern of the self about what is going on, may be here or there as there is need of it, and again is often centered where there is no need of it. Some prominent letter or other form in a preceding or succeeding line may flash into the focus more prominently than the advancing stream of visual forms that the eye is just revealing. The movement of the attention may thus be backward or forward, but of course is usually forward. Doubtless its actual advance has little reference to the sequence of eye-movements and pauses. These are ordinarily indistinguishable to consciousness, and the attention has to do with an unbroken line. The crest of the advancing consciousness seems often to be double or even quadruple, composed of visual, motor, or any other content with which the reader is concerned.

Devices such as the tachistoscope and systems for tracking eye movement were widely used in the early German psychological laboratories. However, it was the American students studying there and later in America who brought technical sophistication to the apparatus—such men as Cattell, Raymond Dodge, and Charles Judd (who were all active in the experimental study of reading). Dodge proved to be the master technician when he constructed the eye-movement camera in 1901 at Wesleyan University. His machine was soon widely used in American psychological laboratories.

Two other early reading specialists had been students at Wesleyan—Judd and Walter Dearborn. Judd then went to Leipzig to obtain his doctorate under Wundt. Dearborn received his from Cattell at Columbia and then studied in several German universities. These men were influential in American psychological circles; Dodge, Judd, and Cattell had all been president of the American Psychological Association by the time of the First World War.

Dodge's device employed a narrow beam of light that was reflected from the cornea to a strip of photographic film. Accurate measurement of fixation-point durations was possible with the film moving at a constant rate and with vibrations of a tuning fork registering on the film at fifty per second. Immediately there were many refinements of the camera, such as the use of two strips of moving film, one recording horizontal movement, the other recording vertical movement. A second beam was reflected from a tiny mirror on a frame placed on a subject's head so that spurious head movements appeared on the film to prevent their confounding with eye movements. At Columbia, Dearborn wrote his dissertation under Cattell on eye movements in reading, and he carried out several of these technical refinements. Later Dearborn and Judd both went to the University of Chicago to set up the reading laboratory there. Judd became simultaneously chairman of the Psychology Department and director of the School of Education. Dearborn went to Harvard as educational psychologist and initiated reading research programs there.

The Chicago laboratory has been the most successful and

productive center for the study of reading skills in this country. In 1915 it was awarded a sizable government grant for the study of reading and writing. Chicago was already a center for educational psychology in America owing to the influence there of John Dewey. Reading research continued to be active and by 1918 Judd was able to publish a lengthy summary of research findings.*

As the research talent concentrated on the refinement of technology, the psychology of reading sometimes became limited to peripheral factors in the reading process. Reading then seemed to be more a matter of muscle movements and retinal stimulation. This is another trend that met the firm opposition of Wundt, whose argument was that the explanation of reading should proceed from a cognitive analysis. His critique in 1900† deemphasized the optical fixation point, duration times, and span of vision. Instead, he believed that the focus of *attention* and span of attention must be understood and that they do not necessarily coincide with retinal stimulation nor with the extent of peripheral vision.

Dodge and Dearborn both held that peripheral retinal stimulation affords "premonitions" of coming words and phrases, as well as a consciousness of the relation of the immediately fixed symbols to the larger groups of phrase and sentence. Dodge thus described the point of clear vision as "an incident somewhere in the middle of the reading process—its effect is to correct, to confirm, and to intensify the premonition. Psychologically its function is selective and definitive." In disagreeing with this analysis William Schmidt (1917) of the Chicago group of reading researchers said it was fallacious to attribute Dodge's "premonition" to peripheral vision. Instead, it occurred because the reader was "immersed in the meaning of that which is being read, be it the sentence, the paragraph, or the selection."‡ For a

* C. H. Judd, *Reading: its nature and development* (Chicago: University of Chicago Press, 1918).

† W. Wundt, Zur Kritik tachistoskopischer Versuche, *Philos. Stud.*, 1900, **16**.

‡ W. A. Schmidt, *An experimental study with the psychology of reading* (Chicago: University of Chicago Press, 1917) p. 52.

while, Judd's group at Chicago was heavily under the influence of Wundt's ideas.

Dearborn in 1906* discovered that the initial pause of the eye on a line was longer in duration than subsequent ones. It seemed that the function of such a pause was to allow the reader a general initial survey of the material. Research was continued in order to find laws governing the location of fixation pauses with respect to syllables, words, phrases, and so on. It met with limited success. Generally connectives, relative pronouns, auxiliary verbs, and other "nonsubstantives" required the most and longest fixations. It is interesting to note that these are the high-frequency words, so that the longer fixation on them is not a matter of unfamiliarity. Rather, it may involve the comprehending of grammatical structure.

In 1917 Thorndike at Columbia University reported the results of his tests of reading-comprehension abilities in 1,000 school children. The reports are titled, "Reading as Reasoning" and "The Understanding of Sentences." In them he described a difference between good and poor readers that may be related to Dearborn's findings, where mature readers had favored fixations on certain grammatical elements. the attentional processes of Thorndike's poor readers were fixed mostly on the act of comprehending individual words, while the good readers observed grammatical relations. Thorndike summarizes the problem of good reading as follows:

> Understanding a paragraph is like solving a problem in mathematics. It consists in selecting the right elements of the situation and putting them together in the right relations, and also with the right amount of weight or influence or force for each. The mind is assailed as it were by every word in the paragraph. It must select, repress, soften, emphasize, correlate and organize all under the influence of the right mental set or purpose or demand.†

Perhaps the most painstaking and thorough laboratory study

---

* W. F. Dearborn, The psychology of reading. *Arch. of philos., psychol., and sci. Methods.*, No. 4, 1906, Chapter 11.

† E. L. Thorndike, Reading as reasoning. *J. educ. Psychol.*, 1917, **8**: 323–332.

of reading performed in the early twentieth century was that of Guy Buswell for his dissertation at Chicago in 1920. To date it has been one of the century's most discussed experimental investigations of reading. With Buswell's work the eye-camera technology reached a peak of development.

Buswell studied the variations in eye-voice span during oral reading. In order to record the voice, he supplemented the usual eye-movement photograph with a Dictaphone recording of oral reading, taken for each subject simultaneously with the photographs. To record the exact relation between eye and voice, the Dictaphone speaking tube was divided, one section being attached to a box containing a tap-bell operated by an electric switch that also operated a shutter interrupting a beam of light. The bell recorded a sharp click on the Dictaphone record, while the shutter recorded on the film; thus it was possible to compare eye and voice records with true precision for the first time.

Buswell made many recordings with subjects who varied over a wide age range and over school grade levels. Further, he sampled populations of good readers and poor readers. Most of his monograph concerns descriptions of data analysis as well as of changes in the behaviors of maturing readers. The following excerpts are some of his conclusions that are directly relevant to questions about the nature of psycholinguistic performance skills. Unfortunately, Buswell's work was to be remembered more for its clever technical achievement than for its characterizations of the reading skill. It illustrates the work and the then prevalent views about reading in the Chicago laboratory.

GUY THOMAS BUSWELL · *Reading Sentences*

Relation of Eye-Voice Span* to Position in Sentence. If the width of the eye-voice span of a single subject is measured at several positions in a selection, it will be found to show considerable variation from point to point. C. T. Gray observed this fact in his study but did not attempt to analyze the variations or explain them.[1] In Quantz's study . . . these variations were also noted, and an explanation proposed in terms of the position of the line.[2] Quantz found an average eye-voice span of 7.4 words at the beginning of a line, 5.1 words in the middle, and 3.8 words at the end of a line. The results of the present study do not agree with those of Quantz. For the fifty-four subjects used, the width of the span at the beginning of the line is 12.7 letter-spaces, in the middle of the line 12.7, and at the end of the line 10.9. The only point of agreement is that the span is slightly narrower at the end of the line than in other positions. Since an analysis of the variations by position in the line does not afford an adequate explanation as to the reason for the variation, it must be concluded that there are other complicating factors. Accordingly, two factors which might complicate the situation were selected for further analysis. The fact that there is a large difference in the width of the span for the good and the poor readers suggested

SOURCE. G. T. Buswell, An experimental study of the eye-voice span in reading. *Supplementary educational monographs*, No. 17 (Chicago: University of Chicago Press, 1920). With permission of the publisher.

* When reading out loud, pronounciation of words generally lags behind the advancing movements of the eye *vis-a-vis* the written line. The eye may be fixated ahead on a certain word while the voice is pronouncing an earlier word in the sequence. The measure of this varying distance between the point of visual fixation and the point of vocal pronunciation is thus the *eye-voice span*.—A.L.B.

[1] C. T. Gray, Types of reading ability as exhibited through tests and laboratory experiments. *Supplementary educational monographs*, No. 5 (Chicago: University of Chicago Press, 1917).

[2] J. O. Quantz, Problems in the psychology of reading. *Psychological review, monograph Supplement*, 1897, No. 5.

the possibility that quality of reading might be related in some way to the variation in width of span within a selection. Also, the fact that oral reading is modified according to the units of thought expressed suggested that position in the sentence might be a more potent factor than position in the line. Accordingly, a detailed analysis was made of the variation in the width of the eye-voice span by the position in the sentence for the good and poor readers separately, and then for all subjects taken together.

. . . .

The averages for each position are given for both good and poor readers. Figure 1 shows a comparison of these averages graphically, for both good and poor readers. The numbers on the horizontal axis refer to the number of the positions in the selection, while the letters *B*, *W*, and *E* are abbreviations for beginning, within, and end of a sentence. The figures on the vertical axis represent the width of the span in letter-spaces. The upper line is that of the good, and the lower line is that of the poor readers. . . .

The most noticeable deviations in the line for the good readers occurred at positions numbers 3 and 5. These are the only positions

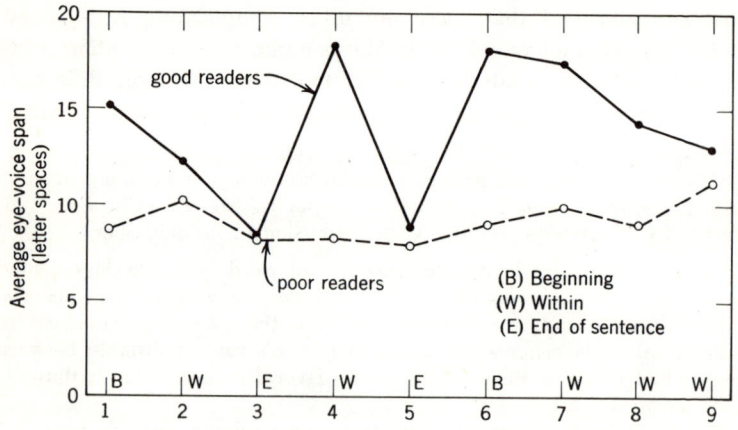

FIG. 1. Average eye-voice span by position in sentence at nine equal intervals of reading. Subjects were seven good and seven poor readers from elementary schools (from Buswell, 1920).

occurring at the end of sentences. The shortening of the eye-voice span here is relatively very great, and is entirely too pronounced to be accidental. The good readers have evidently found that, for the sake of emphasis, a considerable pause must be made at the end of sentences. The time during the pause gives the eye ample opportunity to get ahead and consequently, on the last word before the pause, the eye-voice span is reduced. The relative shortening of the span on the last word of a sentence would therefore indicate an appreciation of the meaning and an attempt to convey it by expressing, through the pause, the fact that a unit of thought had been given. An examination of the record of the poor readers does not indicate any considerable variation in the length of the span at these points. Evidently the eye has travelled right along, the voice has ignored the ending of a unit of thought and has kept its regular distance behind the eye.

A second point of difference between the good and the poor readers is shown by Figure 1 at those positions falling at the beginning of sentences. Positions numbered 1 and 6 show the width of the eye-voice span at the beginning of two sentences. The line for the good readers shows a wider span than the average, at these points, while that of the poor readers varies from the general average by only a very small amount. This gives evidence that when a good reader begins the reading of a new thought, he allows the eye to proceed for a considerable distance before starting to read. This wide initial span gives him an intelligent grasp of the nature of the selection before beginning to read, and enables him to show a proper interpretation through his oral expression. The line for the poor readers shows that the initial span is no wider than the average. This would prevent the reader from obtaining a longer look ahead which is particularly helpful at the beginning of a sentence.

The line for the poor readers differs from that of the good in that it has only a small variation for all positions. For the poor reader, oral reading is evidently a monotonous process of passing over words without any great attempt to emphasize what is read. The good reader varies his span at different positions in the selection in order to bring about a better emphasis. . . . The study indicates, therefore, that for elementary-school pupils a variation in the width of the span for different positions is a characteristic of good reading more than of poor reading, and that for good readers the span is wider at the beginning of a sentence, a little narrower within a sentence, and much narrower at the end of a sentence. The poor readers show less variation and exhibit a tendency to commence reading as soon as the material is put before them, having a narrower span at the beginning than at those positions within the sentence. These data are very suggestive of a causal relationship between width of eye-voice span and the interpretation of meaning as exhibited by the treatment of a sentence as a unit of thought and the modification of the eye-voice span to fit such a unit.

. . . .

The fact that the eye-voice span varies with the position in the sentence is of considerable significance. If the span varied only with the position in the line, as Quantz's study indicated, the determining factors would be entirely mechanical, and would be governed by the printed form of the selection. The control of the span, in that case, would be a matter of the mechanics of book construction, and would be independent of any teaching factor. But if the span varies with with the position in the sentence, it is evident that the content of the meaning is recognized, and that the eye-voice span is determined by thought units rather than by printed line units. Position in the line may be a minor factor, as the results of this study showed a slightly narrower span at the end of a line, but the differences due to position in the sentence are much greater.

For all three classes of subjects, there is agreement among the good readers in that a wide eye-voice span occurs at the beginning of a sentence. The situation at the beginning of a sentence is different from that of any other position. After one has started to read, the meaning of the thought covered will carry him along to some extent, and will enable him to anticipate what is coming. At the beginning of a sentence there is no sequence of words to give one the cue to the content of the new thought. The only way to get this is to look ahead until the meaning of the sentence is partially recognized, and the kind of vocal expression needed is made clear. The good readers recognize this need for a wider span at the outset and inhibit the voice reaction until the eye has gained a considerable lead. The poor readers in the grades above the elementary school have also learned this, but evidently those in the elementary school are not mature enough in reading to recognize any special difficulty at the beginning of a sentence. Instead of making a relatively longer span, they react to the situation by a relatively shorter one. They begin to read as soon as they see the sentence, and have not learned to inhibit their reading until the eye has taken in a larger unit of meaning.

. . . .

Meaning itself is not a unitary and complete sort of thing which occurs instantaneously at certain points through the reading. After a reader has mastered his vocabulary, the recognition of the meanings of words, except in the case of new or difficult ones, doubtless occurs as soon as the eye perceives the words. The recognition of the meaning of words therefore might be said to keep pace with the eye. But the complete meaning of a sentence or a paragraph is not made up by summing together the individual meanings of the words. The meaning of each word in a sentence is modified by what precedes and follows. Phrases, clauses, or whole sentences are the units and the recognition of the complete meaning must be in a liquid state during the reading process, being subject to continual change and being held in the mind in a tentative fashion until the end of the unit of thought is reached. To speak of a location for the recognition of such a developing meaning as this would probably refer to the focal point in the moving state or attention span by which the mind "carries on" in the reading process. That this focal point or the apex of the moving attention span would be nearer the eye than the voice is also indicated by the amount of conscious attention given to these two factors. The motor reaction of the voice ultimately becomes quite automatic. It follows along behind the eye at a distance such that the immediate memory association with the material perceived is kept intact but it is back in the margin of consciousness as long as no special difficulty is encountered. The principal part of the attention span is concerned with the new material which the eye is receiving, and with translating this into the meaning whole. Consequently the focus of attention is centered around the eye and the meaning, while the voice is largely left to pronounce the words automatically with a minimum amount of consciousness accompanying it. . . .

The previous chapters of this study have pointed out that there is a close relationship between a good quality of reading and a wide eye-voice span. The question was raised as to which of the two is cause or effect. It would appear that both are effects, and that causal element is the existence of a general attention span wide enough to hold a large number of words or reading elements in the mind at one time. The preceding evidence shows that a poor, immature reader can hold only a few letters or words in the focus of attention, while more mature readers are the ones who have a wide attention span. Progress in reading would therefore be a matter of the development of the span of attention to such a degree that it would be possible for the eye to keep a considerable distance ahead of the voice and thus provide a wide margin for the interpretation of meaning. The extent to which such a span may be developed, or to which it is dependent of factors of native capacity, will need to be determined by further experimentation.

Following Buswell's work, Clarence Gray who was also at Chicago, tested and interpreted the process of silent reading in a way that was analogous to Buswell's studies of reading aloud.[*] Like Buswell, he also learned much from comparisons of good with poor readers. Gray dealt with the process of attention as it advances ahead of the point of comprehension just as Buswell had considered the forging ahead of the eye in advance of the voice. He found that silent reading skill was not correlated with the span of perception nor with perceptual facility that does not involve connected language sequences. Further, there was no correlation between the rate of recognition of isolated words and the rate of recognition of connected discourse. Nor was reading speed related to individual differences in physiological reaction time. What characterized the differences between efficient and poor readers, according to Gray, was their "strategies of obtaining meaning" from written material. The successful strategy occurs when a reader thinks ahead and tries to anticipate what is coming. Gray suggested that such anticipations are possible because of three factors: (1) grammatical relations that organize each sentence, (2) context (knowledge of the

[*] Gray, C. T. The anticipation of meaning as a factor in reading ability. *The elementary school Journal*, April, 1923.

subject matter, and of the surrounding sentences), and (3) marginal impressions on the retina ("preperceptions" that help initiate the process of anticipation).

American educators early in the century referred to the data obtained with tachistoscopes and eye cameras as evidence supporting changes in public teaching methods. The argument of the progressive educator usually followed this form: Education should be meaningful. Therefore we should not start young readers on senseless sounds or letters. We do not begin to comprehend or to use our native language in that way but instead we start with sounds that indicate demands or assertions. Even in foreign language learning we should not start with elemental sounds. Rather we should learn how to ask, for example in French, for a glass of water—then perhaps in the past and future tenses. After further experience with French we might find ourselves in a situation never before encountered. And we would produce an appropriate utterance—with French sounds, not English ones. But at this point in our experience with French we still might not be able to state the phonetic rules of French. The argument might then continue with the question, "Why then teach the rules of English orthography to the young reader?"

But a logical error occurred when pedagogical techniques were based on psychologists' discussions. It was that the description of the skills of efficient, mature readers was not a description of how the skills were attained. An efficient reader did not start to read with whole phrases in order to avoid smaller elements. He may have acquired the skill by consciously attending to the small parts. The "look-and-say method" is the phrase now used to describe the approach to reading instruction that has recently dominated American schools. It is instruction in the development of sight vocabulary, which has been quite consistent with that aspect of the behaviorist movement concerning the analysis of verbal behavior where the experimental unit or response item was usually the *word*.

In the psychology literature of the past half century there are thousands of word-association investigations, tachistoscopic presentations, paired-associates tests, and verbal conditioning demonstrations. A summary of the psychological support for the sight-word method appeared in 1952 in Irving Anderson and

Dearborn's book *The psychology of teaching reading*. The basis for the approach lies originally in simple associative learning, that is, sight-sound associations acquired through repeated presentations. In 1930 William F. Book of Indiana University was probably the first to describe the process of learning to read in terms of Pavlovian conditioning in which he emphasized a sight-word approach.[*] Later, operant conditioning became the more favored paradigm especially with the appearance of teaching machines.

Anderson and Dearborn concluded that to teach reading one must repeatedly present a visual, printed word, such as FATHER, and simultaneously say it out loud to the child, or present pictures of the object symbolized. Then the child will soon make those "incipient responses" as previously provoked by saying FATHER or by the actual presence of the father. B. F. Skinner has briefly described learning to read in terms of operant conditioning in his *Verbal behavior* (1957). Kantor and Bloomfield had argued that the psychology of language should be purely descriptive without the postulation of any underlying mechanisms or explanations. This was also the spirit of Skinner's writings. He titled reading "textual behavior," that is, verbal behavior that is under the control of textual stimuli. Learning to read, according to Skinner, proceeds as follows:

> Textual behavior, like echoic behavior, is first usually reinforced for explicitly "educational" reasons. Interested persons supply generalized conditioned reinforcers for vocal responses which stand in certain required relations to the marks on a page. If a child responds *cat* in the presence of the marks CAT and not otherwise, he receives approval; if he responds *dog* in the presence of the marks DOG and not otherwise, he also receives approval, and so on.[†]

Recent educational critics have discredited the sight-word method and have suggested that it is causally related to low levels of literacy in some sections of society. Gestalt psychology has been "blamed" for the existence of the sight-word approach

---

[*] W. F. Book, Various methods of mastering new words while learning to read. *Journal of educational Research*, 1930, 21: 81–94.

[†] B. F. Skinner, *Verbal behavior* (New York: Appleton-Century-Crofts, 1957), p. 66.

because of the Gestaltist's concern with "meaningful wholes" (see Hunter Diack's *Reading and the psychology of perception*, 1966). However, nowhere in the Gestalt literature of the Wertheimer, Köhler, and Koffka school, is there any pronouncement about the psychology of reading, and further the rationale of sight-word teaching came from outside the Gestalt school. Some educators (see, for example, G. Hartmann, *Educational psychology*, 1942) may have sought additional support from Gestalt theory for the word method, but this can be considered a misinterpretation of Gestalt notions. A systematic application of Gestalt principles to reading appeared in Brown's *Words and things* (1957) with a result that placed Gestalt psychology in opposition to sight-word methods of reading instruction:

The words "wholist" and "meaningful" are very frequently used by Gestalt theorists to characterize their own position in contrast with that of the associationists. It is not surprising, therefore, that, on a cursory reading, the Gestalt work should seem to favor the reading method that deals in "meaningful" units—*whole* words. I think, nevertheless, that this is a misconstruction of Gestalt theory. Words differ from letters or other phonetic elements in that they have reference to non-linguistic objects or events, and, in this sense, words are "meaningful." In the writings of Gestalt psychologists, however, the word "meaningful" is more nearly synonymous with "systematic" than with "referential." "Meaningful" learning is learning that fits into a structure. Meaningful material is material in which there are systematic relations among the elements. Words are larger units than letters since words are compounded of letters and so, in a sense, words are "wholes." When Gestalt theory calls our attention to "wholes" it is to the system that determines the character of its parts. Are words the relevant "wholes" for someone learning to read? . . .

When material to be learned constitutes a system it is possible to predict some of the materials from knowledge of others. Systematic learning occurs when principles are discovered which make it unnecessary to memorize detailed materials. The relevant whole . . . is not the total series containing the individual (parts) but is, rather, the principle governing the series. Systematic learning gives insight in that it provides principles (not always verbally formulated) from which specific materials can be derived. In learning to read there seems to be more insight provided by phonetic rules than by the look-and-say method. Learning to recognize the total appearance of a given word teaches nothing about recognizing other words. Each part is independent of all others. Learning is a process of memorization. When recurrent sound-letter matchings are learned we acquire a set of principles telling us how to pronounce indefinite numbers of new words; we learn the sound system of English writing. The fact that it is a very complicated and sometimes inconsistent system does not prevent it from being a system. Gestalt theory then would seem to favor the insightful phonetic method.*

However, this view does not necessarily deny the use of whole words in phonics programs. The techniques of the new (1969) *phonic* or *linguistic* methods sometimes proceed with related meaningful words or phrases instead of with unrelated words or nonsense syllables, the latter being what Bloomfield had originally recommended as initial reading material. For instance, by presenting a group of words with the same basic morpheme where pronunciation varies in systematic ways the instructor thereby illustrates phonological rules. For example, observe the varying pronunciations of the root *"sign"* in the following words:

>   *sign*
>   *signal*
> *design*
>   *signature*
> *resign*
> *resignation*

Here the levels of "meaningful" units and "nonmeaningful" units are highly interrelated. The principles that govern such varying pronunciations are quite general, but the rules of the writing system, and their relation to both pronunciation and meaning are complex. One would not expect the child to learn this system in the same sense that a linguist makes it explicit.† However, in being able to speak English a child is already conforming to a highly complex phonological and syntactical system.

---

* Roger Brown, *Words and things* (Glencoe, Illinois: Copyright 1958 by The Free Press, a corporation), pp. 71–72. With permission of the publisher.

† See for example N. Chomsky and M. Halle, *The sound patterns of English* (New York: Harper and Row, 1968).

Regardless of the conflicting viewpoints among educators and psychologists concerning literacy acquisition, most children still learn to read even when instructional methods vary. Statistics of failures have shown that there has always been a surprisingly high rate of functional illiteracy in this country.* Possibly this is more a result of social and cultural influences than of faults in educational technique.

The brief consideration of reading instruction brings this review up to the mid-twentieth century. In the next chapter we shall discuss developments in psycholinguistics that have occurred more recently and that have developed into trends showing striking similarities to the earlier turn of the century *Sprachpsychologie*.

* M. M. Matthews, op. cit.

CHAPTER 5

THE NEW PSYCHOLINGUISTICS
A Renewal of "Sprachpsychologie" in America

The purpose of this book has been to attract attention to an early and active period of psycholinguistics research. One may separate an earlier from a later period by restricting the use of the German term *Sprachpsychologie* as a reference only to the turn of the century and mostly German or German-inspired work. However, the modern American term "psycholinguistics" is a natural translation for *Sprachpsychologie* because it typically refers to the same kind of investigations. Indeed, early users of "psycholinguistics" (such as Kantor and Roback) chose it as a translation of *Sprachpsychologie*. Nevertheless, when the new American work blossomed during the late 1950s there was almost no mention made of the past history. Instead, psycholinguistics was frequently celebrated as an entirely new conception.*

This chapter will present a survey of late developments that have particularly interesting historical implications in the context of what has been reviewed in the previous chapters.

In the 1920s a large quantity of writings on psychology of language had appeared. American, French, and British psychology journals published special issues on language. The *British journal of Psychology* in 1920 reported a conference that was designed to confront the behaviorist Watson with the problems of language and thought. A yearly handbook of research methodology (*Handbuch der biologischen Arbeitsmethoden*), published in Berlin, devoted its sixth volume (1925) to methods in experimental psychology, and one of its eight chapters was a survey of

---

* It is interesting that in 1946 Kantor's student N. H. Pronko wrote an article titled Language and psycholinguistics: a review. *Psychol. Bull.*, Vol. 43, in which a number of the important early works were mentioned, although unfavorably.

methods for experimental study in the psychology of language. Included were techniques for studying sentence structure, speech acoustics, comprehension, word structure, and language acquisition. All this would usually mean a new and productive period in the field. In fact psychologist-linguist interactions and related literature declined in the 1930s and 1940s. In Europe the wars and social upheaval diminished scholarship in general and cut it off further from America where there already was a growing mood of intellectual isolationism; German ceased to be a working language among American psychologists. The notion that the topic of language should have any special status in the purely descriptive study of *behavior* was largely rejected.

Several American reviews of the psychology of language appeared during those decades and they show either no sympathy for the early and foreign work, or an incomplete awareness of it.*
In Vienna, however, Friedrich Kainz began his encyclopedia review of the field with the first volume of his "Psychology of language" (*Psychologie der Sprache*) which appeared in 1941. Over twenty years later this series had reached a length of five volumes. Yet it too has seldom come to the attention of American psychologists. Russian work has only recently come to light in the West (see Dan Slobin, *Soviet psycholinguistics*, 1966).†

Most American linguists in the 1930s followed Bloomfield who formally acknowledged behaviorism in his book *Language* (1933) but then pursued Delbrück's suggestion that linguistics should proceed independently of psychology. Those linguists who later formed the "Bloomfieldian school" brought the antimentalistic, taxonomic study of language to its furthest development. If work in psycholinguistics were to be assessed during this period in the West, it would be more precise to label it the study of "verbal learning and verbal behavior." Psychology of

---

* E. A. Esper, Language. In C. Murchison (Ed.) *Handbook of social psychology* (Worcester: Clark University Press, 1935).

J. R. Kantor, *An objective psychology of grammar* (Bloomington: Indiana University Publications, 1936).

D. V. McGranahan, The psychology of language. *Psych. Bull.*, 1936, 33.

N. Pronko, Language and psycholinguistics. *Psych. Rev.*, 1946, 43.

† In N. O'Connor, *Present-day Russian psychology: a symposium by seven authors* (Oxford: Pergamon Press, 1966).

language research then was likely to be divorced from linguistics. It more generally encompassed investigations concerning notions about the nature of learning, or perception, or motivation, where questions about the nature of language per se were incidental. This may explain in part the lessening of contact with linguists, although the dominant theoretical models in American linguistics were quite compatible with the new orientations in psychology.

By about 1950 interest in language among Western psychologists increased. The sources were many: involvement of psychologists in communications research during the war, development of mathematical models of communication, the appearance of computers, the rediscovery by psychologists and linguists of each other and of each other's similar theoretical models, and increased efforts to analyze verbal learning, word-associations, and speech pathologies. In the United States in 1951 the Social Science Research Council brought together a small group of psychologists and linguists for an informal summer seminar on linguistics and psychology at Cornell University. In the following year the Council formed a "National Committee on Linguistics and Psychology." And in the summer of 1953 the Council sponsored an ambitious interdisciplinary conference on language which was held at Indiana University. That event had at least one lasting effect—it popularized the use of the hybrid term *psycholinguistics*.*

During the 1953 conference there was no thought given to a "renewal" of *Sprachpsychologie,* if indeed there was any attention at all to the early tradition of collaboration between psychologists and linguists. But there was great jubilation over the founding of a new interdisciplinary enterprise. Brown in *Words and things* (1957), p. vii, wrote the following:

Descriptive linguistics was a great find for American psychology. Our first admiration was for the impeccably behavioristic methods of the linguist. Then came the great excitement of finding that this "new" science had turned up phenomena with which psychology was long familiar—perceptual constancy, acquired perceptual distinctiveness,

* The conference report appeared as a special supplement to the *Journal of abnormal and social Psychology,* October, 1954 (C. Osgood and T. Sebeok, Eds.).

sensory generalization, the importance of differential reinforcement, positive and negative transfer in learning. It looked as if the findings of linguistic science could be readily "translated" into psychology, greatly enriching the painfully thin chapter on language behavior.

In the early 1950s there was a heady optimism that communications problems in many areas, including psychotherapy, would soon be resolved. Soon there followed predictions that foreign language instruction would vastly improve through programmed instruction techniques, that technicians would be enabled to build a speech typewriter with consequent savings in human efficiency; it seemed certain that within a few years new efforts would enable computer programmers to devise facile systems for machine translation of language.

Now, after the passing of two decades, the optimism of the early 1950s seems to have been ill-conceived. The speech-typewriter project has been largely unsuccessful; Lindgren discusses the problems in his chapters on "Machine recognition of human language" (in the *I.E.E.E. Spectrum*, 1965).

Language learning with operant conditioning techniques is just as tedious and time-consuming as ever. And after years of intensive support, U. S. government funds have been withdrawn from mechanical translation research owing to the lack of results.* But most important, a number of scholars have been forced to reexamine their views about the fundamental nature of human language, specifically those views that had become dominant in America during the 1925–1955 period.

One theme that grew in prominence during that period was the statistical study of language. The spirit of the times had a notable resemblance to the earlier *Junggrammatiker* era of the 1870s with its emphasis on exact methodology and quantification. Zipf became the patron saint for the modern quantitative study of language. He was certainly not the first to study statistical regularity in language,† but he contributed the most toward

---

* See Bryce Nelson, Machine translation: committee skeptical over research support. *Science*, January 6, 1967, 58–59.

† See also, Kaeding, F. W., *Haufigkeitsworterbuch der deutschen Sprache.* Steglitz, 1897–1898; Markov, A. A., Essai d'une recherche statistique sur le texte du roman "Eugene Onegin," *Bull. acad. imper. Sci.*, St. Petersburg, 1913, 7; Estoup, J. B. *Gammes Stenographique.* Paris: 1916 (4th ed.).

making it a popular pursuit. Although trained in philology in Germany and at Harvard, Zipf was keenly interested in mathematics. His life's work began with simple studies of the frequency of occurrence of individual words, and from that he produced a remarkable array of frequency curves and probability distributions.* But this tradition has very little in common with the trends that have been reviewed here, and it was quite short-lived (see B. Mandelbrot, "Information theory and psycholinguistics," in B. B. Wolman, and E. Nagel (Eds.), *Scientific psychology*, 1965). This field has been extensively reviewed elsewhere,* and no attempt will be made to do so here. Although the mathematics grew more sophisticated, its application to language did not.

In some cases the behavior of speakers had been the object of mathematical interest, in others it was the structure of communications systems or of natural languages. In the 1940s Shannon and Norbert Wiener developed new statistical techniques for the study of communication, borrowing certain ideas from physics. Their work was dubbed "information theory," a procedure for stating degrees of statistical regularity in communication events. This implies a model that conceives of language as a chain of events (usually words or letters), with each such event being assigned a conditional probability of occurrence. It was this implication, more than the mathematical formalism, that was most significant for psycholinguistics. And it is a view which is linked to the behaviorist proposals about language that can be read in Meyer, Watson, Allport, and Kantor.

B. F. Skinner's work *Verbal behavior* (1957) occupies an extremely significant position in behaviorist psychology of language. Though not following the linguistic orientations of Kantor's work, Skinner has been no less devoted to the analysis of verbal behavior. Skinner's ambition after his graduation from Hamilton College had been to become a novelist; thus he moved to Greenwich Village in New York City to enter the

* See G. K. Zipf, *The psycho-biology of language*. (Boston: Houghton Mifflin) 1935; and *Human behavior and the principle of least effort* (Cambridge, Mass.: Addison-Wesley, 1949).

† Miller, G. A. and Chomsky, N. Finitary models of language users. In Luce, R. D., Bush, R. R., and Galanter, E., *Handbook of mathematical psychology* (New York: John Wiley, 1963).

writing profession. Disappointment in this enterprise was a significant force in leading him into graduate school in psychology, but his interest in language performance remained. The writing of *Verbal behavior* began in 1932, shortly after Skinner completed his doctorate at Harvard. Publication was delayed for twenty-five years by the necessity of building a more fundamental behaviorist system and by many revisions of the manuscript. However, early unpublished drafts were widely circulated, and Skinner frequently lectured on the subject. The most influential of these lectures were the invited William James Lecture at Harvard in 1947. The wide acclaim for this event illustrated the eagerness of its audience to receive the program that Skinner offered.

Perhaps no text was more significant than this one in contributing to the background against which the latest phase of psycholinguistic thought has appeared. We may say that its contribution was a more thorough and literal application of the strictly behavioral approach than had been previously attempted. It did not constitute psycholinguistics—it lacked the linguistics. But it did present a behaviorist approach to language in a way that permitted a more precise evaluation of that view.

Skinner argued that the book concerned neither linguistics nor language in any specific way, and least of all in a theoretical way. Critics have nevertheless often read the book as though it were about language, their contention being that any analysis of verbal behavior cannot escape the implication of some theory of language. In any case, the psycholinguist is, along with Skinner, more directly concerned with explaining verbal performance than linguistic theory. And although Skinner began with a commitment to purely descriptive behaviorism, his book seemed to result in many explanatory devices and hypothesized mechanisms.

One section of *Verbal behavior* concerned the stimulus control of grammatical constructions. Skinner claimed that the human talker's potential for speech derives from a verbal response repertoire acquired through conditioning. A repertoire is analogous to a vocabulary list, but the latter concept was not used because he did not wish to restrict the verbal repertoire to any particular unit. Instead, verbal operants could be of any dimension, and were functionally determined. In other words, a verbal operant could be any segment of speech under control of some stimulus condition. The repertoire was constructed synthetically; short verbal segments were generally the first to come under stimulus control, then gradually larger units, such as phrases, sentences, and even whole narratives could become functional units.

Skinner identified an important class of operants within the verbal repertoire and named them "autoclitics," one type of which was the *sentence frame*. This was a response that consisted of ordered verbal segments added to other isolated responses, that imposed a grammatical arrangement on them, and that determined the relations among words. We have already noted (in Chapter Two) that this notion of sentence frames is an old one that had been revived early in the century by James, Marty, Bühler, Selz, and some of their colleagues. The difficulties they encountered are still present in Skinner's approach.

This view asserted that there were a fixed number of sentence patterns, or frames, consisting of grammatical elements or function words. During the acts of verbal performance other words were placed into the slots of the frame in order to form a sentence. The frame held words together and determined relations among them, according to James and to Skinner. In studies similar to the earlier ones of Bühler, Selz in 1922 had obtained verbal protocols and then had segregated them according to several types of sentence scheme. For instance, defining statements always employed "is-sentence" schemes. Likewise, there were schemes for questions, imperatives, and so forth. In contrast to Skinner, Selz was a mentalist, claiming that schemes were controlled by the idea underlying each sentence, whereas for Skinner the schemes were controlled by the relational properties of the environmental stimuli.

The sentence-frame approach to the psychology of the sentence has remained vague, whether or not it has involved the issue of mentalism. The possible variety of different sentence schemes simply becomes so large (theoretically infinite, since there is no absolute limit on sentence length) that it is difficult to conceive of them all being learned as one learns a vocabulary list. Miller, Galanter, and Pribram in *Plans and the structure of behavior* (1960) illustrated the astronomical numbers one might obtain in attempts to estimate the number of different sentences available to speakers. And recently the sentence-frame theory has been confounded with further problems. "Autoclitics," or frames, are far from sufficient to capture the relations between words that people comprehend and to which they respond. Consider the following autoclitic:

The . . . was . . . to . . . by . . . .

We could insert five separate verbal responses and have

The picture was given to John by Picasso.

But the same frame produces

The picture was given to John by mistake,

where the relations among words are different. In the latter, *mistake* is not "giving the picture" as is *Picasso* in the first sentence. One might propose another supplementary autoclitic to take care of this special case. For example, the phrase *by mistake* might be considered functionally as one operant. Its syntax is then responded to in a way that is different from the syntactic response to *by Picasso*, which would be *two* functional units where *by* is part of the sentence frame. However, we could go on endlessly producing such sentence-frame contradictions where each requires some sort of *ad hoc* adjustment of the sentence-frame notion.*

The psychology of the sentence was a new puzzle for a number of psychologists in America during the 1950s. In one particularly ambitious attempt, O. H. Mowrer (once a student under Meyer) analyzed the sentence as a conditioning device and employed the terms of Pavlovian conditioning for his analysis. The importance of Mowrer's work came from its emphasis on

---

* In a paper cited in the European psychology of language literature, Bruno Sonneck (1935), a student of Bühler's, analyzed the notion of sentence types in terms of Bühler's functionalism. He suggested that the problems surrounding sentence scheme explanations may be avoided through discerning two levels of sentence analysis: that of sentence structure and that of the actual verbal performances. The notion of sentence types is intelligible only in the latter case. If a person's utterances can be classified at all according to sentence schemes, then this would be a result of situational performance factors and not some inherent characteristic of grammatical structure (see B. Sonneck, Der Satz als Einheit und die Satzarten. *Arch. f. d. ges. Psychol.*, 1953).

the propositional, or the subject-predicate basis of human discourse. This had been fundamental a few generations earlier.

According to Mowrer (1954),† the subject of a sentence was originally a neutral, unconditioned stimulus. But the sentence was a device that paired the subject with another verbal segment, the predicate, which had the power to provoke a response automatically somewhere in a person's muscle system or glands. The pairing of these two constituents permitted the visceral response for the predicate to transfer to the sentence subject. Unfortunately, Mowrer's analysis applied only to simple declarative sentences that had contiguity of subject and predicate constituents. It is common knowledge that determination of *subject* and *predicate* is not made on the basis of the left-to right order contiguous elements. Mowrer's explanation ran into hopeless difficulty with complex sentences that had widely separated subjects and predicates.

Mowrer, in contrast to Skinner, explained "linguistic responses" more on the basis of hypothetical physiological mechanisms. There is thus the postulation of unobserved mediating responses and inner reactions to linguistic signs that make those signs meaningful for the reacting organism. This approach, sometimes called *neo-behaviorism*, has been applied to the psychology of language in the writings of Charles Osgood (see Osgood's "On understanding and creating sentences," *Amer. psychol.*, 1963). His assumption that linguistic meaning consists of fractional or unobserved partial responses had been proposed explicitly in Ogden and Richard's *The meaning of meaning*, 1923. And this, of course, had always been a strong American theme. It was clearly represented in the turn of the century writings of Holt and Münsterberg at Harvard (see Chapter Two). For example, Holt attributed linguistic meaning to slight or fractional muscle movements that had become associated with words. The meaning of the word *bottle* was thus considered to be some reduced or "implicit" gestures that were part of the behavior of manipulating, using, or responding to bottles. Osgood's writings inspired the more recent assertions of this view.

† O. H. Mowrer, The psychologist looks at language. *American psychologist*, 1954, **9**: 660–694. (1953 presidential adress delivered before the American Psychological Association.)

The more strict behaviorists, such as Skinner, have agrued that Osgood's "mediation theory" simply reintroduces the mind into psychology, or at least relies on events that one cannot profitably observe. But then Skinner apparently does just that in his own book, particularly in the chapter titled "Thinking." The neo-behaviorist reconsideration of internal mediating events was offered in response to the inadequacy of the strict peripheralist views within the behaviorist movement. But still another type of criticism suggests that the more complicated speculations of the Osgood approach are *logically* no different from, and reduce to, the more simplistic description of the earlier behaviorist program, and that the implicit or fractional responses add no power to the neo-behaviorist explanations (Fodor, 1965).*

The logical critique by Fodor represents the culmination of a series of attacks on what was a strongly established approach to the psychology of language in the English speaking world. It is not surprising then that acrimonious debate has marked this field in recent times. How, then, did this new challenge come about? What in all of this amounts to a renewal of *Sprachpsychologie*?

There is one classic paper that foreshadowed the revolution in thought in some American quarters among the mid-twentieth century psycholinguists—Karl Lashley's *The problem of serial order in behavior* (1951).† Though Lashley's article has now been reprinted several times, the present historical review would stand as incomplete without presenting it at least in part. In 1948, the year following Skinner's successful William James Lectures, Lashley read his paper before a conference on brain mechanisms and behavior. For several years it received little attention, but later it was widely reproduced and circulated.

During an intense and dramatic career Lashley came to be recognized as America's leading physiological psychologist. His training came from eminent physiologists as well as from Watson, who influenced his decision to become a psychologist. However, he emerged as one of the strongest iconoclasts of American psy-

---

* Fodor, J. A. Can meaning be an r_m? *J. verb. learn. and verb. Behav.*, 1965, pp. 73–81. See also replies and rebuttal in that Journal.

† In L. A. Jeffress (Ed.) *Cerebral mechanisms in behavior* (New York: John Wiley, 1951).

chological thought, and his work has been described as a series of destructions of physiological and psychological theories, including his own, by means of clever experimental demonstrations.* The major thrust of this work went against associationism. He later discounted the prevailing behaviorism as a form of "pseudo-objectivity," and near the end of his life he made statements reflecting his own depressed feelings about the state of knowledge among psychologists.† Indeed, he felt that the field had made little progress during his lifetime.

Just before his death, Lashley had planned to undertake an extensive study of linguistics with the hope that solutions to the problem of brain function—which had eluded him throughout his career—would be illuminated through the study of language. But he died suddenly in 1957.

The following excerpts are from Lashley's only published statements about language where he outlined a class of problems that psychologists and linguists would soon profitably approach together. His aim was to show how the production of an utterance was not a matter of stringing together a sequence of responses under the control of external stimuli or of mediating S-R chains, and further that the syntax of an utterance was only indirectly related to its sequential form. What is most striking, in the present context, is Lashley's revival of Wundtian psycholinguistic notions such as the simultaneity of the sentence as a mental event. However, although he gives a few references to early literature, there is no evidence that he was directly acquainted with Wundt's psycholinguistics. He does cite the work of Pick who was acquainted with Wundt's writings.

* See F. A. Beach, Karl Spence Lashley. In *Biographical memoirs, national academy of science*, Vol. 35, 1961.
† *Ibid.*

KARL SPENCE LASHLEY · *The Problem of Serial Order in Behavior*

My principal thesis today will be that the input is never into a quiescent or static system, but always into a system which is already actively excited and organized. In the intact organism, behavior is the result of interaction of this background of excitation with input from any designated stimulus. Only when we can state the general characteristics of this background of excitation, can we understand the effects of a given input.

The unpronounceable Cree Indian word "kekawewechetushekamikowanowow" is analyzed by Chamberlain (1911)[1] into the verbal root, *tusheka*, "to remain," and the various particles which modify it as follows: *ke(la)wow*, the first and last syllables, indicating second person plural; *ka*, a prefix of the future tense; *we*, a sort of imperative mode expressing a wish; *weche*, indicating conjunction of subject and object; *mik*, a suffix bringing the verb into agreement with a third person subject and second person object; and *owan*, a suffix indicating that the subject is inanimate and the object animate. A literal translation: "You will I wish together remain he-you it-man you" or, freely, "May it remain with you." This difference in structure between Cree and English illustrates an outstanding characteristic of verbal behavior; the occurrence of predetermined, orderly sequences of action which are unique for each language. In English the adjective precedes, in French it follows the noun which it modified. In English the movement or action of the subject is expressed as early as possible after the subject; in German the expression of action may be postponed until all qualifying thoughts have been expressed. In a sentence discussing this subject, Pick (1913)[2] in-

SOURCE. Karl S. Lashley, The problem of serial order in behavior. In *Cerebral mechanisms in behavior*, L. A. Jeffress (Ed.) (New York: John Wiley, 1951).

[1] A. F. Chamberlain, Indians, North American. *Encyclopedia Britannica*, 1911, 14: 452–482.

[2] A. Pick, *Die agrammatischen Sprachstörungen* (Berlin, 1913).

troduces fifty-five words between the subject and the principal verb. Each Chinese word, and to a lesser extent, each English word, stands as an unchanging unit. In the highly inflective languages, such as Sioux, the form of almost every word in the sentence may be altered, according to some attribute of the subject, as when two objects rather than one or several are discussed.

The study of comparative grammar is not the most direct approach to the physiology of the cerebral cortex, yet Fournié (1887)[3] has written, "Speech is the only window through which the physiologist can view the cerebral life." Certainly language presents in a most striking form the integrative functions that are characteristic of the cerebral cortex and that reach their highest development in human thought processes. Temporal integration is not found exclusively in language; the coordination of leg movements in insects, the song of birds, the control of trotting and pacing in a gaited horse, the rat running the maze, the architect designing a house, and the carpenter sawing a board present a problem of sequences of action which cannot be explained in terms of successions of external stimuli.

Associative Chain Theories

In spite of the ubiquity of the problem, there have been almost no attempts to develop physiological theories to meet it. In fact, except among a relatively small group of students of aphasia, who have had to face questions of agrammatism, the problem has been largely ignored. It is not even mentioned in recent textbooks on neurophysiology or physiological psychology, nor is there any significant body of experimental studies bearing upon the problem. The spinal animal scarcely exhibits serial activity, so the physiologist may be excused for overlooking the phenomenon. On the other hand, psychologists have been concerned chiefly with the question of whether or not the organizing processes displayed in serial action are conscious, and very little with the organization itself. I have chosen to discuss the problem of temporal integration here, not with the expectation of offering a satisfactory physiological theory to account for it, but because it seems to me to be both the most important and also the most neglected problem of cerebral physiology. Temporally integrated actions do occur even among insects, but they do not reach any de-

---

[3] Fournié. *Essai de psychologie* (Paris, 1887).

gree of complexity until the appearance of the cerebral cortex. They are especially characteristic of human behavior and contribute as much as does any single factor to the superiority of man's intelligence. A clearer formulation of the physiological problems which they raise should be of value, even though a solution of the problems is not yet in sight.

I shall consider first some of the questions raised by the structure of language, then turn to other forms of serial action for indications of the nature of the nervous mechanisms involved.

To the best of my knowledge, the only strictly physiological theory that has been explicitly formulated to account for temporal integration is that which postulates chains of reflexes, in which the performance of each element of the series provides excitation of the next. This conception underlays the "motor theories" of thinking which were advocated by several psychologists early in this century. Watson (1920)[4] sought to identify thought with inaudible movements of the vocal organs, linked together in associative chains. The peripheral chain theory of language was developed in greatest detail by Washburn (1916).[5] She distinguished what she called "successive movement systems" and, although she drew her examples from memorized series of nonsense syllables her implication was that such series are typical of all language behavior. She defined a movement system as "a combination of movements so linked together that the stimulus furnished by the actual performance of certain movements is required to bring about other movements." She described speech as a succession of vocal acts in which the kinesthetic impulses from each movement serve as a unique stimulus for the next in the series (1916 pages 11 ff.). Attempts to confirm these peripheral theories by mechanical (Thorsen, 1925)[6] or electrical (Max, 1937)[7] recording of muscular tensions have given no valid evidence in support of them. It should be noted that, at the time when the theories were proposed,

---

[4] Watson, J. B. Is thinking merely the action of the language mechanism? *Brit. J. Psychol.*, 1920, **11**: 86–104.

[5] Washburn, M. F. *Movement and mental imagery* (Boston: Houghton Mifflin, 1916).

[6] Thorsen, A. M. The relation of tongue movements to internal speech. *J. exp. Psychol.*, 1925, **8**: 1–32.

[7] Max, L. W. Experimental study of the motor theory of consciousness. IV. *J. comp. Psychol.*, 1937, **24**: 301–344.

it was generally believed that conduction in the nervous system is always downstream from sense organ to muscle, and that muscular contraction must always follow promptly on stimulation. The existence of reverberatory circuits which could maintain central activity was scarcely suspected.

The introspective psychology which objected to such peripheral theories did not explicitly formulate an alternative neurological theory, but there is implicit in it a view that verbal thought is a simple chain of central processes in which each element serves to arouse the next by direct association. Titchener, for example, maintained that the meaning of a word (or of an auditory image in his system) consists of the chain of associations which it arouses; that it has no meaning until such a sequence has occurred. From this it must be inferred that he was thinking in terms of a simple associative chain, since no other relating process is suggested.*

Objections to the Associative Chain Theory

A consideration of the structure of the sentence and of other motor sequences will show, I believe, that such interpretations of temporal organization are untenable and that there are, behind the overtly expressed sequences, a multiplicity of integrative processes which can only be inferred from the final results of their activity. There is an extensive controversial literature dealing with this inferred integrative activity. Pick (1913) devotes almost his entire book, *Die agrammatischen Sprachstörungen*, to reviewing discussions of the subject. Most of this literature deals with the question of whether or not the integrative processes are conscious. Much of this is irrelevant to the present topic, but the advocates of so-called imageless thought did present a great deal of material indicative of the complexity of the problem of thought structure. From this, and other evidence which I shall present, I believe that the production of speech involves the interaction of at least three, possibly four, major neurological systems which are interrelated but somewhat independently variable.

Let us start the analysis of the process with the enunciation of the word. Pronunciation of the word "right" consists first of retraction

---

* Notice that in referring to "the introspective psychology" Lashley was citing Titchener, not Wundt. Wundt made the same type of objection to associative chaining as Lashley did here (see Chapter Two).—A.L.B.

and elevation of the tongue, expiration of air and activation of the vocal cords; second, depression of the tongue and jaw; third, elevation of the tongue to touch the dental ridge, stopping of vocalization, and forceful expiration of air with depression of the tongue and jaw. These movements have no intrinsic order of association. Pronunciation of the word "tire" involves the same motor elements in reverse order. Such movements occur in all permutations. The order must therefore be imposed upon the motor elements by some organization other than direct associative connections between them. So, for the individual movements in writing or typing the word, finger strokes occur in all sorts of combinations. No single letter invariably follows *g*, and whether *gh*, *ga*, or *gu* is written depends upon a set for a larger unit of action, the word.

Words stand in relation to the sentence as letters do to the word; the words themselves have no intrinsic temporal "valence." The word "right," for example, is noun, adjective, adverb, and verb, and has four spellings and at least ten meanings. In such a sentence as "The mill-wright on my right thinks it right that some conventional rite should symbolize the right of every man to write as he pleases," word arrangement is obviously not due to any direct associations of the word "right" itself with other words, but to meanings which are determined by some broader relations.

It has been found in studies of memorization of nonsense syllables that each syllable in the series has associations, not only with adjacent words in the series, but also with more remote words. The words in the sentence have, of course, associations with more remote words as well as with adjacent ones. However, the combination of such direct associations will not account for grammatical structure. The different positions of the word "right" in the illustrative sentence are determined by the meanings which the positions in relation to other words denote, but those meanings are given by other associations than those with the words in the spoken sentence. The word can take its position only when the particular one of its ten meanings become dominant. This dominance is not inherent in the words themselves.

From such considerations, it is certain that any theory of grammatical form which ascribes it to direct associative linkage of the words of the sentence overlooks the essential structure of speech.

The individual items of the temporal series do not in themselves have a temporal "valence" in their associative connections with other elements. The order is imposed by some other agent.

This is true not only of language, but of all skilled movements or successions of movement. In the gaits of a horse, trotting, pacing, and single footing involve essentially the same pattern of muscular contraction in the individual legs. The gait is imposed by some mechanism in addition to the direct relations of reciprocal innervation among the sensory-motor centers of the legs. The order in which the fingers of the musician fall on the keys or fingerboard is determined by the signature of the composition; this gives a *set* which is not inherent in the association of the individual movements.

The Determining Tendency

What then determines the order? The answer which seems most in accord with common sense is that the intention to act or the idea to be expressed determines the sequence. There are, however, serious difficulties for this solution. There is not much agreement among psychologists concerning the nature of the idea. The structuralist school, under the leadership of Titchener, held that the idea consists of mental images, often the auditory images of words, and the meanings are nothing but sequences of such images. Describing the role of images in his lecturing, Titchener wrote (1909),[8] "When there is any difficulty in exposition, a point to be argued *pro* and *con* or a conclusion to be brought out from the convergence of several lines of proof, I hear my own voice speaking just ahead of me." What solution of the lecture problem for the lazy man! He need not think but only listen to his own inner voice, to the chain of associated auditory images. A behaviorist colleague once remarked to me that he had reached a stage where he could arise before an audience, turn his mouth loose, and go to sleep. He believed in the peripheral chain theory of language. (This clearly demonstrates the superiority of behavioristic over introspective psychology. The behaviorist does not even have to listen to his own inner voice.)

Seriously, such positions offer no solution for the problem of temporal integration. Titchener finds his grammar ready made and does

---

[8] Titchener, E. B. *Lectures on the experimental psychology of the thought processes* (New York: The Macmillan Co., 1909).

not even raise the question of the origin of the succession of images. The chain-reflex theory, while definite, is untenable.

The third view of the nature of the idea was developed by a group known as the "Würzburg School" (see Boring, 1929),[9] exponents of imageless thought. It held that some organization precedes any expression that can be discovered by introspective or objective means. Thought is neither muscular contraction nor image, but can only be inferred as a "determining tendency." At most, it is discovered as a vague feeling of pregnancy, of being about to have an idea, a *Bewustseinslage*. It is not identical with the words which are spoken, for quite frequently no word can be recalled which satisfactorily expresses the thought, and we search a dictionary of synonyms until a word or phrase is found which does seem appropriate.

In his discussion of the relation of thought to speech, Pick (1913) accepts this point of view, but he asserts further that the set or the idea does not have a temporal order; that all of its elements are contemporal. Evidence in support of this conclusion comes, for example, from translation of one language into another which has a different sentence structure. I read a German sentence, pronouncing the German words with no thought of their English equivalents. I then give a free translation in English, without remembering a single word of the German text. Somewhere between the reading and free translation, the German sentence is condensed, the word order reversed, and expanded again into the different temporal order of English. According to Epstein[10] the polyglot shifts readily from one language to another, expressing the same thought in either, without literal translation. The readiness with which the form of expression of an idea can be changed, the facility with which different word orders may be utilized to express the same thought, thus is further evidence that the temporal integration is not inherent in the preliminary organization of the idea.

The Schema of Order

The remaining alternative is that the mechanism which determines the serial activation of the motor units is relatively independent,

---

[9] Boring, E. G. *A history of experimental psychology* (New York: Century Co., 1929).

[10] Epstein, I. *La pensée et la polyglossie* (Paris Payot et Cie. (no date)).

both of the motor units and of the thought structure. Supporting evidence for this may be found in the mistakes of order, the slips and interferences which occur in writing and speaking. For some time I have kept records of errors in typing. A frequent error is the misplacing or the doubling of a letter. *These* is typed t-h-s-e-s, *look* as l-o-k-k, *ill* as i-i-l. Sometimes the set to repeat may be displaced by several words. The order is dissociated from the idea. Earlier, in preparing this paper, I wrote the phrase, "maintain central activities." I typed *min*, omitting the *a*, canceled this out and started again; *ama*. The impulse to insert the *a* now dominated the order. I struck out the *a* and completed the phrase, only to find that I had now also dropped the *a* from *activities*. This example suggests something of the complexity of the forces which are at play in the determination of serial order and the way in which conflicting impulses may distort the order, although the primary determining tendency, the idea, remains the same.

The polyglot, who has become proficient in a secondary language, who thinks in it and even dreams in it, may still tend to use the grammatical structure of his native tongue. If, as in French, that tongue applies gender to inanimate things, the English pronouns referring to them may take the gender of the French equivalents, though the French nouns are not thought. The German postponement of the verb or the Magyar use of the past infinitive may be incorporated in the new language. In such cases, the structuring seems to be dissociated both from the content and from the simple associative connections of the words themselves.

The ease with which a new structure may be imposed on words is illustrated by the quickness with which children learn hog Latin. The form which I learned involved transposing the initial sound of each word to the end of the word and adding a long *a*. Thus—at-thay an-may oes-gay own-day e-thay eetstray. Some children become very facile at such inversions of words, and re-structure new words without hesitation. From such considerations it seems to follow that syntax is not inherent in the words employed or in the idea to be expressed. It is a generalized pattern imposed upon the specific acts as they occur.

"Priming" of Expressive Units

There are indications that, prior to the internal or overt enunciation of the sentence, an aggregate of word units is partially activated or readied. Evidence for this comes also from "contaminations" of speech and writing. The most frequent typing errors are those of anticipation; the inclusion in the word being typed of some part of a word or word structure which should properly occur later in the sentence. It may be only a letter. Thus I wrote, *wrapid* writing, carrying the *w* from the second word to the first. Not infrequently words are introduced which should occur much later in the sentence, often five or six words in advance.

In oral speech, Spoonerisms illustrate the same kind of contamination. The Spoonerism is most frequently an inversion of subject and object: "Let us always remember that waste makes haste." But it may be only a transposition of parts of the words: "Our queer old dean" for "our dear old queen." The frequency with which such contaminations occur is increased by haste, by distraction, by emotional tension, or by uncertainty and conflict as to the best form of expression. In some types of aphasia the tendency to disordered arrangement of words is greatly increased, and, in extreme cases, the attempt to speak results in a word hash with complete loss of grammatical organization. Professor Spooner, after whom such slips are named, was probably suffering from a mild form of aphasia. In these contaminations, it is as if the aggregate of words were in a state of partial excitation, held in check by the requirements of grammatical structure, but ready to activate the final common path, if the effectiveness of this check is in any way interfered with.

In his *Psychopathology of everyday life*, Freud has given numerous examples of similar contaminations of action outside the sphere of language. We do not need to accept his theories of censorship and suppression to account for such slips. They are of the same order as misplacements in typing and represent contaminations of co-existing, determining tendencies to action.

Such contaminations might be ascribed to differences in the relative strength of associative bonds between the elements of the act, and thus not evidence for the pre-excitation of the elements or for simultaneous pre-excitation. However, the understanding of speech involves essentially the same problems as the production of speech and definitely demands the postulation of an after-effect or after-discharge of the sensory components for a significant time following stimulation. Thus, in the spoken sentence, "Rapid righting with his uninjured hand saved from loss the contents of the capsized canoe," the associations which give meaning to righting are not activated for at least 3 to 5 seconds after hearing the word. I shall refer later to other evidence for such long after-discharge of sensory excitation. The fact of continued activation or after-discharge of receptive elements and their integration during this activation justifies the assumption of a similar process during motor organization. The processes of comprehension and production of speech have too much in common to depend on wholly different mechanisms. . . .

Generality of the Problem of Syntax

I have devoted so much time to discussion of the problem of syntax, not only because language is one of the most important products of human cerebral action, but also because the problems raised by the organization of language seem to me to be characteristic of almost all other cerebral activity. There is a series of hierarchies or organization; the order of vocal movements in pronouncing the word, the order of words in the sentence, the order of sentences in the paragraph, the rational order of paragraphs in a discourse. Not only speech, but all skilled acts seem to involve the same problems of serial ordering, even down to the temporal coordination of muscular contractions in such a movement as reaching and grasping. Analysis of the nervous mechanisms underlying order in the more primitive acts may contribute ultimately to the solution even of the physiology of logic.

It is possible to designate, that is, to point to specific examples of, the phenomena of the syntax of movement that require explanation, although those phenomena cannot be clearly defined. A real definition would be a long step toward solution of the problem. There are at least three sets of events to be accounted for. First, the activation of the expressive elements (the individual words or adaptive acts) which do not contain the temporal relations. Second, the determining tendency, the set, or idea. This masquerades under many names in contemporary psychology, but is, in every case, an inference from the restriction of behavior within definite limits. Third, the syntax of the act, which can be described as an habitual order or mode relating the expressive elements; a generalized pattern or schema of integration which may be imposed upon a wide range and a wide variety of specific acts. This is the essential problem of serial order; the existence of generalized schemata of action which determine the sequence of specific acts, acts which in themselves or in their associations seem to have no temporal valence.

. . . .

This is as far as I have been able to go toward a theory of serial order in action. Obviously, it is inadequate. The assumptions concerning spatial representation and temporal representation may even beg the question, since no one can say whether spatial or temporal order is primary. Furthermore, such determining tendencies as the relation of attribute to object, which gives the order of adjective and noun, do not seem to be analyzable into any sort of spatial structure or for that matter, into any consistent relationship. I have tried a number of assumptions concerning the selective mechanism of grammatical form (spatial relations, the relative intensity or prominence of different words in the idea, and so on) but I have never been able to make an hypothesis which was consistent with any large number of sentence structures. Nevertheless, the indications which I have cited, that elements of the sentence are readied or partially activated before the order is imposed upon them in expression, suggest that some scanning mechanism must be at play in regulating their temporal sequence. The real problem, however, is the nature of the selective mechanism by which the particular acts are picked out in this scanning process, and to this problem I have no answer.

The same selective scanning mechanism that had eluded Lashley was also the central theme in Wundt's psychology—namely, Wundt's notion of apperception. Lashley had described the act of language production as involving some internal nonlinear (perhaps spatial) representation that was somehow transformed into an external temporal sequence. The problem then was how and by what mechanism this was accomplished.

Thus Lashley's approach to language was radically different from that of his contemporaries. The linguist Zellig Harris, for example, at the University of Pennsylvania, continued in the Bloomfieldian program with the most ambitious effort to restrict linguistics to the study of external sequential events. His book *Methods in structural linguistics* (1951) is a maze of methods and procedures for segmenting, classifying, and distributing speech elements.

While an undergraduate at Pennsylvania, Chomsky helped Harris prepare this text for publication, and later completed his graduate studies under Harris. In related work, Chomsky further studied modern British linguistic philosophy with Nelson Goodman who successfully nominated him for a position in the Society of Fellows at Harvard in 1951. Arriving at Harvard, Chomsky was deeply immersed in the optimism of the early 1950s which promised so much for the behaviorist procedures in linguistics and for such engineering enterprises as machine translation. His first publication ("Systems of syntactic analysis," *Journal of symbolic Logic*, 1953) was an attempt to further sharpen the techniques of the taxonomic and behaviorist approach to linguistics, which he later abandoned. It was natural that after completing his dissertation, he should take a position at M.I.T.'s Research Laboratory of Electronics which was then heavily involved in the mechanical processing of language. Simultaneously, however, Chomsky was deeply impressed by Lashley's paper.

Chomsky has since remarked that the fundamental view of language inherited from Bloomfield had been strained and pushed to its limits. In a lengthy doctoral dissertation (900 pages) he formulated a radical departure from behaviorist or taxonomic linguistics. Because of his extreme change of view, he was unable to find a publisher who would accept the manuscript, and it was thus never published. Chomsky eventually found a European publisher who printed a short monograph based on lecture notes from his introductory linguistics class at M.I.T. This appeared as *Syntactic structures* (1957), and it is now popularly described as the first major document of a modern "revolution in linguistics."*

Chomsky was among the first to take a strong interest in Lashley's paper on serial order, and he continued Lashley's final efforts, with respect to language, by working out a new model for syntactic structure. Through that work the Humboldtian

---

* See Robert Sklar, Chomsky's revolution in linguistics. *The Nation*, Sept. 9, 1968, 213–217.

and Wundtian views, with their emphasis on the creative nature of language productive processes, were revitalized. However, the relationship to the earlier views had not been immediately apparent because in America those particular historical movements were either largely forgotten or had never been widely accepted nor understood.*

As a logician and linguist, Chomsky relied on formal logic for his methodology. One of his earliest concerns was to investigate the distinction between *semantics* and *syntax*. But wider initial recognition came from a formal demonstration of the inadequacy of statistical and Markovian conceptions of language structure. Essentially, the argument Chomsky proposed was that human language structure permitted the occurrence of unbounded and novel constructions. Finite state (Markovian systems) did not. In fact, it can be shown that it is impossible to construct a statistical model that produces all the sentences of English word by word. A description in terms of higher levels apparently avoids this consequence. (See Chomsky's "Three models for the description of language." *I.R.E. Transactions on information theory*, Vol. IT-2, No. 3, 1956.)†

Critical analyses of behaviorism in psychology and a reconsideration of mentalism then appeared. Chomsky's critical review of Skinner's *Verbal behavior* (in *Language*, Vol. 35, No. 1, 1959) constituted his entrance into psychology, and it has subsequently become a popular critique of the assumptions of behaviorist psychology. The classic confrontation between the views of these two men—the empiricist confronting the rationalist—has since drawn wide comment, yet Skinner has expressed a strong disinterest in forming any reply. Nevertheless, Skinner did recently make the following brief remark in print concerning Chomsky's assertion that language behavior is governed by abstract rules.

The behavior of one who speaks correctly by applying the rules of a grammar merely resembles the behavior of one who speaks cor-

---

* The earlier work did survive to some degree in Europe. See for example, M. Sandmann's book *Subject and predicate* (Edinburgh Univ. Press, 1954), which contains detailed allusions to the psycholinguistics of Wundt, Paul, Marty, and so on.

† See also G. A. Miller's discussion of this phase of Chomsky's work in *Mathematics and psychology* (New York: John Wiley, 1964).

rectly from long experience in a verbal community. The efficiency may be the same, but the controlling variables are different and the behaviors are therefore different. Nothing which could be called following a plan or applying a rule is observed when behavior is a product of the contingencies alone. To say that "the child who learns a language has in some sense constructed the grammar for himself" (Chomsky, 1959) is as misleading as to say that a dog which has learned to catch a ball has in some sense constructed the relevant part of the science of mechanics. Rules can be extracted from the reinforcing contingencies in both cases, and once in existence they may be used as guides. The direct effect of the contingencies is of a different nature.*

But Chomsky did not use the term "rule of grammar" in the sense criticized here by Skinner. The activity of a linguist who constructs a grammar and of a child who acquires language are certainly quite different. That people can speak grammatically without being able to describe their grammar is as obvious as their capacity to learn without being able to state principles of reinforcement, or that they can see without being perceptual theorists.

Although Skinner usually restricts his comments to observations of *speech*, Chomsky has been more fundamentally concerned with *language*; the distinction corresponds to de Saussure's separation of *la parole* and *la langue*. And although Skinner would remain with empiricist practicality, Chomsky would construct theories and explanations. Yet the schism cannot be dismissed that easily, because Chomsky chose Skinner's work as a paradigm case for a critique of the entire behaviorist and empiricist trend, a trend that he viewed as a particular Anglo-American mythology that constituted the true basis of its widespread acceptance rather than any empirical support, persuasive reasoning, or absence of a plausible alternative. Further, Chomsky argued that when Skinner described the "higher mental processes" the result was a *reductio ad absurdum* of behaviorist assumptions.

---

* B. F. Skinner, Operant behavior. In W. K. Honig, *Operant behavior: areas of research and application* (New York: Appleton-Century-Crofts, 1966), p. 29.

In Chomsky's mentalistic approach to language study, the *sentence* once again assumes the position as the fundamental unit of language. Smaller speech segments or imperfectly formed utterances can be understood only in terms of the sentences in which they occur or that underlie them. This again is "analytic" and mentalistic approach in opposition to the "synthetic" methodologies of taxonomic linguistics and behaviorism. Chomsky has described his views on *mentalism* with the following statement:

To accept traditional mentalism . . . is not to accept Bloomfield's dichotomy of "mentalism" versus "mechanism." Mentalistic linguistics is simply theoretical linguistics that uses performance as data (along with other data, for example, the data provided by introspection) for the determination of competence, the latter being taken as the primary object of its investigation. The mentalist, in this traditional sense, need make no assumptions about the possible physiological basis for the mental reality that he studies. In particular, he need not deny that there is such a basis. One would guess, rather, that it is the mentalistic studies that will ultimately be of greatest value for the investigation of neurophysiological mechanisms, since they alone are concerned with determining abstractly the properties that such mechanisms must exhibit and the functions they must perform.

In fact, the issue of mentalism versus antimentalism in linguistics apparently has to do only with goals and interests, and not with questions of truth or falsity, sense or nonsense. At least three issues are involved in this rather idle controversy: (a) dualism—are the rules that underlie performance represented in a nonmaterial medium?; (b) behaviorism—do the data of performance exhaust the domain of interest to the linguist, or is he also concerned with other facts, in particular those pertaining to the deeper systems that underlie behavior?; (c) introspectionism—should one make use of introspective data in the attempt to ascertain the properties of these underlying systems? It is the dualistic position against which Bloomfield irrelevantly inveighed. The behaviorist position is not an arguable matter. It is simply an expression of lack of interest in theory and explanation. . . . Perhaps this loss of theory, in the usual sense, was fostered by certain ideas (e.g., strict operationalism or strong verificationism) that were considered briefly in positivist philosophy of science, but rejected forthwith in the early nineteen-thirties. In any event, question (b) poses no substantive issue. Question (c) arises only if one rejects the behaviorist limitations of (b). To maintain, on grounds of methodological purity, that introspective judgements of the informant (often, the linguist himself) should be disregarded is, for the present, to condemn the study of language to utter sterility.*

Chomsky's innovation, which surpassed earlier ideas, was the formalization of the notion of *grammatical rule* and in such a way that it accounted for the possibility of an infinite variety of sentences, that is, the capacity for creation of novel utterances. The new formal tool, transformational analysis, was a technique that transformed abstract relational structures (analogous to Wundt's analyzed *Gesamtvorstellung*) into the sequential orderings of speech. This procedure described our understanding of the relations between constituents of the speech string more explicitly than before.†

Half a century earlier when many linguists became incensed because a brazen psychologist and outsider, Wundt, attempted to discredit their work; the same events worked in reverse when the linguist Chomsky made pronouncements about psychology. Yet the comparison between Chomsky and Wundt goes further. Chomsky did what Wundt surely would have wished to do. Wundt's analysis of sentences, tree diagrams, and discussions of grammatical relations and underlying structures was an initial attempt; but at the time of Wundt's death, a formalization of the notion of *grammatical rule* was lacking, although he certainly had appreciated its significance. In 1957 Brown expressed the significance of this notion for the more recent psycholinguists:

. . . it has taken psychologists a long time to realize that the linguist means something when he says: "Language is a system." Very simply, he means that when someone knows a language he knows a set of rules: rules of phonology, morphology, reference, and syntax. These rules can generate an indefinite number of utterances. Learning a language is more than the rehearsal of particular sentences. From

---

* Reprinted from *Aspects of the theory of syntax* (1967, p. 193) by Noam Chomsky by permission of The MIT Press, Cambridge, Massachusetts. See also J. J. Katz, Mentalism in linguistics. *Language,* Vol. 40, 1964.

† For the formalisms see *Aspects of the theory of syntax*. Ibid.

particular sentences we induce a governing set of rules and the proof is that we can say new things, never heard and never rehearsed, which nevertheless conform to the rules and are comprehensible to people who know the rules. The most important thing psychology is likely to get from linguistics is the reminder that human behavior includes the response that is novel but appropriate.*

In 1962, the Ninth International Congress of Linguists met in Cambridge, Massachusetts, and on that occasion Chomsky read a paper on "current issues in linguistic theory" in which he spelled out his radical proposals for revisions of linguistic theory. The paper constituted a long and complex comparison of the *taxonomic model* of language with the *transformational model*. The taxonomic one was simpler, more "concrete," and more "atomistic." It essentially attempted to specify all the contexts in which each linguistic element of some language inventory could occur. In sharp contrast, the transformational model was more complex and highly structured. It consisted of ordered sets of rules that related phonetic representations to semantic representations, both being potentially infinite sets of events, although the transformational rules themselves would constitute a relatively small and manageable finite set.

Chomsky's discussion was quite detailed in its examination of these models, and he concluded that the taxonomic model did not account for the facts of human language. This inadequacy was then traced to impoverished conceptions of human cognitive processes. These formal arguments are not presented in the excerpts that follow below because to appreciate them the reader needs familiarity with linguistic terminology and symbolism. (Indeed, linguistic analysis has advanced so rapidly that not only have laymen been left behind, but also linguists of different backgrounds often have trouble communicating with each other.) Rather than lose the reader at this point, several less technical sections of the paper were selected that illustrate the relevance of Chomsky's thought to the historical traditions already considered here and also to the fundamental issues concerning the study of human mental capacities.

* R. Brown, *Words and things* (Glencoe, Ill.: Copyright 1958 by The Free Press, a corporation), p. viii. With permission of the publisher.

NOAM CHOMSKY · *Transformational Generative Grammar*

1. Goals of Linguistic Theory[1]

1.1 The central fact to which any significant linguistic theory must address itself is this: a mature speaker can produce a new sentence of his language on the appropriate occasion, and other speakers can understand it immediately, though it is equally new to them. Most of our linguistic experience both as speakers and hearers, is with new sentences; once we have mastered a language, the class of sentences with which we can operate fluently and without difficulty or hesitation is so vast that for all practical purposes (and, obviously, for all theoretical purposes), we can regard it as infinite. Normal mastery of a language involves not only the ability to understand immediately an indefinite number of entirely new sentences, but also the ability to identify deviant sentences and, on occasion, to impose an interpretation on them. . . .[2]

SOURCE. Noam Chomsky, Current issues in linguistic theory. In Jerry A. Fodor and Jerrold J. Katz (Eds.) *The structure of language: readings in the philosophy of language,* © 1964. Reprinted by permission of Prentice-Hall, Inc., Englewood Cliffs, N.J. A revised and expanded version of a report presented to the session: *The logical basis of linguistic theory,* Ninth International Congress of Linguists (Cambridge, Mass.), 1962.

[1] The account of linguistic structure sketched below in part incorporates, and in part developed in response to many stimulating ideas of Zellig Harris and Roman Jakobson. Its present form is to a large extent a product of collaboration over many years with Morris Halle, to whom (along with Paul Postal and John Viertel) I am indebted for much helpful criticism of this paper.

[2] Apparently many linguists hold that if a context can be constructed in which an interpretation can be imposed on an utterance, then it follows that this utterance is not to be distinguished, for the purposes of study of grammar, from perfectly normal sentences. Thus, e.g. "colorless green ideas sleep furiously," "remorse felt John," "the dog looks barking," etc., are not to be distinguished, in this view, from "revolutionary new ideas appear infrequently," "John felt remorse," "the dog looks frightening," though the distinction can clearly be both stated and motivated on syntactic grounds.

On the basis of a limited experience with the data of speech, each normal human has developed for himself a thorough competence in his native language. This competence can be represented, to an as yet undetermined extent, as a system of rules that we can call the *grammar* of his language. To each phonetically possible utterance . . . the grammar assigns a certain *structural description* that specifies the linguistic elements of which it is constituted and their structural relations (or, in the case of structural ambiguity, several such structural descriptions). For some utterances, the structural description will indicate, in particular, that they are perfectly well-formed sentences. This set we can call the *language generated by the grammar*. To others, the grammar will assign structural descriptions that indicate the manner of their deviation from perfect well-formedness. Where the deviation is sufficiently limited, an interpretation can often be imposed by virtue of formal relations to sentences of the generated language.

The grammar, then, is a device that (in particular) specifies the infinite set of well-formed sentences and assigns to each of these one or more structural descriptions. Perhaps we should call such a device a *generative grammar* to distinguish it from descriptive statements that merely present the inventory of elements that appear in structural descriptions, and their contextual variants.

The generative grammar of a language should, ideally, contain a central *syntactic component* and two *interpretive components*, a *phonological component* and a *semantic component*. The syntactic component generates strings of minimal syntactically functioning elements (following Bolinger, 1948, let us call them formatives)[3] and specifies the categories, functions and structural interrelations of the formatives and systems of formatives. The phonological component converts a string of formatives of specified syntactic structure into a phonetic representation. The semantic component, corespondingly, assigns a semantic interpretation to an abstract structure generated by the syntactic component. Thus each of the two interpretive com-

---

Thus grammar reduces to such matters as government, agreement, inflectional paradigms, and the like. This decision seems to me no more defensible than a decision to restrict the study of language structure to phonetic patterning.

[3] D. L. Bolinger, On defining the morpheme. *Word*, 1948, IV: 18–23.

ponents maps a syntactically generated structure onto a "concrete" interpretation, in one case phonetic, and in the other, semantic. The grammar as a whole can thus be regarded, ultimately, as a device for pairing phonetically represented signals with semantic interpretations, this pairing being mediated through a system of abstract structures generated by the syntactic component. Thus the syntactic component must provide for each sentence (actually, for each interpretation of each sentence) a semantically interpretable *deep structure* and a phonetically interpretable *surface structure*, and, in the event that these are distinct, a statement of the relation between these two structures. (For further discussion, see Katz and Postal, 1964.)[4] Roughly speaking, it seems that this much structure is common to all theories of generative grammar, or is at least compatible with them. Beyond this loose and minimal specification, however, important differences emerge.

The generative grammar internalized by someone who has acquired a language defines what in Saussurian terms we may call *langue* (with a qualification to be specified below). In performing as a speaker or hearer, he puts this device to use. Thus as a hearer, his problem is to determine the structural description assigned by his grammar to a presented utterance (or, where the sentence is syntactically ambiguous, to determine the correct structural description for this particular token), and using the information in the structural description, to understand the utterance. Clearly the description of intrinsic competence provided by the grammar is not to be confused with an account of actual performance, as de Saussure emphasized with such lucidity (cf. also Sapir, 1921; Newman, 1941).[5] Nor is it to be confused with an account of potential performance.[6] The actual use of language obviously involves a complex

[4] J. Katz and P. Postal, *An integrated theory of linguistic descriptions* (Cambridge: M.I.T. Press, 1964).

[5] E. Sapir, *Language* (New York: Harcourt, Brace & World, Inc., 1921). S. S. Newman, Behavior patterns in linguistic structure: a case study. In *Language, culture, and personality*, Spier, Hallowell, and Newman (Eds.) (Menasha, Wisconsin: Sapir Memorial Publication Fund, 1941).

[6] The common characterization of language as a set of "verbal habits" or as a "complex of present dispositions to verbal behavior, in which speakers of the same language have perforce come to resemble one another" (Quine, *Word and object*. 1960, p. 27) is totally inadequate. Knowledge of one's language is not reflected directly in linguistic habits and dispositions, and

interplay of many factors of the most disparate sort, of which the grammatical processes constitute only one. It seems natural to suppose that the study of actual linguistic performance can be seriously pursued only to the extent that we have a good understanding of the generative grammars that are acquired by the learner and put to use by the speaker or hearer. The classical Saussurian assumption of the logical priority of the study of *langue* (and the generative grammars that describe it) seems quite inescapable.

. . . .

1.2 It would not be inaccurate to regard the transformational model as a formalization of features implicit in traditional grammars, and to regard these grammars as inexplicit transformational generative grammars. The goal of a traditional grammar is to provide its user with the ability to understand an arbitrary sentence of the language, and to form and employ it properly on the appropriate occasion. Thus its goal is (at least) as far-reaching as that of a generative grammar, as just described. Furthermore, the rich descriptive apparatus of traditional grammar far exceeds the limits of the taxonomic model, though it is largely, and perhaps fully formalizable within the framework of the transformational model. However, it is important to bear in mind that even the most careful and complete traditional grammar relies in an essential way on the intuition and intelligence of the user, who is expected to draw the correct inferences from the many examples and hints (and explicit lists of irregularities) presented by the grammar. If the grammar is a good one, the user may succeed, but the deep-seated regularities of the language that he somehow discovers escape explicit formulation, and the nature of the abilities that enable him to perform this task remain a complete mystery. The vastness of these gaps can be appreciated only when one makes an attempt to construct explicit rules to account for the full range of structural information available to the mature user of a language.

Focusing on the notion of "creativity," one can distinguish two conflicting views regarding the essential nature of language in nineteenth-century linguistic theory. On the one hand, we have the

---

it is clear that speakers of the same language or dialect may differ enormously in dispositions to verbal response, depending on personality, beliefs and countless other extra, linguistic factors.

Humboldtian view that "one should not view language as a lifeless *product*, but rather view it as a *productive activity*."* (1836, Section 8, p. LV).[7] The essence of each language is what Humboldt designates as its characteristic *Form* (not to be identified with "inner form"). The form of language is that constant and unvarying factor that underlies and gives life and significance to each particular new linguistic act. It is by having developed an internal representation of this form that each individual is capable of understanding the language and using it in a way that is intelligible to his fellow speakers. This characteristic form determines and inheres in each separate linguistic element. The role and significance of each individual element can be determined only by considering it in relation to underlying form, that is, in relation to the fixed generative rules that determine the manner of its formation. It is this underlying generative principle that the linguist must seek to represent in a descriptive grammar.

. . .

In sharp contrast to the Humboldtian conception, in the general linguistics of the nineteenth century, is the view that is perhaps expressed most clearly by Whitney (1872),[8] namely, that "language in the concrete sense . . . [is] . . . the sum of words and phrases by which any man expresses his thought" (372); that study of speech is no more than study of a body of vocal signs; and that study of the origin and development of language is nothing more than study of origin and development of these signs. The problem of accounting for the acquisition of language, so conceived, disappears. ". . . the acquisition of language by children does not seem to us any mystery at all." It is not at all astonishing "that a child, after hearing a certain word used some scores or hundreds of times, comes to understand what it means, and then, a little later, to pronounce and use it. . . ."

This narrowing of the scope of linguistics to the study of an inventory of elements was occasioned not only by the dramatic successes of comparative linguistics, which operated within these limita-

---

* Chomsky's quotation was in German. This translation is by A. L. Blumenthal.—A.L.B.

[7] W. von Humboldt, *Ueber die Verschiedenheit des menschlichen Sprachbaues.* (Berlin, 1836), Facsimile edition (Bonn, 1960).

[8] W. D. Whitney, Steinthal and the psychological theory of language *North American Review,* 114, (1872).

tions, but also by the unclarities and obscurities of formulation of Humboldt ("a man whom it is nowadays the fashion to praise highly, without understanding or even reading him"—Whitney, 1872, 333) and his successors. Furthermore there were some serious confusions concerning the notion of "creativity." Thus it is significant that the comments of Paul's [concerning creativity, 1886][9] are from a chapter that deals with analogic change. He makes no distinction (just as Humboldt makes no clear distinction) between the kind of "creativity" that leaves the language entirely unchanged (as in the production—and understanding—of new sentences, an activity in which the adult is constantly engaged) and the kind that actually changes the set of grammatical rules (e.g., analogic change). But this is a fundamental distinction. In fact, the technical tools for dealing with "rule-governed creativity," as distinct from "rule-changing creativity," have only become readily available during the past few decades in the course of work in logic and foundations of mathematics. But in the light of these developments, it is possible to return to the questions to which Humboldt addressed himself, and to attempt to represent certain aspects of the underlying "Form of language," insofar as it encompasses "rule-governed creativity," by means of an explicit generative grammar.

Saussure, like Whitney (and possibly under his influence—cf. Godel, 1957, 32–33),[10] regards *langue* as basically a store of signs with their grammatical properties, that is, a store of wordlike elements, fixed phrases, and, perhaps, certain limited phrase types (though it is possible that his rather obscure concept of "mecanisme de la langue" was intended to go beyond this—cf. Godel, 1957, 250). He was thus quite unable to come to grips with the recursive processes underlying sentence formation, and he appears to regard sentence formation as a matter of *parole* rather than *langue*, of free and voluntary creation rather than systematic rule (or perhaps, in some obscure way, as on the border between *langue* and *parole*). There is no place in his scheme for "rule-governed creativity" of the kind involved in the ordinary everyday use of language. At the same time,

---

[9] H. Paul, *Prinzipien der Sprachgeschichte*. 2nd ed. (1886). Translated into English: Longmans, Green & Co., London (1890).

[10] R. Godel, *Les sources manuscrites du cours de linguistique générale* (Geneva-Paris: Librairie E. Droz—Librairie Minard, 1957).

the influence of Humboldtian holism (but now restricted to inventories and paradigmatic sets, rather than to the full-scale generative processes that constitute *Form*) is apparent in the central role of the notions "terme" and "valeur" in the Saussurian system.

Modern linguistics is much under the influence of Saussure's conception of *langue* as an inventory of elements Saussure, 1916, 154, and elsewhere, frequently)[11] and his preoccupation with systems of elements rather than the systems of rules which were the focus of attention of traditional grammar and of the general linguistics of Humboldt. In general, modern descriptive statements pay little attention to the "creative" aspect of language; they do not face the problem of presenting the system of generative rules that assign structural descriptions to arbitrary utterances and thus embody the speaker's competence in and knowledge of this language. Furthermore, this narrowing of the range of interest, as compared with traditional grammar, apparently has the effect of making it impossible to select an inventory of elements correctly, since it seems that no inventory (not even that of phonemes) can be determined without reference to the principles by which sentences are constructed in the language. To the extent that this is true, "structural linguistics" will have suffered from a failure to appreciate the extent and depth of interconnections among various parts of a language system. By a rather arbitrary limitation of scope, modern linguistics may well have become engaged in an intensive study of mere artifacts.

In summary, a comparison of Humboldtian general linguistics with typical modern views reveals quite a number of basic differences. Thus Humboldt's belief that the instrumental function of language is derivative, and that it is the characteristic property only of parasitic special purpose systems, contrasts with the view of, for example, Bloomfield (1933, p. 22f.)[12] and Wittgenstein (1958, p. 16–17)[13] that this instrumental function is paradigmatic and basic, and that (for Wittgenstein) its study "is the study of primitive forms of language or primitive languages." Furthermore, Humboldt's conception of underlying form as a system of generative rules that defines the

[11] F. de Saussure, *Cours de linguistique générale* (Paris: C. Bally & A. Sechehaye, 1916).

[12] L. Bloomfield, *Language* (New York: Holt, 1933).

[13] Wittgenstein, L., *The blue and brown books* (New York: Harper & Row, 1958).

role of each element differentiates his approach strikingly from that of modern structural linguistics, with its emphasis on element and inventory. In the same vein, one may compare his account of how a rich system of generative principles is involved in understanding a particular utterance with the late view of Wittgenstein (1958, p. 42) that there is no necessity to suppose the whole "calculus of language" to be present to the mind as a permanent background for each act of language use. Correspondingly, Humboldt's account of perception in terms of a schematism involving a system of rules contrasts with the elementary data-processing approach characteristic of modern linguistic theory. . . . Finally, it is interesting to compare Humboldt's views on language-learning (which might, with certain reservations, be called "Platonistic"; cf., in this connection, Leibniz, *Discourse on metaphysics*, Section 26) with the typical modern notion expressed, for example, in Wittgenstein's claim (1958, p. 12–13, 27) that the meanings of words must not only be learned, but also taught (the only means being drill, explanation, or the supplying of rules that are used consciously and explicitly), or in the claim (cf., e.g., Quine, 1960, p. 9f.) that sentences are, typically, "learned" by some sort of process of stimulus-sentence conditioning or sentence-sentence association (with analogic extension of some elementary sort playing a marginal, and in principle dispensable role).

. . . .

2. Models of Perception and Acquisition

A concern with perception and acquisition of language has played a significant role in determining the course of development of linguistic theory, as it should if this theory is ever to have broader scientific significance. But I have tried to show that the basic point of view regarding both perception and acquisition has been much too particularistic and concrete. It has failed totally to come to grips with the "creative" aspect of language use, that is, the ability to form and understand previously unheard sentences. It has, in general, failed to appreciate the degree of internal organization and the intricacy of the system of abstract structures that has been mastered by the learner, and that is brought to bear in understanding, or even identifying utterances. With regard to perceptual models, these limitations reveal themselves in such conditions as linearity, invariance, and biuniqueness; with regard to models of acquisition, in such methodological conditions as the principle of separation of levels, the attempt to define grammatical relations in terms of co-occurrence, and, in general, in the emphasis on elementary procedures of segmentation and classification that has dominated modern linguistic theory.

These taxonomic models of acquisition are not far removed from the extremely limited paradigms of learning and concept formation, based exclusively on some notion of matching or similarity or possession of a common property from some fixed set of available properties, that are to be found in recent cognitive psychology. But it does not seem plausible that the kind of generative grammar that seems to be descriptively adequate might be acquired in a reasonably brief time (if at all) by an organism that brings to the learning task only a "quality space" and a "distance measure" along these dimensions. Evidence suggests that each natural language is a simple and highly systematic realization of a complex and intricate underlying model, with highly special and unique properties. To the extent that this observation can be substantiated, it suggests that the structure of the grammar internalized by the learner may be, to a presently quite unexpected degree, a reflection of the general character of his learning capacity rather than the particular course of his experience. It seems not unlikely that the organism brings, as its contribution to acquisition of a particular language, a highly restrictive characterization of a class of generative systems (potential theories) from which the grammar of its language is selected on the basis of the presented linguistic data. There is no a priori reason to expect that these potential theories are of the highly simple taxonomic variety with which modern linguistics has been preoccupied, and the linguistic evidence seems to show, in fact, that they are not.

In the case of perception of language, the step-by-step models of taxonomic linguistics are not in the least convincing. The process of coming to understand a presented utterance can be quite naturally described, in part, as a process of constructing an internal representation (a "percept") of its full structural description. There is little reason to doubt that the full apparatus of the generative grammar that represents the hearer's linguistic competence is brought to bear immediately in carrying out this task. In particular, much of the perceived phonetic shape of an utterance (e.g., in English, the complex arrangements of reduced and unreduced vowels and stress contours) is a reflection of its syntactic structure. It would not be surprising to find that what the hearer (or the phonetician) perceives is an ideal pattern, not incompatible with the signal that actually reaches his ears, that is projected by the phonological component of his grammar from the syntactic description that he has assigned to this signal.

In part, these questions belong to theoretical psychology. But purely linguistic research can play a fundamental role in adding substance to these speculations. A perceptual model that does not incorporate a descriptively adequate generative grammar cannot be taken very seriously. Similarly, the construction of a model of acquisition (whether a model of learning, or a linguistic procedure for discovery of grammars) cannot be seriously undertaken without a clear understanding of the nature of the descriptively adequate grammars that it must provide as output, on the basis of primary linguistic data. . . . It presupposes, in other words, a general linguistic theory that achieves the level of explanatory adequacy. It is clear that we have descriptively adequate grammars, and underlying theories that reach the level of explanatory adequacy, only for a rather narrow range of linguistic phenomena in a small number of languages. It seems to me that present theories of transformational generative grammar provide a basis for extending and deepening our understanding of linguistic structure. In any event, whether or not this hope is ultimately justified, it seems clear that to pursue the goals of Section 1 in any serious way, it is necessary to go far beyond the restricted framework of modern taxonomic linguistics and the narrowly-conceived empiricism from which it springs.

As linguistics struggled with the challenge to a tradition that had once seemed established beyond doubt, psychologists who were interested in language approached the new views more timidly. Strong interpreters were present who had been equally close to both areas. George Miller, through his writings, introduced the new linguistics to the English-speaking psychology community.

A list of Miller's publications, which begins in the 1940s, reads almost like a history of the mid-twentieth century psycholinguistics movements. He began with a strict commitment to communication engineering and behaviorism and in the course of twenty years shifted to a view of psychology as "the science of the mind" and also to a view, similar to many in the nineteenth century, that the study of linguistics was one of the best ways to understand the mind. Along with his students, Miller has been one of the pioneers in the experimental investigation of psychological implications of linguistic theory. In the *Handbook of mathematical psychology* (Bush, Luce, and Galanter, Eds., 1963) Miller and Chomsky coauthored chapters that surveyed the quantitative approaches to language study and the models of language users.

In a presidential address delivered before the Eastern Psychological Association in 1962, Miller described several early experimental investigations that had been inspired by the newer linguistics. It is worth quoting here, not for the pilot work it describes, but to show parallels between the proposals and programs it proclaims and the work of the earlier *Sprachpsychologie* era. First, in Miller's discussion is found an echo of the dispute between Wundt and Paul when Miller contrasts "categorial grammar" (synthetic) with "generative grammar" (analytical). He then argues that psychologists have not been enough concerned with the internal processes of comprehension. The tree diagram is one device that has been used to illustrate how we comprehend sentences: to understand a sentence would involve inducing some structure that the diagram suggests. As pictured it would be dominated by the holistic symbol S (for sentence). And like Wundt, he uses such diagrams for a similar purpose, that is, for discussions of sentence comprehension. However, Wundt's diagrams represented sentences at the "base" or conceptual level and were not mere parsings of utterances.

Miller spoke of abstract cognitive structures, as did Wundt. And his article concluded with a Wundtian appeal for serious consideration of the phenomena of *minds*, with the suggestion that they may profitably be studied through the systems of human language. In contrast to Wundt, Miller was more optimistic about the value of experimental investigations for psycholinguistics.

The excerpt that follows omits sections that give details of several pilot investigations concerning language performance, which have since been improved and extended.

GEORGE ARMITAGE MILLER · *The Psychology of the Sentence*

Language is a topic that psychologists have long discussed from many points of view. We have treated it as a system of cognitive categories, as a medium for self-expression or for persuasion, therapy, and education, as a tool for ordering and controlling our other mental operations, and in many other ways. The approach I want to take here, however, is to regard language as an extremely complicated human skill. My aspiration is to examine that skill in detail in the hope of learning something more about what it consists of and how it functions.

When psychologists talk about language as a skill they frequently emphasize problems of *meaning*. Learning what different utterances mean is, of course, a fundamental skill that any user of a language must acquire. But meaning is too large a problem to solve all at once; we are forced to analyze it into more manageable parts. Consequently, there is in psychology a long tradition of defining meaning in terms of *reference*—in terms of an arbitrary association between some referent and a vocal utterance—and then reducing reference in turn to a simple matter of *conditioning*. In that way many difficult problems of human language are transformed into simpler processes that can be studied in lower animals as well as in man, so the general similarities, rather than the specific differences between linguistic and other skills are emphasized.

I have no quarrel with that approach as long as we recognize that it treats only the simplest 1% of the psycholinguistic problem, and that our crucially important human skill in arranging symbols in novel and useful combinations is largely ignored by the successive reduction of language to meaning to reference to conditioning.

SOURCE. G. A. Miller, Some psychological studies of grammar. *American Psychologist*, Vol. 17, 1962, 748–762. Copyright 1962 by the American Psychological Association and reproduced by permission.

Our combinatorial power, which is so characteristically human, provides the psychological foundation for something that linguists usually call "grammar." I use the term defiantly, for I am fully aware that it is a grim and forbidding subject. It still reeks of the medieval trivium of grammar, logic, and rhetoric; it still reminds us vividly of all those endless and incomprehensible rules that our teachers tried to drum into us in grammar school. I wish I could gloss over it with some euphemism about "communication theory" or "verbal behavior," but, alas, I have no honest alternative but to admit that it is grammar that concerns me. It is grammar that is so significantly human, so specific to our species, so important for psychologists to understand more clearly. I do not in any sense wish to criticize psychological studies of the referential process, or of the intricate associative network that supports the referential process. My goal is rather to persuade psychologists, by argument and illustration, that there is much more to our linguistic skills than *just* the referential process. I do not see how we are going to describe language as a skill unless we find some satisfactory way to deal with grammar and with the combinatorial processes that grammar entails.

In order to illustrate what our linguistic skills are, I need to draw on certain basic concepts of modern linguistics. Fortunately, modern linguists have a somewhat different conception of grammar—a more scientific conception—than your English teacher had years ago. If I can communicate this newer conception of grammar well enough, perhaps it will revive some spark of interest that you may still have.

Consider a brief sample of the scientific approach to grammar. Let us choose a sentence so simple that we can have no trouble in analyzing it or in understanding the principles of analysis that are being used. Interesting sentences are much more complicated, of course, but the same principles are involved.

Take the sentence *Bill hit the ball*. To native speakers of English it is intuitively obvious that this sequence of words has a kind of structure, that some pairs of adjacent words are more closely related than others. For instance, *the ball* feels like a more natural unit than, say, *hit the*. One way to express that fact is to say that it is very easy to substitute a single word for *the ball*, but it is difficult to think of a single word for *hit the* that would not change the underlying structure of the sentence.

On the first line at the top of Table 1 is the original sentence, *Bill* hit the ball. On line 2 is the derived sentence, *Bill hit it*, which is formed by substituting *it* for *the ball*. On line 3 there is another substitution—*acted* instead of *hit it*—and so we obtain the sentence *Bill acted*.

TABLE 1
Illustrating Constituent Analysis of a Simple Sentence

1	Bill	hit	the	ball
2	Bill	hit	it	
3	Bill	acted		

Bill	hit	the / T	ball / N
	V	NP_2	
NP_1	VP		

This process, in one form or another, is called "constituent analysis" by modern linguists (Harris, 1946; Nida, 1948; Pike, 1943; Wells, 1947).[1] As described so far, it may sound as though it depends on your perseverance in searching for alternative words to substitute for each constituent. We can generalize the procedure, however, by introducing specific names for the various kinds of constituent units. Such a use of names is indicated in the lower half of the table. *The*

[1] Harris, Z. S. From Morpheme to utterance. *Language*, 1946, **22**: 161–183. Nida, E. A. The analysis of immediate constituents. *Language*, 1948, **24**: 168–177. Pike, K. L. Taxemes and immediate constituents. *Language*, 1943, **19**: 65–82. Wells, R. S. Immediate constituents. *Language*, 1947, **23**: 81–117.

is an article (symbolized T) and *ball* is a noun (symbolized N); together they form a noun phrase (symbolized NP). The verb *hit* combines with the noun phrase to form a verb phrase (symbolized VP). And, finally, the initial noun phrase *Bill* combines with the verb phrase to form a grammatical sentence. Thus each type of constituent has its own name.

As soon as we try to deal abstractly with grammatical sentences, we become involved with these kinds of structured patterns. Obviously, we need some formal system to keep track of them. Several theoretical possibilities are currently available.

One way to deal with the constituent structure of a sentence is to use what linguists have come to call a *generative grammar* (Chomsky, 1956).[2] The central idea was first developed for combinatorial systems in the study of formal logic (Post, 1936, 1944).[3] Starting from a basic axiom, we apply rules of formation that permit us to rewrite the axiom in certain acceptable ways until we have finally derived the desired sentence. If the rules are formulated properly, only the grammatical sentences will be derivable; all other sentences will be ungrammatical.

Figure 1 illustrates how a small fragment of English grammar might be expressed in this manner. The basic axiom is S. The rewriting rules F1-7 permit us to form the sentence *Bill hit the ball* in a sequence of steps. First S is rewritten as NP + VP according to rule F1. Then we can rewrite NP as *Bill* according to rule F4. Since there is not any rule available for rewriting *Bill*, we are forced to stop at this point. We can, however, rewrite VP according to rule F3, thus getting *Bill* + V + NP. In this way we can proceed as indicated by the tree graph on the right until the desired sentence is derived. Note that the diagram of the derivation corresponds to the constituent structure that we saw in Table 1.

The set of rewriting rules on the left of Figure 1 can be conveniently referred to as the grammar, and the set of sentences that the grammar generates defines the language. It is an important feature of this kind of grammar that there are terminal symbols, symbols that

[2] Chomsky, N. Three models for the description of language. IRE *Trans. inform. Theory*, 1956, IT-2, 113–124.

[3] Post, E. L. Finite combinatory processes: Formulation I. *J. symb. Logic*, 1936, **1**: 103–105; and, Recursively enumerable sets of positive integers and their decision problems. *Bull. Amer. math. Soc.*, 1944, **50**: 284–316.

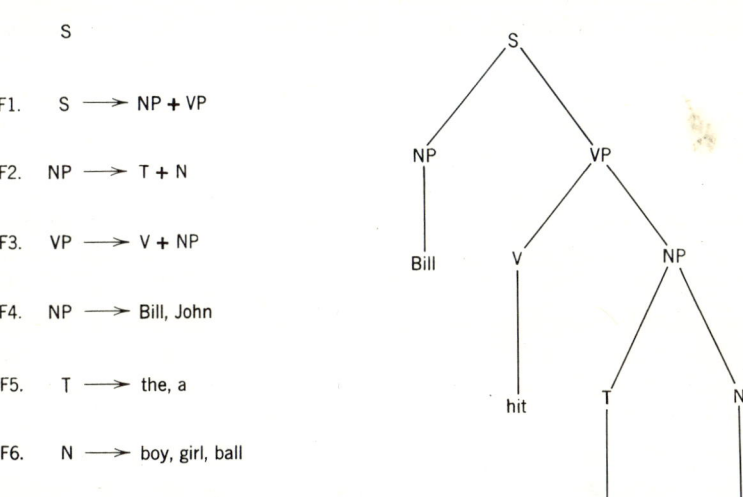

FIG. 1. A fragment of English grammar, phrased in terms of rewriting rules, illustrating a generative grammar.

cannot be rewritten, and these comprise what we ordinarily recognize as the vocabulary of the language. According to this way of representing it, the vocabulary is included in the grammar.

Most people, when they encounter a generative grammar for the first time, get an impression that it means we must always form our sentences from axiom to terminal symbols, that we must always decide what phrases we want before we can decide what words we want to use. That is not a necessary assumption, however. These rules of formation, and the trees that represent the structures of the grammatical sentences, are purely formal devices for representing word groupings. How a sentence is actually manufactured or understood by users of the language—what particular cognitive processes he performs—is not a linguistic problem, but a psychological one.

Just to suggest how the same structural properties can be formalized in a different manner, therefore, consider briefly something that linguists have come to call a *categorial grammar* (Bar-Hillel, 1953;

Lambek, 1958).[4] This alternative was also borrowed from symbolic logic (Cf. Ajdukiewicz, 1935).[5] According to this way of thinking about grammar, all the words and constituents must be classified into syntactic categories—corresponding roughly to what you may once have learned to call *parts of speech*—that, like chemical elements, are characterized by the ways they can combine with each other. I can make the reasoning clear most quickly, I think, by an example. In Figure 2 on the left is a small segment of the English vocabulary, alphabetized as it would be in any proper dictionary. Listed after each entry are a set of symbols that indicate the syntac-

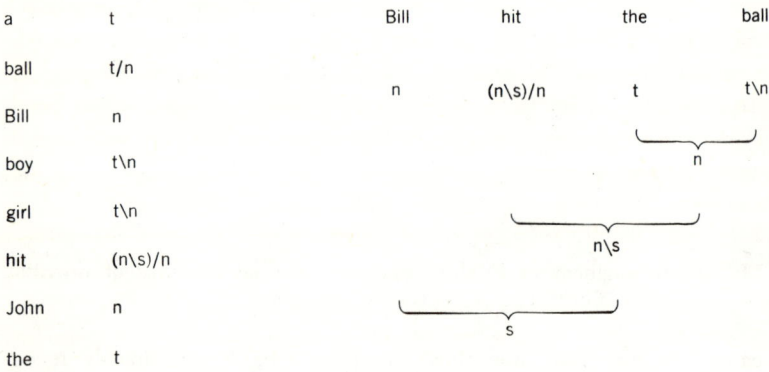

FIG. 2. A fragment of English grammar, phrased in terms of rules of cancellation, illustrating a categorial grammar.

tic categories that the word belongs to. In order to use those category markers you must understand a simple fact about the way they cancel, namely, that left and right cancellation are distinct. The word *ball* belongs to the category $t \backslash n$ (read "t under n") and has the characteristic that when a member of t is placed to its left, the ts cancel, much as in ordinary algebra, leaving simply n. According

---

[4] Bar-Hillel, Y. A quasiarithmetical notation for syntactic description. *Language*, 1953, **29**: 47–58. Lambek, J. The mathematics of sentence structure, *Amer. math. Mon.*, 1958, **65**: 154–169.

[5] Adjdukiewicz, K. Die syntaktische Konnexität. *Stud. Phil.*, 1935, **1**: 1–27.

to this way of representing the grammar, each word in the sentence is first replaced by its category symbol, then the category symbols are combined by left and right cancellation in all possible ways. If any result includes the single symbol S, then we know that we are dealing with a grammatical sentence; the order of cancellations indicates its underlying constituent structure. In the case of *Bill hit the ball*, the successive cancellations are shown on the right half of Figure 2.

There are obvious differences between categorial grammars and generative grammars. A categorial grammar starts with the words and works toward a single symbol that represents a grammatical sentence; a generative grammar seems to move in the opposite direction. Notice also that the categorial system seems to have all its grammatical rules included in the dictionary, whereas the generative system does just the opposite and includes the dictionary in its grammatical rules. In spite of these superficial differences, however, it has been possible to show—by stating each type of system precisely and studying its formal properties—that they are equivalent in the range of languages that they are capable of characterizing (Bar-Hillel, Gaifman, and Shamir, 1960).[6]

That is enough grammatical theory for the moment. It is time now to stop and ask whether there are any psychological implications to all this. Are these systems of rules nothing more than a convenient way to summarize linguistic data or do they also have some relevance for the psychological processes involved? If human speech is a skilled act whose component parts are related to one another in the general manner that the linguists have been describing, what measurable consequences can we expect to find? What measurable effects would such skills have on our other psychological processes?

First, we might ask if there is any solid empirical evidence for the psychological reality of syntactic categories. One clear implication of these linguistic hypotheses would be that we must have our memory for the words of our language organized according to syntactic categories. Is there any evidence that such an organization exists? There is, of course. For example, psychologists who work with word associations have always claimed—although until recently

[6] Bar-Hillel, Y., Gaifman, C., and Shamir, E. On categorial and phrase-structure grammars. *Bull. res. council Israel,* 1960, **9F**: 1–16.

they have done relatively little to explore the claim—that responses from adult subjects on a word-association test have a marked tendency to be members of the same syntactic category as are the stimuli that evoke them (Ervin, 1961).[7] Certainly there is *some* lawful relation between the syntactic category of the stimulus word and the syntactic category of the response word, but exactly what the relation is may not be quite as simple as originally advertised. . . .

I believe that the case for the psychological reality of these grammatical conventions might be strengthened if we would focus on the process of comprehension, rather than on the processes of learning and memory. In order to phrase the matter in a strong form, consider the following proposition: *We cannot understand a sentence until we are able to assign a constituent structure to it.*

Perhaps the simplest way to illustrate what I have in mind is to examine a sentence that is syntactically ambiguous. In Figure 3 we have an example of the sort that linguists like to consider: *They are eating apples* is really two sentences, even though both of them consist of exactly the same sequence of words. The sentence on the left

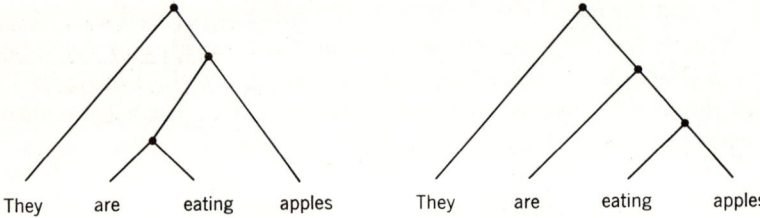

FIG. 3. Syntactic ambiguity arises when two different sentences are expressed by the same string of words.

would answer the question, *What are your friends doing?* The one on the right would answer the question, *Are those apples better for eating or for cooking?* On the basis of linear sequence of words alone, however, we cannot tell which meaning is intended. Somehow, from the context, we must decide which syntactic structure is appropriate. Until we have decided on its structure, however, the sentence is ambiguous and we cannot completely understand its meaning. Thus,

---

[7] Ervin, S. M. Changes with age in the verbal determinants of word-association. *Amer. J. Psychol.*, 1961, 74: 361–372.

the proper functioning of our syntactic skill is an essential ingredient in the process of understanding a sentence. Again I emphasize that the problem of meaning involves a great deal more than the matter of reference.

. . . .

I believe that sentences are not just arbitrary chains of vocal responses, but that they have a complex inner structure of their own. How we perceive them, understand them, and remember them depends upon what we decide about their structure. Just as we induce a three-dimensional space underlying the two-dimensional pattern on the retina, so we must induce a syntactic structure underlying the linear string of sounds in a sentence. And just as the student of space perception must have a good understanding of projective geometry, so a student of psycholinguistics must have a good understanding of grammar.

There is much more to grammar, however, than just the system of syntactic categories and constituent structure. Let me lapse once again into linguistics long enough to introduce the transformational rules of grammar . . . . Go back to the simple sentence *Bill hit the ball*. But now observe that there are a large number of other sentences that seem to be closely related to it: the negative, *Bill didn't hit the ball*; the passive, *The ball was hit by Bill*; various interrogative forms, *Did Bill hit the ball?*, *What did Bill hit?*, and so on.

Linguists disagree about the best way to describe these different kinds of relations among sentences. One opinion is that we learn "sentence frames" that we keep filed away in a sort of sentence-frame dictionary. The declarative, interrogative, affirmative, negative, active, passive, compound, complex, etc., sentence frames are all supposed to be learned separately and to have no intrinsic relation to one another. A second opinion agrees with the first in seeing no intrinsic relations among the various types of sentences, but argues that there are too many different frames to learn them all separately. The advocates of this second view say that there must be rules, . . . that the talker can use actively to manufacture a grammatical frame as it is needed. But, according to this view, there is one set of rules for manufacturing active, declarative, affirmative sentences, etc.

On the other side of the argument are linguists who wish to describe the relations among these sentences in terms of explicit rules of transformation. One version of this view, which I favor, says that we do indeed have a scheme for manufacturing simple, active, declarative sentences, but we can apply rules of transformation to change them from active to passive, or from declarative to interrogative, or from affirmative to negative, or to combine them, etc. This transformational scheme shortens the statement of a grammar considerably, since many rules need be stated only once and need not be repeated for each separate type of sentence. And once you have admitted such rules to your grammar you quickly discover many uses for them.

Transformational rules are both complicated and powerful, however, so many linguists are reluctant to use them. There has been some esthetic disagreement about which kind of simplicity is more desirable in a linguistic theory. Is it better to have a long list of short rules, or a short list of long rules?

The arguments among linguists—who seem to rely heavily on their linguistic intuitions on logical counter examples, and on appeals to the economy and elegance of simplicity—can get rather bitter at times. And it is by no means obvious a priori that the most economical and efficient formal description of the linguistic data will necessarily describe the psychological process involved when we actually utter or understand a grammatical sentence.

. . . .

My colleagues and I now see syntactic structure as an important variable to explore. The logicians and linguists are currently defining the theoretical issues with great precision, so that the full range of our experimental and psychometric methods can be brought to bear. I am enthusiastically convinced that such studies have an important contribution to make to the science of psychology.

In the course of this work I seem to have become a very old-fashioned kind of psychologist. I now believe that mind is something more than a four-letter, Anglo-Saxon word—human minds exist and it is our job as psychologists to study them. Moreover, I believe that one of the best ways to study a human mind is by studying the verbal systems that it uses. But what I want most to communicate here is my strong conviction that such a program is not only important, but that it is also possible, even now, with the relatively crude and limited empirical weapons that we have already developed. In the years ahead I hope we will see an increasing flow of new and exciting research as more psychologists discover the opportunities and the challenge of psycholinguistic theory and research.

Early psychological interpreters of transformational grammar had failed to appreciate the depth of its implications. Its power did not hinge on the fact that it merely extended the variety of sentences described in a grammar by converting simple "kernel" sentences into more complex form. Rather, transformational rules were necessary to account for the grammatical relations underlying most sentences because these relations cannot be depicted by the parsing of utterances.

A proof of this situation can be illustrated by ambiguous syntactic constructions. Chomsky originally studied such phenomena with sentence constructions involving the morpheme *-ing*.* Consider his example sentence *I don't approve of John's cooking* (or *drinking, driving*, etc.). This may be comprehended as disapproving of the way John cooks, or as disapproving of the fact that he cooks. The ambiguity is in the phrase *John's cooking*. This construction may be understood either as a modifier-plus-noun or as a subject-plus-predicate (*John cooks*) embedded into the verb phrase *approve of X*. The origin of the ambiguity stems from the fact that two superficially identical sentence constructions, that is, utterances, may be derived from two different underlying cognitive configurations. The two sentences are generated by two different paths in the grammar that in fact describe the two different ways in which the sentence may be understood. The goal of this type of analysis was, according to Chomsky, "to explain why sentences are what we intuitively know them to be; that is, to give a kind of rational reconstruction of this intuitive knowledge."

An early interpretation had been to view language as a set of kernel sentences—simple declaratives—from which all other

---

* Noam Chomsky, Logical structures in language. *American Documentation*, Vol. III, 1957, pp. 284–291. (Paper presented to the joint meeting of A.A.A.S. and A.D.I., New York, December, 1956.)

more complex sentences derived. But this misses what was actually implied. The "base" on which transformational rules operate is a cognitive structure, a system of propositional judgments. And the base is not depicted as a sequential structure, but rather as a complex, simultaneous configuration which is dominated, in the formal symbolism, by the symbol "S" designating a closed whole or sentence unit. This is the abstract level of language which Chomsky holds as universal for all human languages.

The Humboldtian notion concerning universal form had been corrupted during the nineteenth century (as Wundt pointed out, above) whenever one of the classical languages (usually Greek) was taken as the universal "pure" form and considered to be the abstraction underlying all other languages. Similarly, in recent times a misconception has arisen whenever a universal base of all languages is thought of as consisting of simple *sentences*, for example, simple (English-type) declaratives. But the universal base of human language lies in the human ability to make abstract judgments in analyzing cognitions. Each individual language then constitutes a different set of transformational rules for converting these cognitive structures into physical manifestations in sound. And there are apparently still strong restrictions on how this process may occur, which makes this skill a characteristic possession of *homo sapiens*.* A strong proposal that the human language skill largely rests upon an innate component obviously would have an impact on the study of language acquisition and on the study of the biological basis of language.

Two other notable modern interpreters of these views have been Brown and Eric Lenneberg. Similar to Miller, they were also close psychological observers of the development of transformational grammar. Brown came to Harvard in 1953 and immediately initiated a program to administer a joint degree in psychology and linguistics. The first person to complete a dissertation under this plan was Lenneberg, who subsequently became known for his studies of the biological bases of language. Brown had studied language primarily within the interests of

---

* For examples see J. H. Greenberg (Ed.) *Universals of language* (Cambridge: M.I.T. Press, 1963).

social psychology. But more recently he and his students have focused their attention on the problem of initial language acquisition. It is striking how a renewal of earlier ideas has emerged in this area just as it has for psycholinguitics in general. Ten years after the first psycholinguistic conference at Cornell, the Social Science Research Council once again sponsored a meeting of psychologists and linguists (at Dedham, Massachusetts, 1961). But this time its purpose was more restricted in examining the question of how children learn language. However, as it developed, the issues were much more basic than could have been imagined at the earlier conference, and it is interesting to examine the difference between the reports of the 1953 and the 1961 meetings.* At the later conferences, linguists did not present a united front but instead were caught in the midst of querulous disagreements about the basic nature of their field. The excitement that psychologists had expressed in 1953 at having found independent linguistic confirmation of their views was now transformed into a defensiveness against a threatened disconfirmation by linguists. And the age-old philosophical dispute between empiricism and rationalism had never been more alive. Brown and his research group were heavily involved in the 1961 meeting, and linguists and psycholinguists from M.I.T., including Chomsky, also participated.

Examples of the similarities between recent pronouncements about first language learning and those in the earlier, turn-of-the-century literature are obvious. For instance, David McNeill (1966) arrived at the following premise: "The process of acquisition . . . is one of invention. On the basis of a fundamental capacity for language, each generation creates language anew, and does so with astonishing speed."† McNeill based his conclusions on summaries of asquisition reports on Japanese, Russian, and American children. Brown and Bellugi (1964) concluded their report of a biographical study of infant language with the following statement:

---

* The 1961 conference report appeared in the *Society for research in child development, Monographs*, 1964 (U. Bellugi and R. Brown, Eds.).

† D. McNeill, The creation of language by children. In *Psycholinguistics papers*. J. Lyons and R. Wales (Eds.) (Chicago: Aldine, 1966), p. 99.

The very intricate simultaneous differentiation and integration that constitutes the evolution of the noun phrase is more reminiscent of the biological development of an embryo than it is of the acquisition of a conditioned reflex.*

Essentially that same analogy of embryonic development was either explicitly argued or implied by Wundt, Preyer, Meumann, Dewey, Stern, Guillaume, and others. Some of the early theorists were perhaps more nativistic, with their suggestions of innate ideas, than Brown and Bellugi would care to be. But recently nativism has also been reborn in proposals by Chomsky and, more recently, by the language philosopher Jerrold Katz (1966) who suggested that linguistic theory described the child's inborn capacity for language.†

The kind of empiricism that has dominated twentieth century psychology has been heavily under the influence of the *phylogenetic* model of Darwin's evolutionary biology. Some behaviorists have made analogies between the history of the *individual* and that of the *species*. Such views yield explanations of development based on selective adaptational adjustment. Osgood expressed this well in his *Method and theory of experimental psychology* in 1953:

Both receptive and motivational processes bear the stamp of Darwinian principles. Selective modifications of this order result from experiences of the *species*: prolific multiplication of kind, accompanied by mutational variation in structure, and the endless competitive struggle for survival eventuate in selection according to adaptive capacity. . . . In repeated situations of similar character, the individual organism varies and multiplies its behaviors, selection among competing responses depending upon their adaptiveness.‡

In contrast to this analogy, late nineteenth-century psychologists gave at least as much attention to the *ontogenetic* biolog-

---

* R. Brown and U. Bellugi, Three processes in child's acquisition of syntax. In E. Lenneberg, *New directions in the study of language* (Cambridge: M.I.T. Press, 1964), p. 161.

† J. Katz, *The philosophy of language* (New York: Harper & Row, 1966).

‡ C. Osgood, *Method and theory in experimental psychology* (New York: Oxford University Press, 1953), p. 299.

ical model, or to the development of the individual through the predetermined elaborative growth of the embryonic cell. Then there was more consideration given to innate mechanisms. But nothing was inherent in these biological models that made one more appropriate to psychology than the other. It might be argued that the development of an individual biological cell into a complex organism is a closer analogy, in a physical sense, to the development of an individual's behavior, than is the analogy of the *phylogenetic* history of a species. This was precisely Wundt's argument—he adapted this approach to the study of development and gave it the title of "genetic psychology." Preferences for a *phylogenetic* model, however, were more characteristic of the Zeitgeist in American psychology.

Wundtian genetic psychology was represented in America to a certain degree by Heinz Werner who emmigrated from Germany during the 1930s. However, his influence went little beyond his students at Clark University, and the link with the "classical" European tradition remained isolated and largely ignored by the mainstream of the American psychological community.*

There were still other reasons that supported a modern nativist view of language acquisition. First, there was the observation that language appeared quite universally in healthy infants at nearly the same age, and expanded and progressed through the same stages regardless of language or culture. Not only was it impossible to teach a child to speak before a certain age, but to some investigators it appeared that it would even be difficult to suppress the emergence of language after a certain age. And the recent disclosures of the structural complexity of language raised the question of just how a child could possibly learn such a thing at all. Another related discovery was that certain unique language disorders were inherited sex-linked traits where in

---

* See H. Werner, *The comparative psychology of mental development* (Chicago: Follet, 1948); also H. Werner and B. Kaplan, *Symbol formation: an organismic-developmental approach to language and the expression of thought* (New York: John Wiley, 1963). The latter work is a good source for other topics in the earlier European literature concerned with psychology of language, which have not been mentioned in the present volume.

such cases intelligence or other cognitive functions were not affected. Lenneberg summarized this evidence in his *Biological foundations of language* (1967).

For the final illustrative selection to appear in this book we turn to Eric Lenneberg. His text on biological foundations encompasses a huge range of topics. However, the section on normal language acquisition furnishes another good example of the modern trend in psycholinguistics and its relevance to past ideas. The one-word sentence, the progressive stages of infant language, and the ontogenetic creative abilities of children, and other notions are described with modern data. All these ideas, as Lenneberg discusses them, are mostly based on recent observations, yet they clearly restate early *Sprachpsychologie* descriptions.

ERIC HEINZ LENNEBERG · *Language Acquisition*

The first feature of natural language to be discernible in a child's babbling is contour of intonation. Short sound sequences are produced that may have neither any determinable meaning nor definable phoneme structure, but they can be proffered with recognizable intonation such as occurs in questions, exclamations, or affirmations. The linguistic development of utterance does not seem to begin by a composition of individual, independently movable items but as a whole tonal pattern. With further development, this whole becomes differentiated into component parts; primitive phonemes appear which consist of very large classes of sounds that contrast with each other. . . .

1. *Primitive One-Word Utterances*

Between the twelfth and eighteenth months the toddler is heard to utter unmistakable single words. There is evidence that at first these words serve quite a different function from that of mature

SOURCE. Eric H. Lenneberg, *Biological foundations of language* (New York: John Wiley & Sons, 1967), excerpts from Chapter Seven, "Primitive stages in language development."

speech. The difference is on all levels: phonological, syntactic, and semantic. The acoustic shape is merely a crude replica of the adult word, and it is only by means of our capacity to see pattern similarities that we can recognize the child's word. This is common enough knowledge. But perhaps it has not been stressed sufficiently that it is not merely the adult who must be able to equate the child's utterance to an English word; the child must have similar skills in pattern recognition and equation. For almost a whole year children are satisfied with general pattern similarity and dispense, so to speak, with segment by segment phonetic identity. Surely this has to do with their initial clumsiness and thus with maturational factors.

If this were not so, we might expect that many children would choose a different strategy toward language acquisition, namely, first to perfect their phonetic skills and only when they can reproduce a word with phonetic perfection, go on with syntax and semantics. This is what parrots do, and in fact, it is the usual strategy of teachers who want to train nonspeaking children (the retarded or the deaf) or animals to speak. It is also the strategy that most adults adopt in learning or teaching a second language. Therefore, the infant's initial lack of concern for phonetic accuracy is by no means a trivial or logically necessary phenomenon. It points to a fundamental principle in language acquisition: what is acquired are patterns and structure, not constituent elements.

There are also dramatic deviations in the realm of semantics during the first stage of single words. This is true of reference as well as of meaning. At the beginning, a word such as *daddy* covers a different and wider range of objects than later. There is overgeneralization. However, at no time does the multitude of reference relationships and the multilevel overlap of synonymy, homonymy, metonymy or the names of particulars as against the names of generalities, of aspects, qualities or objects to which the language-learning child is exposed from the beginning cause a chaotic use of words. The reference classes of objects in the beginner's language are merely less differentiated than in adult language, but from the start there is something which we might call an "understandable logic" to the word-object relationship. It is as if the child did *in principle* the same as adults do, only on a more general level.

It has already been pointed out that meaning is intimately related to syntax, because the meaning of the sentence is never equivalent to an unordered summation of the reference of words contained in the sentence.

A short elaboration on a certain aspect of the grammatical structure of adult utterances is necessary here. Is it correct to say that the unit of discourse is the *sentence*? Two objections are often raised in this connection. First, in adult speech we frequently hear single words uttered; in what respect are these sentences? Second, the transcripts of conversations always show drastic infringements upon grammar; can we call these distortions "sentences?"

Take the first point. Someone may hold out an opened pack of cigarettes and ask, "*Smoke?*" or a person may answer the question "Do you smoke?" by means of the one-word utterance "*Yes!*" or the question "Which one of these boys was seen to smoke?" by "*Johnnie!*" and so on. Countless other examples are possible. In every instance, we are clearly dealing with ellipsis. The single word utterances are only interpretable by virtue of the listener's ability to supplement the omitted parts of the sentence. The first instance is interpreted as the sentence, "Do you smoke?", the second as "I smoke" (or, "I do smoke"; hence "Yes, I do smoke"); and the third as "Johnnie has been seen to smoke." There may, in some instances, be ambiguity because not enough context is given to enable the listener to place the single word into the intended sentence. But generally it is correct to say that the meaning of words is uninterpretable in social commerce, unless we have enough clues with which to construct a sentence for that word.

The second point is factually correct: utterances heard in colloquial English (or any language, for that matter) do not conform to what we know to be correct grammar. We must make here a distinction. There are indeed utterances that are totally "ungrammatical," but they are also uninterpretable—we do not know what the speaker was trying to say. On the other hand, much more often we do know what the speaker wanted to say even though his utterances are clearly ungrammatical. This may be because he omitted part of the sentence or because a sentence is begun as if it were to end in one way but is actually concluded by using the second half of a different type of construction. (Several variations of this are possible.) Our capacity to understand such semi-sentences can only be due to a facility to supplement the omitted part of incomplete sentences. Thus, the interpretation of semisentences is not simpler than the understanding of grammatical sentences but actually requires a special ability: to supplement the missing parts of a partially concealed pattern (analogous to pattern-completion in visual perception). If a sentence is remodeled under certain circumstances [Osgood (1957)[1] cites the example, "Garlic I taste!"], this is not necessarily a sign that syntax may be abandoned at will but rather of the existence of possible rules of correspondence that do not ordinarily enter into the writing of normative grammars. The rule of correspondence in this case relates the form of the "Garlic" sentence to the form of such sentences as "I taste garlic!" The example cited is not necessarily an instance of agrammatism but merely that of an admissible rule. That the types of such rules are limited (or that the rules have a psychological reality) is seen in the fact that the words in this sentence cannot be permuted in *all* possible ways.

In the light of this discussion, how do we explain the onset of language development where it is a universal finding that children begin with one-word utterances? Does this mean that the observations on adult language are false? or that they are irrelevant? I do not believe that either is the case. To the contrary, if we assume that the child's first single word utterances are, in fact, very primitive, undifferentiated forms of sentences, and that these utterances actually incorporate the germs of grammar, a number of phenomena may be explained.

There is a period at which an infant may have a repertoire of up to 50 words including such items as *daddy, here, milk, up, baby,* etc. He will utter any one of these words in isolation and they may mean: Daddy, come here; Daddy went by-by; I want to be picked up; thanks, no milk; more milk, please; etc. But even though the child's memory is sufficient to know all of the 50 words, and even though he hears such phrases as *here is your milk, shall daddy take you by-by,* etc., he will neither join together any two words he knows nor can he be induced to do so upon request. This cannot be explained by assuming that he makes himself better understood this way, or that the reference of the words (that is, the association with the object) is still too narrow and fixed; or that he has no need for putting words

[1] C. Osgood, Motivational dynamics of language behavior. In *Nebraska symposium on motivation*, M. Jones (Ed.) (Lincoln, Nebraska: Univ. of Nebraska Press, 1957).

together; or that he cannot vocalize for that long a period of time; or that this is due to poorly developed general memory. All of these assumptions are refutable by observations. Nor would any of these assumptions make it clear why the child suddenly and spontaneously *does* begin to join words into two-element phrases.

The assumption that the early single word utterances are primitive syntactic units—in a sense primitive sentences—finds support in the following considerations. Semantically, and in terms of communication, the single words seem to function in the same way that sentences come to function later on: they cover a complete proposition; for instance, they may stand for a statement such as, *Daddy is coming down the street*. Phonologically they may be operated upon by a given rule, much the way a whole string of symbols is operated upon later on; for example, one of a variety of intonation patterns influences the utterance—such as declarative, interrogative, or hortative pitch-contours. It is reasonable to assume that the formal processes that regulate the perception and production of sounds are essentially the same as those that enter into syntax and that the one-word stage is simply a transitional stage during which the rules are extended from the interaction of articulatory movements to the interaction of larger language units, namely morphemes and words, and that the eventual acquisition and mastery of grammar has its origin right at the beginning of language development; otherwise we would have to assume that some day the child "discovers" grammar and makes an effort to learn this phenomenon, which seems farfetched.

2. Theoretical Considerations

Understanding-Speaking. It is easier to construct a theory that explains why adults understand sentences the way they do, than a theory that explains why or how a given sequence of words is produced by a specific person at a specific time. This is not to say that understanding language is based on a separate mechanism from producing language. Both are based on the same apparatus of principles. But if we test an individual's understanding of sentences, we are more exclusively exploring this apparatus than when we survey the utterances that he produces. In order to say something at a certain occasion it takes more than a knowledge of the language. There must be certain motor capacities, memory, motivation, a specific train of thoughts, given social conditions and other factors.

It is easier to study general capacities for behavior than the specific forms that behavior will take at any one time, and it is easier to predict the capacity for understanding than the capacity for speaking, because there are fewer factors affecting the former than the latter. A similar point, but with further refinement, is made by Chomsky . . . under the headings of *competence* and *performance*.

The distinction made here is relevant to many types of behavioral studies. Suppose we wanted to make a psychobiological study of chess playing. For instance, we wanted to know, "What are the mental characteristics necessary for this game?" or, "Can a chimpanzee learn to play it?" The empirical questions that would be asked in this research are: can a given subject learn the various moves? Can he develop a strategy? Does he see the implications of his adversary's moves? and so on. We would want to know whether he can comprehend the game. If we had nothing but a catalogue of his moves without a report of what his opponent was doing (that is, how he understood his opponent's game), we should have an imperfect idea of his competence as a chess player.

That the understanding of language is more relevant to an estimation of language capacities may also be seen from the following: we can learn to understand a language without ability to speak it. This is true of primary language acquisition, as well as the acquisition of a second language. In these cases, the underlying principles of the language are acquired, but the development of the skills for production are lagging.

There is an interesting situation here which would be a paradox unless we were willing to make assumptions on the nature of the learner: as investigators of the nature of language, it is preferable to concentrate on understanding; the objects that are to be understood are sentences; the sentences that are actually heard are frequently "degraded specimens" from a grammatical point of view—they are semisentences at best; on the other hand, the understanding of semisentences is apparently more difficult than proper sentences. We first seem to learn the rules and principles underlying grammatically correct sentences, and only by virtue of having acquired these can we begin to understand semisentences. (This becomes particularly evident in the acquisition of a second language by an adult person; we understand correct sentences, for instance, uttered by a good lecturer or presented in print, long before we can understand a conversation which is heavily loaded with semisentences.) The paradox is this: if the child's task is to abstract principles that generate correct sentences, but is presented indiscriminately with semi- and proper-sentences, how can the correct principles be established, and why or how does his understanding of sentences become fairly explainable in terms of a grammatical theory? The assumption that we have to be willing to make here concerns the cognitive meachinery that we must suppose to be developing in the child. . . .

3. *Structural Characteristics of Children's Primitive Sentences*

In the absence of systematic research on children's understanding of adult sentences, and hence of their developing "analytic equipment" for syntax, we can only make educated guesses at how grammar actually develops. The study of adult syntax makes it clear that discourse could not be understood, and that no interpretable utterances could be produced, without syntactic development *pari passu* with lexical and phonological development. Syntax is the calculus, so to speak, of functional categories, and the categories are arranged hierarchically from the all-inclusive to the particular.

The child whose language consists of nothing but single word utterances has obviously a more primitive syntactic understructure than the mature speaker. Syntactic categorization is the speaker's act of superimposing structure; he assigns given lexical items to parts of speech. The child's syntax is primitive because all of his words have the same syntactic function: they may be used as a self-sufficient utterance. There is just one undifferentiated syntactic category, and any word heard or produced is assigned to it. If we wish to introduce Chomskian notation already at this primitive stage, we might use the equation or *rewriting instruction* as he calls it,

$$S \rightarrow W$$

which reads, in this grammar, a sentence S is formed by the use of any word that belongs to the class W, and all of the child's words do belong to it.

Notice that it would make no sense to ask whether the child, at this stage, knows more adjectives than nouns or whether he has any verbs. Strictly speaking, *adjectives, nouns, verbs* are modes of functioning, given a complex syntax. But since the syntactic conditions for such functioning are not yet present, we cannot ask whether the infant has verbs. We do not ask whether a fertilized human egg thinks or what the social order among chicks is before they have hatched.

The joining of two words in a single utterance is a sign that the initial global category, labeled W, is splitting up into two functionally distinct categories. The following examples, collected from Braine (1963), Brown and Fraser (1963), Brown and Bellugi (1964), and Ervin (1964),[2] show that the two words are not random concatenations but that a functional distinction is emerging.

"find it"	"here sock"	"more milk"
"fix it"	"here allgone"	"more nut"
"drink it"	"here is"	"more up"
etc.	etc.	etc.

A paradigm is clearly being formed.

One of the two words has a higher frequency of occurence and seems to be a grammatical functor, whereas the other word appears to come from a large pool of lexical items with a great variety of meanings. Braine (1963) has called the functor words the *pivot* of these two-word sentences. The entire utterance seems to "turn around them."

It is not always easy to recognize the pivot of the two-word utterances, and we cannot always be sure how to characterize the sentences formally. For instance, "mommy sandwich," "baby highchair," "throw daddy," "pick glove" are all quite typical productions. At present, there are no reliable procedures to demonstrate that the two elements of these sentences belong to two different syntactic categories, although such an assumption is not unreasonable. We may have the primitive subject-predicate distinction.

The structure of these second-stage sentences might be characterized formally by diagrams such as these:

---

[2] M. Braine, The ontogeny of English phrase structure: the first phase. *Language*, 1963, 39: 1–13; R. Brown and U. Bellugi, Three processes in the child's acquisition of syntax. In E. Lenneberg (Ed.), *New directions in the study of language* (Cambridge: M.I.T. Press, 1964); R. Brown and C. Fraser, The acquisition of syntax. In *Verbal behavior and learning*. C. Cofer and B. Musgrave (Eds.) (New York: McGraw-Hill, 1963); S. Ervin, Imitation and structural change in children's language. In E. Lenneberg, *New directions in the study of language* (Cambridge: M. I. T. Press, 1964).

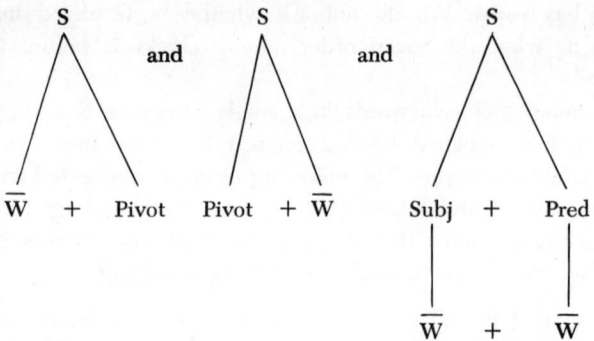

By the time he uses three-word sentences, further differentiations of categories have taken place. We now find utterances such as these:

"fix a Lassie"   "my horsie stuck"
"here two sock"   "poor Kitty there"
"More nice milk"   "that little one"

At this stage, many types of utterances are heard, and it becomes increasingly difficult to describe the child's syntactic skills by an exhaustive catalogue of phrase-markers. Instead we endeavor to discover the principles by which these structures are recognized and produced.

The last examples cited illustrate, however, the progressive differentiation of syntactic categories. The structure of these sentences may be characterized by postulating a splitting of the earlier category W into two, namely a modifier m and a noun N. A tree diagram might look like the following:

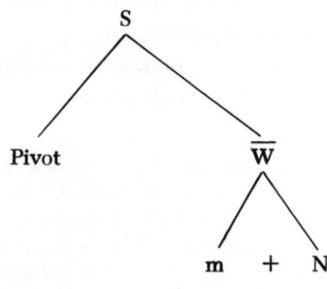

The process of differentiation, seen during ontogeny, becomes a process of specification or elaboration in the mature speaker. The string

> That man thinks.

is a complete and mature sentence. We can specify or elaborate on the main elements of this sentence, a process which is formally similar to the differentiation process of categories during ontogeny. We may elaborate on *man* by saying

> That old man thinks.

This expansion comes about by "applying an elaboration principle." We may apply this principle as often as we wish. For instance, we may say

> That old old man thinks.

The repetitive application of the identical principle is called *recursiveness*. Obviously, the sentence may be expanded in many ways not only by reapplying the same principle just introduced, but also by applying other, similar but not identical principles of elaboration or specification. Thus we may produce a sentence.

> That old, old, hoary man who is well known by all who were folk-music lovers as far back as the early twenties thinks he is the great Italian opera singer Caruso.

In this sentence, elements were being differentiated progressively and/or repeatedly. As a consequence of these differentiations, the elements *man* and *thinks* have become physically separated although they continued to be related or dependent upon one another, and the same is true of other elements interposed between these two words, for instance, the words *known* and *lovers*. This phenomenon of splitting up elements by introducing other elements, which in turn may be split up, is called *nested dependencies*. Both recursiveness and nested dependencies are simply consequences of differentiation or specification.

. . . .

We are discovering a basic process that is reflected in language as well as in many other aspects of behavior. It consists of first grasping a whole that is subsequently further differentiated, each of the specifics arriving at a different time and being subordinated to the whole by a process of temporal integration. In productive behavior a plan for the whole is differentiated into components, and the temporal integration results in ordering of movements (or thoughts). Organization of phrase structure with the resulting phenomenon of recursiveness and nested dependencies appears as a "natural phenomenon" once we assume that a ubiquitous process is influencing a specific behavior.

CHAPTER 6

RETROSPECT

In the history of psychology the study of psycholinguistics should be regarded as an early established enterprise, not a recent development. It is true that interest in it has fluctuated, but as times change, ideas come and go and then reappear. Some problems continue unsolved, and for other problems new solutions are found. This history might not unfairly be described as a continual struggle of ideologies—rationalism against empiricism, holism against atomism, and so forth, or even as nationalist controversies—for example, German thought vs. English thought. Such ideological controversies have too often obscured the immediate problems at hand. But at other times, they have lead to great advances in thought.

We have reviewed some major trends in what has been called "psycholinguistics," or "Sprachpsychologie" from Leipzig, Prague, Vienna, and Paris to Indiana, Harvard, and M.I.T. This is by no means a complete survey—the topic of "language and psychology" is too formidable for that. We have scarcely touched on the early work concerning the sound patterns of language, or the study of semantics, or the study on language pathologies. But we have examined some very fundamental issues.

We are now almost forced to reconsider Wundt—the amazingly prolific scholar whose crowning achievement was his work in psycholinguistics, a work that was a continuation of a consistent and systematic psychology. It was his psychological system that was the basis for many of the above selections. Wundtian psychology may be characterized as a development of the "constructivist" view of cognition and perception. His psycholinguistics was configurational, not atomistic. For all the recognition he is accorded today as the founder of experimental psychology, he is one of the least understood and least accurately reported of the early psychologists.*

---

* An accurate and comprehensive review of Wundt's work is non-existent

When we consider the historical events, there can be little reason to wonder at the schism in psychology between the schools. The break stems from at least three major situations: the antagonism between James and Wundt; the dominance of the empiricist-positivist tradition in the English-speaking world; and Titchener's influence in America.

First, the styles of James and Wundt were incompatible. James preferred poetic description and abhorred formal analysis. Wundt was a formalist. The contrasting quotations from Wundt and James in the above selection from Huey (Chapter 4) illustrate this well. The split between Wundt and James came at the midpoint of both men's careers (about 1890). Originally James had sent students to Wundt and had proclaimed the gospel of Germany's "new psychology" to America. But then the clash of temperaments occurred. After reading James' *Principles of psychology* (1890) Wundt had said, "It is literature, it is beautiful, but it is not psychology." When in 1894 Judd, then an American student in Leipzig, inquired about the possibility of translating James' works into German, he was told that James was considered a second-rate philosopher and would not be studied there. A reciprocal reaction against Wundt set in at Harvard. James indulged in sarcastic remarks about patient laboratory work "in a land where they do not know what it means to be bored." At that point "diplomatic relations" between the Harvard and the Leipzig groups were promptly suspended. After the turn of the century, American psychologists with few exceptions followed James, instead of Wundt.

It is true that Wundt never oversimplified. His work is com-

---

in English. Shortly after his death some assessments by those who were closest to him appeared in Germany, but they are not cited in American texts. In citing books about Wundt, E. G. Boring in his *History of experimental psychology* refers only to three that were published around the turn of the century when Wundt was still in the midst of his career. There were several others that came later. See especially P. Peterson, *Wilhelm Wundt und seine Zeit* (Stuttgart: Frommanns, 1925); also Arthur Hoffman (Ed.) *Wilhelm Wundt, Eine Würdigung* (Erfurt: Stenger, 1924), also published separately as sections 3 and 4, Vol. II, of *Beiträge zur Philosophie des Deutschen Idealismus*. This latter work includes papers by those Wundt chose to succeed him at the Psychological Institute in Leipzig.

plex. In contrast, the early American movements in psychology seemed to flourish because they had reduced psychology to a few simple formulas whose comprehension required no serious mental effort. In reviewing the turn-of-the-century psychology J. J. Sullivan described it this way: "This period in the history of psychology, which focused exclusively on the analysis of consciousness, has been the despair of students, with the result that the simple clarities and easy confirmations of the Behaviorist doctrines have been studied with relief."*

The German-American schism came at the point in Wundt's career when his physiological psychology period was drawing to a close and the social psychology and philosophy period began. He moved away from the positivism and Darwinian biology that had influenced him when working under Helmholtz at Heidelberg. However, in most modern American textbook accounts only the early physiological period is described—the period that preceded the break with James and the development of an independent American psychology.

Second, a situation related to the above events was the dominance of empiricist and pragmatist philosophies in England and America, forming an ingrained cultural tradition. It perhaps led Esper in his *History of psychology* (1965) to state that Wundtian psychology was "an interruption in the development of the natural science of man." Wundt did hold *natural science* apart from psychology, because in psychology we have the unique situation of intelligence studying itself. Indeed, Wundt lamented the rise of positivism and the narrow academic specialization that it bred. He feared this would lead academic scholarship into a "dark age." He repeatedly and dramatically emphasized that psychology must not be separated from philosophy.†

---

* J. J. Sullivan, in B. Wolman (Ed.) *Historical roots of contemporary psychology* (New York: Harper & Row, 1968), p. 255.

† See W. Wundt, *Die Psychologie im Kampf ums Dasein* (Leipzig: Englemann, 1913). Wundt's views on positivism, academic specialization, and related matters reflected what were very broad movements of opinion in the German academic community around the turn of the century. This topic has been thoroughly documented recently by Fritz Ringer in his *The decline of the German mandarins: the German academic community, 1890–1933* (Cambridge, Mass.: Harvard University Press, 1969).

Third, the Englishman Titchener's influence in America was partly responsible for misinterpretations of Wundt (see Chapter 2). His influence carried into the present through his student's (E. G. Boring's) *History of experimental psychology* (1950), which has been the predominant account. For example, Boring described Wundt as a sensationist and associationist in the English tradition; and concerning apperception, Boring asserted "that Wundt attached rather less importance to it" (p. 338). He further described Wundt's psychology as diffuse and resisting summarization. On the contrary, Wundt was a supreme systematizer who wished to join all the branches to a common trunk. If his psychology is to be faulted, it should be for its overzealous parsimony, not diffuseness. Wundt's works on logic, philosophy, and anthropology were consistent extensions of his psychological (apperception) system. And for this reason, reading Wundt is not as difficult as Boring claims. But if one omits the center of Wundt's system, namely apperception processes, then indeed it would be diffuse and difficult to describe.

There are a number of other situations having an indirect effect on the reception of Wundt that are difficult to classify—his vocal opposition to British and American politics, which had apparently embarrassed his English-speaking students.* But perhaps the strongest factor was the unfortunate and confused issue of mind-body dualism. Contrary to popular description, Wundt expressly opposed the type of dualism that has been ascribed to him lately (see Chapter 2). Wundt's fundamental *method* had always been logic, not experiment. He arrived at the notion of experimentation only by way of logic, and then on the basis of logical argument, restricted its use. Logic had always led the way. Boring agrees on this point.

These, then, are some situations that contributed to the decline of Wundt's psychology in the West. The result today is that contradiction abounds in the folklore about Wundt that has grown up during the course of the twentieth century.

Wundt's earliest American student, Hall, was in Leipzig when the first experimental laboratory was organized. Later in 1912,

* See Memories of Wundt by his former students. *Psychological Review,* 1921, **28**: 153–188.

Hall had thoroughly alienated Wundt by misrepresenting Wundt's psychology in a volume titled *Founders of modern psychology*. Their earlier disagreement centered on Wundt's lack of interest in certain schools of psychiatry. Yet in 1912 Hall could still make the following prophetic statement about his old professor:

But if Wundt is to suffer eclipse or fall away from the fovea to the indirect field or even to the blind spot of attention, it can surely be but for a time, and when his successors shall have reached certainty and agreement on the main questions he experimented on, and when they shall have seen a little more clearly what can and what cannot be done in the laboratory, then Wundt will "come back" . . . .*

A later student of Wundt's, Judd (Ph.D., Leipzig, 1896), had the unusual opportunity of working with Wundt in Leipzig on an English translation of one of Wundt's texts. This gave Judd the advantage of close contact and frequent meetings with Wundt. In his own autobiography in 1932, Judd sums up his survey of Wundt's work.

Wundt's two volumes of *Die Sprache* (Language) will, I believe, come to be thought of as his most important single contribution to psychology.†

We must stop here because this volume concerns only psycholinguistics, an area within the broader scope of cognitive psychology. In that broader field, the decade before and after the publication of Wundt's *Die Sprache* was a momentous period. The many other volumes on psycholinguistics that soon appeared all revolved around Wundt, including such arguments as those that involved Wundt with Paul, Marty, Delbrück, and Bühler (to mention only the more prominent ones). After the First World War there was another brief surge of European interest

---

* G. S. Hall *Founders of modern psychology* (New York: Appleton, 1912) p. 421.

† In C. Murchison (Ed.), *A history of psychology in autobiography* (Worcester, Mass.: Clark University Press, 1932) vol. 2, p. 219. Many of Wundt's students followed him in his work in language. In 1909, former students presented him with a two-volume *"Festschrift"* commemorating his seventieth birthday. About one-third of the articles in these volumes concerned language.

in the psychology of language with Bühler as the commanding figure.

We might now ask, what is the historical relevance of the new American psycholinguistics as a discipline today, assuming it to be heavily under the influence of the developments in generative grammar. It is, in fact, in an analogous position to that of Wundt and his followers who in the 1880s opposed the *Junggrammatiker* (or narrow empiricist) tradition in linguistics because of its strict limitation of linguistics study to descriptions of utterances. The *Junggrammatikers* had studied only the physical shape of inventories. Wundt then revived the Humboldtian notions about language, essentially the same notions that were recently revitalized in overcoming the limitations of American behaviorist linguistics. Chomsky pointed out, as did Wundt, that "language has an inner and an outer aspect. A sentence can be studied from the point of view of how it expresses a thought or from the point of view of its physical shape."

The real successes of both the comparative linguistics in the nineteenth century and of the behaviorist linguistics in the twentieth century were concerned with methodology, procedures, and techniques. Those times in both centuries were perhaps paralleled by similar movements within psychology in general. The Wundtians, no less than some recent psychologists, discovered that positivistic psychology was in need of explanatory theory, of a more sophisticated cognitive psychology, a psychology of attention and judgment and short-term memory. In Wundt's view, one reason for this was the apparent necessity of a consistent distinction between cognition and expression—a prerequisite for an adequate explanation of human language. One must understand the nature of attention and its specific cognitive functions (once called "apperception") if one is to explain such language performances as speaking, describing, reading, or comprehending. Those skills include the ability to receive and store language utterances and at the same time to make anticipatory decisions about sentence structure in order to interpret the utterances. Many present techniques of experimental psychology may not be appropriate to some important problems that those skills entail. Today a number of leading experimental psychologists are still directly concerned with the nature of the mental representation that underlies the sentence. This too was also a central theme in Wundt's time and has not advanced significantly since then. Formalizations in recent linguistic work has forced us to return to the problem.

There are yet further signs that Wundt's views have been revived. In 1966, the psychologist J. J. Jenkins brought the role of experimentation in psycholinguistics into serious question in arguing that only language *performance* and not *competence* can be studied experimentally.* In 1969, psychologist James Deese radically revised his thinking and rejected experimental techniques for all aspects of cognitive psychology.† Deese's appeal seemed to imply a reunion of psychology with philosophy. He thus described the value awaiting psychologists in a reexamination of the Kantian tradition in philosophy. Moreover, Deese's proposals were thoroughly Wundtian in their reasoning. Both Deese and Jenkins had been leaders in the neo-behaviorist movement within the experimental psychology of mid-twentieth-century America, especially as it concerned the study of verbal behavior. Their changes in course were the direct result of the impact of developments in theoretical linguistics.

Much modern work in the psychology of language may then truly be viewed as related to the earlier *Sprachpsychologie*. However, today there are both richer logical and procedural tools for elaborating the ideas of Wundt and his commentators. Yet no matter how we approach language it remains the intellectual living space of those who use it. It is a fascinating object of study. What could be more enticing to the inquisitive student of human skills than this phenomenon of human language?

---

* J. J. Jenkins, The role of experimentation in psycholinguistics. Invited address, American Psychological Association meeting (New York, September, 1966).

† J. Deese, Behavior and fact. *American Psychologist,* 1969, **24**: 515–522.

INDEX

Pages of selections are shown in boldface type.

Ajdukiewicz, K., 216
Allport, F. H., 131–132, **133–140,** 141, 176
Ament, W., 83, 93–94, 99, 102
Anderson, I., 167–168
Aquinas, T., 41
Aristotle, 41

Baldwin, J. M., 64, 131
Bar-Hillel, Y., 215–217
Beach, F. A., 182
Bellugi, U., 223–224, 233
Bever, T. G., 54, 142
Binet, A., 49, 53, 79–80, 113, 116, 108–110
Blanton, M. & S., 111, 133
Bloch, O., 114, 128
Bloomfield, L., 8, 40, 168, 170, 173, 193–194, 197, 206
Blumenthal, A. L., 54
Bolinger, D. L., 201
Bolzano, B., 63
Book, W. F., 168
Bopp, F., 3
Boring, E. G., 85, 189, 238, 240
Braine, M., 233
Brentano, F., 5, 41, 44, 84, 116
Brett, G. S., 41
Broens, O., 43
Brown, R., 67, 169–170, 174–175, 198–199, 222–224, 233
Brunot, F., 75–76, 114
Buckman, S. S., 107, 110, 111
Bugental, J., 63
Bühler, K., 41, 46, 49–57, **58–63,** 64, 71, 78, 178, 179, 241–242
Buswell, G. T., 160, **161–166**

Carmichael, L., 115, 127
Carroll, J., 146
Cattell, J. M., 65, 145, 157

Chamberlain, A. F., 102, 183
Chomsky, N., 8, 170, 194–199, **200–209,** 210, 214, 221–224, 231–232, 242
Cofer, C., 233
Cohen, M., 114–115, 128
Condon, E. V., 48

Dale, E., 141
Darwin, C., 3, 10, 58, 81, 100, 224, 239
Dearborn, W. F., 157–159, 168
Decroly, O., 114
Dedekind, R., 63
Deese, J., 68, 243
Delacroix, H., 64, 113–114
De Laguna, G., 64, 71
Delbrück, B., 39–40, 46, 58, 60–61, 67, 72, 173, 241
Dempe, H., 63
de Saussure, F., 6–8, 78, 202, 205–206
Descartes, R., 14, 78
Deville, G., 94
Dewey, J., 65, 114, 127–129, 158, 224
Diack, H., 169
Dittrich, O., 22–23, 47, 61, 92
Dodge, R., 145, 157–158

Ebbinghaus, H., 54, 68, 83–84
Egger, E., 81
Epstein, I., 189
Erdmann, B., 145, 147
Ervin, S., 218, 233
Esper, E. A., 40, 43, 67, 69–70, 78, 173, 239
Estoup, J. B., 175

Fechner, G., 6
Feldman, H., 81
Feyeux, J., 142
Fichte, J. G., 13
Fodor, J. A., 181, 200
Forchhammer, E., 112
Fournié, E., 184

245

NAME INDEX

Franke, C., 100
Fraser, C., 233
Freud, S., 104, 191

Gabelentz, G. von der, 34
Gaifman, C., 217
Galanter, E., 178, 210
Galton, F., 65
Gardiner, A. H., 64, 78
Garvin, P. L., 57, 78
Geiger, L., 65
Gheorgov, I., 79, 93–94
Ginneken, J. van, 48
Godel, R., 205
Goldscheider, A., 147–148, 151
Goodman, N., 194
Gray, C. T., 161, 166
Greenberg, J. H., 222
Gregoire, A., 114, 141–142
Grimm, J., 2, 4–5
Guillaume, P., 115–116, **117–127**, 128, 141, 224
Guthrie, E. R., 136
Gvozdev, A. N., 141–142

Hale, H., 102, 109, 111
Hall, G. S., 79, 82, 104–105, 127, 146, 240–241
Halle, M., 170, 200
Harris, Z., 193, 200, 213
Hartmann, G., 169
Helmholtz, H., 9, 239
Henri, V., 53
Herbart, J., 6, 12, 19, 32, 39, 61, 72, 80
Herodotus, 100
Heyse, L. & K., 61
Hoffman, A., 238
Hollingsworth, L. S., 137
Holt, E. B., 65, 131, 180
Honig, W. K., 196
Huey, E. B., 144, 146, **147–156**
Hull, C. & B., 129–130
Humboldt, W. von, 4, 8, 10, 30–31, 42, 47, 85, 194, 204–206, 222, 242
Hume, D., 4
Humphrey, G., 49

Idelberger, H., 93–94

Jakobson, R., 48, 82, 142, 200

James, W., 12–13, 46, 64, 147, 155, 178, 238, 239
Javal, E., 145, 147
Jenkins, J. J., 243
Jespersen, O., 73, 103–104
Judd, C. H., 157–159, 238, 241

Kaeding, F. W., 175
Kainz, F., 9, 63, 173
Kant, I., 4, 12–13, 243
Kantor, J. R., 70–71, **72–78**, 168, 172–173, 176
Kaplan, B., 55, 225
Katz, J. J., 198, 200, 202, 224
Kessen, W., 105
Koffka, K., 50, 169
Köhler, W., 50, 115, 169
Kolers, P., 146
Krueger, F., 50
Külpe, O., 49

Lalande, A., 117
Lambek, J., 216
Langer, S., 64, 80
Lashley, K., 181–182, **183–193**, 194
Lazarus, M., 7, 81, 83, 87
Learned, W. B., 67
Leibniz, G. W., 4, 207
Lenneberg, E., 222, 224, **226–236**
Leopold, W. F., 80, 141
Leskien, A., 9
Lewis, M. M., 142
Lindgren, N., 175
Lindner, G., 93–94, 99
Locke, J., 4, 12
Logeman, W. S., 33
Lukens, H., 127, 129

McCarthy, D., 115, 127
McGranahan, D. V., 173
McNeill, D., 223–224
Major, D. R., 94, 97–98, 107, 109, 112
Mandelbrot, B., 176
Mandler, G., 49, 69
Mandler, J. M., 49
Marbe, K., 67–69
Markov, A. A., 48, 175, 195
Marty, A., 40–43, **44–46**, 47–48, 54–55, 59, 63–64, 178, 195, 241
Mathesius, V., 48

NAME INDEX

Mathews, M. M., 143, 171
Max, L. W., 185
Meader, C. L., 64
Messmer, O., 149
Meumann, E., 83, 224
Meyer, M., 65–66, 71, 176, 179
Mikloshich, F. von, 5
Miller, G. A., 6, 178, 195, 209–210, **211–221**, 222
Moore, K., 128–129
Morris, E. P., 40
Mowrer, O. H., 179–180
Müller, M., 3, 101
Müller, R., 147–148, 151
Münsterberg, H., 64, 131, 180
Murchison, C., 80, 241
Musgrave, B., 233

Nagel, E., 176
Nagy, L., 79
Neisser, U., 13
Nelson, B., 175
Newman, S. S., 202
Newton, I., 2
Nice, M. M., 105–106, **107–112**
Nida, E. A., 213

O'Connor, N., 173
Oertal, H., 40
Ogden, R. M., 64, 71, 180
Osgood, C., 16, 174, 180–181, 224, 229

Paget, R., 64
Paul, H., 6, 32–33, **34–37**, 38–39, 43, 46, 60–63, 67–68, 71, 88, 89, 100, 129, 195, 205, 210, 241
Pavlov, I., 66, 168, 179
Perez, B., 81
Peterson, P., 238
Piaget, J., 115
Pick, A., 46, 182–183, 186, 189
Pike, K. L., 213
Pillsbury, W., 64, 146
Plato, 207
Post, E. L., 214
Postal, P., 200, 202
Preyer, W., 81–83, 93–95, 102, 152, 224
Pribram, K., 178
Pronko, N. H., 172, 173
Psammeticus, 100

Quantz, J. O., 144, 161, 164
Quine, W., 202, 207

Rask, R., 2, 4–5
Richards, I. A., 64, 71, 180
Richter, F., 84
Ries, J., 57
Ringer, F., 239
Roback, A. A., 105, 172
Robins, R. H., 1
Romanes, G., 102, 140
Rousseau, J. J., 79–80

Sander, F., 50
Sandmann, M., 195
Sapir, E., 76
Schlauch, M., 78
Schleicher, A., 3–4
Schmidt, W., 158
Sebeok, T., 174
Sechehaye, C. A., 48
Selz, O., 46, 178
Shamir, E., 217
Shannon, C., 48, 176
Sheffield, A. D., 40
Shinn, M., 111–112
Sigismund, B., 81
Skinner, B. F., 168, 176–178, 181, 195–196
Sklar, R., 194
Slobin, D., 142, 173
Smart, B. H., 5
Smith, S., 136
Sonneck, B., 179
Spinoza, B., 13
Stählin, W., 52–53
Steinthal, H., 7–8, 19, 34, 43, 61, 81, 204
Stern, C. & W., 83–85, **86–100**, 108, 110, 112, 125, 141, 224
Stout, G. F., 49, 152
Stricker, S., 65
Strong, H., 33
Strümpell, L., 81
Stumpf, C., 66, 83–84, 98, 102, 104, 107–108, 110, 112
Suci, G., 16
Sullivan, J. J., 239
Sully, J., 94, 102
Sütterlin, L., 47–48

Taine, H., 79, 81, 94

NAME INDEX

Tannenbaum, P., 16
Tanner, A., 102
Terman, L. M., 130
Thorndike, E. L., 69, 136, 159
Thorsen, A. M., 185
Thumb, A., 67–69
Tiedeman, D., 80
Titchener, E. B., 9, 12, 49, 65, 186, 188, 238, 240
Tögel, H., 93–96, 99
Tomb, J. W., 113
Town, C. H., 107, 109, 112
Tracy, F., 94, 102, 127
Trubetzkoy, N. S., 48

Vachek, J., 57
Vendryes, J., 72, 74
Vierordt, K., 81
Viertel, J., 200
Volkelt, H., 50
Vossler, K., 48
Vygotsky, L. S., 115

Ward, J., 84–85
Washburn, M. F., 65, 185

Watson, J. B., 65–66, 70–71, 172, 176, 181, 185
Weaver, W., 48
Weber, E., 6
Wegener, P., 63–64, 120
Weis, A. P., 66–67, 73
Weksel, W., 54, 142
Wells, R. S., 213
Werner, H., 55, 84, 225
Wertheimer, M., 50, 169
Wheeler, B. I., 33
Whitney, W. D., 6, 111–112, 204–205
Wiener, N., 176
Wittgenstein, L., 206–207
Wolman, B. B., 176, 239
Woodworth, R. S., 49, 142
Wundt, W., 5, 8–19, **20–31,** 37–50, 53–54, 57–58, 60–65, 68, 70–72, 78, 80–84, 88, 91, 92, 96, 98–103, 116, 129, 144–147, 152–154, 158–159, 182, 186, 193–195, 198, 210, 222, 224–225, 237–243

Yerkes, R. M., 67

Zeitler, J., 149, 152
Zipf, G. K., 48, 175, 176

LIBRARY